# ECO'S CHAOSMOS
## From the Middle Ages

While Umberto Eco's intellectual itinerary was marked by his early studies of post-Crocean aesthetics and his concentration on linguistics, information theory, structuralism, semiotics, cognitive science, and media studies, what distinguishes his critical and fictional writing is the tension between a typically medieval search for a code and a hermeneutic representative of deconstructive tendencies. This tension between *cosmos* and *chaos*, order and disorder, is reflected in the word *chaosmos*.

In this assessment of the philosophical basis of Eco's critical and fictional writing, Cristina Farronato explores the other distinctive aspect of Eco's thought – the struggle for a composition of opposites, the outcome deriving from his ability to elicit similar contrasts from the past and replay them in modern terms. Focusing principally on how Eco's scholarly background influenced his study of semiotics, Farronato analyses *The Name of the Rose* in relation to William of Ockham's epistemology, C.S. Peirce's work on abduction, and Wittgenstein's theory of language. She also discusses *Foucault's Pendulum* as an explicit comment on the modern debate on interpretation through a direct reference to early modern hermetic thought, correlates *The Island of the Day Before* as a postmodern mixture of science and superstition, and reviews *Baudolino* as a historical/fantastic novel that again situates the Middle Ages in a postmodern context. Demonstrating Eco's use of semiotic theory, *Eco's Chaosmos* shows how critical models of the past map contemporary literature and culture.

(Toronto Italian Studies)

CRISTINA FARRONATO is an assistant professor in the Department of Romance Languages and Literatures at Colgate University.

# ECO'S CHAOSMOS

## From the Middle Ages to Postmodernity

*Cristina Farronato*

UNIVERSITY OF TORONTO PRESS
Toronto Buffalo London

© University of Toronto Press Incorporated 2003
Toronto Buffalo London
Printed in Canada

ISBN 0-8020-8789-2 (cloth)
ISBN 0-8020-8586-5 (paper)

Printed on acid-free paper

Toronto Italian Studies

---

**National Library of Canada Cataloguing in Publication**

Farronato, Cristina
   Eco's chaosmos : from the Middle Ages to postmodernity /
   Cristina Farronato.

   (Toronto Italian studies)
   Includes bibliographical references and index.
   ISBN 0-8020-8789-2 (bound).   ISBN 0-8020-8586-5 (pbk.)

   1. Eco, Umberto – Criticism and interpretation.   I. Title.
   II. Series.

   PQ4865.C6Z645      853'.912      C2003-903967-6

---

This book has been published with the help of a grant from the Italian
Foreign Ministry and the Istituto Italiano di Cultura, Toronto.

University of Toronto Press acknowledges the financial assistance to its
publishing program of the Canada Council for the Arts and the Ontario Arts
Council.

University of Toronto Press acknowledges the financial support for its publishing activities of the Government of Canada through the Book Publishing
Industry Development Program (BPIDP).

*To Sylva and Dario*

# Contents

# Figures

# Preface

This book focuses on the philosophical background at the basis of Umberto Eco's critical writings and novels. It investigates how Eco's early study of medieval philosophy (his dissertation was an analysis of Thomas Aquinas' aesthetics) and profound interest in the postmodern hermeneutics of interpretation come together in a unique way in the formulation of his thought. Although Eco's itinerary was marked by his early studies of post-Crocean aesthetics and his spectacular concentration on linguistics, information theory, structuralism, semiotics, cognitive science, and media studies, what constitutes the peculiarity of his critical and fictional writings is a tension between a typically medieval search for a code and a hermeneutics representative of deconstructive tendencies. This tension between *cosmos* and *chaos*, order and disorder, is reflected in the word *chaosmos*.

As an outcome, the other distinctive aspect of Eco's thought is the struggle for a composition of opposites, which derives from his ability to elicit similar contrasts from the past and to replay them in modern terms. The worldwide success of *The Name of the Rose* is, due, I argue, to the application of this critical procedure.

In the first part of this study, I focus principally on these philosophical aspects of Eco's theory, and I accompany my discussion of them with an analysis of how Eco's background has influenced his studies of semiotics, mass communication, and popular culture. Further, I consider his interest in founding the philosophical possibility of laughter. In the second part, I address Eco's fiction in connection with his philosophy. I analyse his first novel, *The Name of the Rose*, in relation to William of Ockham's epistemology, the work on abduction by the American philosopher C.S. Peirce, and Wittgenstein's theory of language; I discuss *Foucault's Pendulum* as an explicit comment on the modern debate on interpretation through a direct reference to early modern hermetic thought; I correlate *The Island of the Day Before* to a postmodern mixture of science and superstition; and I review *Baudolino* as a historical/fantastic novel that once again situates the Middle Ages in a postmodern context.

I attempt to identify precise factors in Eco's complex works in order to highlight the vibrancy of his semiotics in today's intellectual world, and to show how the critical models of the past map the contemporary world.

# Acknowledgments

First of all I would like to thank Umberto Eco, who inspired and encouraged me from the moment I met him. The seriousness with which he is dedicated to his role of mentor will influence my career forever. My deepest thanks go to Professor Alain Cohen, who has followed my project and guided and supported me over the years, and to the patient readers of my manuscript, Professor Steven Cassidy, Professor Donald Wesling, Professor Oumelbanine Zhiri, Professor Jack Greenstein, and Professor Peter Bondanella, whose intelligent suggestions and comments have offered me fresh perspectives.

I would also like to thank my friends in the Department of Communication Sciences at the University of Bologna, especially Nicola Dusi, for our illuminating discussions. I thank Paola and Andrea for their support, and my husband, Jeff, for debating ideas with me and for always being there.

ECO'S CHAOSMOS
From the Middle Ages to Postmodernity

# 1 Introduction

Umberto Eco was born in Alessandria, a town in the Northern Italian region of Piedmont, on 5 January 1932. He was therefore a child when first Fascism and later the Resistance movement swept over Italy. His Piedmontese roots remain at the core of his personality, both as a man and as an intellectual; in fact, they often surface in his essays and fiction, which comment on the raw and matter-of-fact character of his ancestors and his people, on their indifference to opposing factions' sudden changes of front, and on the political decisions made by a faraway and obsolete Italian government.

Eco moved to the city of Turin when he was nineteen and attended the University of Turin, where he received a *laurea* in philosophy and wrote a thesis on the aesthetics of Thomas Aquinas. The University of Turin at the time was a rich and stimulating environment, animated by personalities such as Luigi Pareyson, who influenced Eco's conception of aesthetics, and Augusto Guzzo, who authorized the publication of Eco's thesis on Thomas Aquinas.

Having worked with RAI, the Italian national television network, for a few years, Eco went on to teach in universities in different parts of the world and was awarded numerous honorary degrees. He established the first chair of semiotics at the University of Bologna in 1972. He is now head of the Department of Communications at the University of Bologna and has recently founded the Scuola Superiore di Studi Umanistici. Eco has produced many theoretical works and gained world-wide renown as a novelist. In this regard, he is one of those rare intellectuals (Sartre comes to mind) who have combined two different kinds of production, theory and fiction, so thoroughly that it is impossible to evoke the writer without mentioning the critic, the two being equally important and firmly interconnected. It is one of my tasks in this study not to treat the theory and fiction separately but to highlight their interconnections. The challenge is not to write an intellectual biography of the writer Eco (such as has been done brilliantly by Peter Bondanella and by Michael Caesar) but to reflect on the founding philosophical conception at the basis of all of Eco's work, the fundamental tension that has made him different from any other intellectual in either the European or the American literary scene. This tension was made possible by the peculiarity of Eco's formation, which is characterized by the encounter of his knowledge of medieval philosophy with three 'events' that dominated the cultural and intellectual life of the 1960s and 1970s: the structuralist movement, French deconstruction, and the growing importance of the media. This encounter bears fruit in Eco's thought in a brilliant intellectual synthesis, which surpasses in a unique way the elements that contribute to it. His vast literary enterprise, furthermore, distinguishes him from his peers of the great French wave of philosophical research in the second half of the twentieth century (which includes the thinkers Barthes, Lacan, Foucault, Derrida, and Deleuze).

This study was provoked by a suggestion from Eco himself. In the preface to the 1970 Italian edition of *Il problema estetico in Tommaso d'Aquino*, Eco discusses the importance of republishing his very first theoretical book, his dissertation, and acknowledges his indebtedness to the Thomistic method, which in its rigour and lucidity was exemplary for him. In an aside, Eco suggests a direction for research. He writes, 'It would be interesting to show how and to what extent I am still indebted to him.' A chief purpose of this inquiry is to show the influence of medieval philosophy in Eco's semiotic theory. But it is also my contention that the scholastic method intersects with a whole line of other influences that, for convenience, can be categorized under the label 'postmodernism.' Just as Eco defines correspondences between the scholastic method and structuralism in the conclusion of *The Aesthetics of Thomas Aquinas*, so is it possible to identify connections among scholasticism, Renaissance and baroque hermeticism, and postmodern hermeneutics.

This analysis also reveals that, even more than his theory, what is masterful in Eco is his style, which, like Aquinas', shows a tension towards the composition of opposites and the establishment of a harmony always disrupted by extremes. The most fundamental tension in both Eco's criticism and his narratives is that between the hermeneutics

of deconstruction and the kind of search for a code that was characteristic of medieval thought. These paradigms are constantly investigated
and compared with contemporary theories in Eco's work, and his tendency to refer to the past and learn from it allowed him to develop his
unique message.

In the early part of the study, I analyse Eco's theory of communication and semiotic method in contraposition with some aspects of the
philosophy of Thomas Aquinas, William of Ockham, and Nicholas of
Cusa. I suggest a parallel between the evolution of Eco's thought and
the development of James Joyce's writings, showing striking similarities
but also differences in their theories of aesthetics. As an introduction to
Eco's semiotic theory in chapter 3, chapter 2 presents an excursus on
medieval and early modern logic from Nicholas of Cusa to Emanuele
Tesauro.

Chapter 3 returns to Eco's early years at the University of Turin and
to the influence of his thesis adviser, Luigi Pareyson, one of the innova-
tors in aesthetic theory in Italy after the almost complete preponderance of the philosophy of Benedetto Croce. Here I argue that these
years, devoted to the study of Aquinas' aesthetics, were fundamental in
establishing the trajectory of Eco's work, in leading him to the writing
of his first important theoretical book, *Opera aperta* (1962), and from
there to his defining studies on media and mass culture. In books such
as *Apocalittici e integrati* (1964) and *Il superuomo di massa* (1976), the
influence of the rigorous Thomistic method is evident, and constant
parallels are established between the contemporary and the medieval
world. I consider Eco's theories of culture in the context of today's
discipline of cultural studies, and show how the exponents of this discipline have often unjustly criticized or disregarded his methodology.

Chapter 4 is an extensive study of Eco's reflections on the Reader
and on his theory of interpretation, largely based on his *Lector in fabula*
(1979), *The Limits of Interpretation* (1990), and *Interpretation and
Overinterpretation* (1992). These theories become most interesting when
discussed in connection with Eco's own novels. In line with his study of
signs, Eco's theory of interpretation reflects the balance he has tried to
create between modern hermeneutics and a search for a code inspired
by the medieval theory of signs.

Chapter 5, on intertextuality, analyses the use of citations in
postmodern literature and compares Eco's technique with that of other
major authors of intertextual works, especially the two most influential
writers for his fiction, Borges and Calvino. I argue that the use of

quotations, far from being unique to postmodern literature, was very much in vogue among medieval authors, and I suggest similarities and differences between the two periods' use of the technique.

Chapter 6 is one of the most important in this study, as it deals with a highly significant aspect of Eco's thought and personality: his wit, his humour, and his taste for laughter. The investigation concludes that Eco's humour is a metaphysical answer to the limitations imposed on humankind by Being. More similar to medieval scholars than to Nietzsche, Eco sees laughter as reflecting our defensive mechanism while we search and interrogate Being, testing its resistances.

Chapter 7 considers the *whodunit* as the ideal postmodern genre, since postmodern authors quickly turn the detection process into a metaphysical search for truth. Eco's four novels, all more or less detective stories, follow the same trajectory, but generic categorization is rendered difficult by the independent variables that Eco introduces and that make them unique. *The Name of the Rose* (1980) is characterized by the presence of a medieval Sherlock Holmes who adopts a method of investigation based on medieval and Peircian semiotics. *Foucault's Pendulum* (1989) once again derives the pleasure of its narrative from a blending of contemporary hermeneutics and deconstruction theory with a historical dimension that takes the detection back to the founding of the Templars in the Middle Ages. *The Island of the Day Before* (1994) has as its hero a baroque character, whose Bildung and philosophy can easily be connected with postmodern theories. This hero represents the union of a medieval taste for scientific discovery and a typically hermetic belief in magical forces. In *Baudolino* (2000), the *whodunit* story line is even less imperative – a development that characterizes a shift in Eco's narrative and semiotic interest.

Finally, chapter 8 discusses *Baudolino*, Eco's most recent novel, with particular attention to its historical/fantastic medieval setting and its postmodern philosophical references.

It is difficult to do justice to Eco's work, because of the great quantity of his writings and because his theories are very much works in progress. The large intention of this work is to identify in Eco's itinerary a symbolic line of research and to raise important questions regarding the past, the present, and the future of semiotics. Eco has many admirers, but also some detractors, who have attacked various aspects of his theory. Most of the criticisms are those usually made about semiotics, concerning, for example, its focusing on the spatial dimension and disregarding of the temporal one, or its incapacity to extend its criticism and analysis beyond the text. I demonstrate in chapter 3, dedicated to the study of culture, that these attacks are inappropriate in the case of Eco. Cultural studies exponents have regarded semiotics as a dated theory, inadequate to study of the contemporary world. In this work I argue instead that Eco offers precious tools for such study, and that disregarding his position handicaps contemporary theory.

When 'thrown' in front of extremely complex phenomena, it is wise to dispense with all the useful criteria we have in our possession. Some positions seem irreconcilable, but Eco has given us many examples of how we can reconcile opposites to reach a higher solution.

Beyond his theory, what Eco has taught is that we must never disregard the lessons of the past and that, as we review human history, we see repeated mistakes and many similar situations that time and again have been resolved in the wrong direction. His message, therefore, is to learn from the ancients, to see ourselves as dwarfs on the shoulders of giants, and to look beyond the immediate, in the words of Michael Caesar, to that horizon 'by which we are contained, to which we reach out.'[1]

# 2 From Cosmos to Chaosmos: Eco and Joyce

Eco's omnivorous interest is manifested throughout his writings. The reading public knows him as the author of four successful novels, but his narrative talent ought not to obscure his scholarly accomplishments, as he has produced an immense quantity of ground-breaking critical work.

In spite of Eco's success as an internationally known author and his cutting-edge critique, he remains, as he likes to designate himself, 'a medievalist in hibernation.' The phrase certainly does not imply a turning back of his theory to the medieval past, which would be unthinkable; instead, it casts light on his intellectual position with respect to the world. While others have assumed critical distance in their theory of culture by projecting their critiques into the future or by dissociating themselves geographically from their areas of study, Eco has established his critical distance by identifying himself as a medieval scholar in hibernation who looks at the contemporary world with ecstatic eyes. Despite its connection to the past, this position is thoroughly postmodern, in that links between past and present are quickly established in a fragmentation of the chronological narrative line of history, and contemporary events become repetitions of episodes that have already occurred. Only the ironic observation of the shrewd intellectual can identify the hidden associations that tie together in an unlimited semiosis the most disparate occurrences.

Eco's statement about his role as a medievalist in hibernation also represents an acknowledgment of indebtedness to a method that, with its rigour and clarity, has deeply influenced him since his earliest years; furthermore, it represents a recognition that scholastic methodology has influenced contemporary thought, in particular the work of writers such as James Joyce, Gerard Manley Hopkins, and Marshall McLuhan. Contrasting the rigour of medieval theory with the complex web of postmodern theory creates new insights, and in the same way in which this opposition has produced interesting results in Eco's thought, it can offer new stimuli in our study of philosophy, literature, and culture.

Some critics, John Deely, for example, have seen Eco's theory as reaching the boundary between modernity and postmodernity without quite crossing that boundary. I believe that this criticism, although legitimate in a sense, is based on a misunderstanding of the tendencies that brought Eco to the formulation of his principles. I would argue that, instead of occupying a place on the border between modernity and postmodernity, Eco's theory is a postmodern accomplishment that has a significant and peculiar tie to the methodology of scholastic philosophers such as Thomas Aquinas and of early modern thinkers such as Nicholas of Cusa.

The tension between the principles of medieval philosophy and the philosophical and cultural debates of postmodernity, of which Eco's approach is conscious most of the time, has produced a fruitful struggle in almost every one of his works, whether criticism, fiction, or philosophical or cultural divertissement, and that tension is at the foundation of his originality and sensibility. We can therefore characterize Eco's thought as a fruitful clash between the principles of medieval philosophy and those philosophical and cultural debates that define postmodernity.

**Between Order and Chaos:** *A Theory of Semiotics*

Eco's theory can be said to develop from a theory of signification and sign production to a theory of network. In the foreword to *A Theory of Semiotics*, he explains how he uses the principle of Ockham's razor, *non sunt multiplicanda entia praeter necessitatem*, in the first part of his treatise in order to propose a restricted and unified set of categories on which a *theory of codes* can be based. Later, he explains that, in the second part of his book, devoted to a *theory of sign production*, he was forced to adopt an anti-Ockhamistic principle: *entia sunt multiplicanda propter necessitatem*. He discovered that the categories he had identified for the *theory of codes* were not sufficient to explain many of the phenomena occurring in the *theory of sign production*.

This idea reflects a characteristic of Eco's work. From its beginning, his semiotic theory is grounded in medieval philosophy, but later it is forced to evolve from the strict principles of the pre-modern theory of signs and to *open* to a wider spectre, that of unlimited semiosis. Unlimited semiosis seems to constitute a middle ground between the linearity of medieval logic (pre-Aquinas) and the analogic, non-linear thinking of the hermetic tradition.

This idea is reflected not only in Eco's critical writings, but also in his fiction, from *The Name of the Rose* to *Baudolino*. In the evolution of these works as a body, we see Eco beginning with a book about the Middle Ages that argues for the *openness* of interpretation; then, worried by the excessively aimless drift of interpretation, continuing with a novel about contemporary culture that warns about the dissemination of language; and then, to fill the space between these two opposites, writing a novel about the seventeenth century, an epoch that presents clear similarities to ours but that most of all constitutes a middle ground between the Middle Ages and modernity (see chapter 7); and finally, once again writing a novel that takes place in the Middle Ages but in fact focuses on postmodern concerns. Eco's fiction is interested in mixing the principles of medieval philosophy and ideas with contemporary theoretical debates and cultural characteristics. It could be argued that the explorations of the past are just excuses to enable him to deal with the present. This theory would precisely validate the fact that the development that characterized the beginning of modernity is similar to the development that characterized the beginning of postmodernity: from scholastic logic to early modernity, from structuralist theory to post-structuralism,[1] from the Porphyrian tree to the idea of network or *rhyzome*.[2]

In *Le poetiche di Joyce. Dalla 'Summa' al 'Finnegans Wake'* (1962; *The Aesthetics of Chaosmos*, 1982), Eco writes that there is 'a radical opposition between the medieval man, nostalgic for an ordered world of clear signs, and the modern man, seeking a new habitat but unable to find the elusive rules and thus burning continually in the nostalgia of a lost infancy.' He asserts that 'the definitive choice is not made,' and that there is 'a development of a continuous polarity between Chaos and Cosmos, between disorder and order, liberty and rules, between the nostalgia of the Middle Ages and the attempts to envisage a new order' (*The Aesthetics of Chaosmos*, p. 3).

The complexity of this idea is expanded with specific historical references in the analysis Eco develops in *Semiotics and the Philosophy of Language* (1984), but it is in *A Theory of Semiotics* (1976) that it finds its precise theoretical explanation, and it lies at the basis of every writing on the limits of interpretation. What we discover in the end is not a simplistic separation between linear and analogical thinking, but a continual tension between them: this tension is what informs Eco's idea of unlimited semiosis and his passage from the concept of dictionary to the concept of encyclopaedia.

This chapter analyses the elements that characterize Eco's tension between order and disorder, between cosmos and chaos, and that bring him to find a middle theory that characterizes his chaosmos. These elements belong particularly to semiotic theory, but also to his philosophy and his fiction (if the three can be separated).

**The Middle Ages of Umberto Eco**

Umberto Eco began his career as a medievalist philosopher, with a dissertation on Thomas Aquinas at the University of Turin in 1954. Over the last forty years, this work, *The Aesthetics of Thomas Aquinas*, has been published several times and translated;[3] Eco has made corrections and additions but has refused to rewrite the book. In the different prefaces to the various editions, he explains that although his project might appear dated, the problems discussed and the conclusions reached are still very current.

In the preface to the 1970 Italian edition, Eco indicates that what inspired him to write about Aquinas was his adhesion to the religious universe of the medieval philosopher, but that, while writing, he distanced himself more and more from the spiritual content and was left with a methodological experience, a method 'that I would apply even today to any research in the history of philosophy' (*Il problema estetico in Tommaso d'Aquino*, p. 6).

Eco's experience did not leave him simply with a theoretical approach. On the contrary, Aquinas' methodology and philosophical system left a well-defined imprint on many aspects of Eco's work. It is possible to analyze Eco's own Middle Ages in the same way in which Eco studies the medieval features of James Joyce's aesthetics in *The Aesthetics of Chaosmos: The Middle Ages of James Joyce*.

When Eco tries to define what aspects of the Middle Ages are embodied in Joyce's theoretical approach, he identifies a series of connections that can easily be reversed and applied to Eco himself. The interest in Catholicism is fairly obvious, given Eco's early activism,[4] and is admitted by Eco in the preface to his work on Aquinas. Like Joyce, Eco detached himself more and more from spiritual motifs, but a 'Catholic thread' survives, especially in his interest in interpretation of the scriptures and in gnosticism. The fascination with the sacred is evident in *The Name of the Rose*, where, as in Joyce's writings, the narration 'is tuned to liturgical time' ( *The Aesthetics of Chaosmos*, p. 4).

Second, Eco identifies in Joyce a tendency towards abstraction, which he considers one of the premises of scholasticism. The same tendency is manifest in Eco's thought, primarily in his taste for debating questions of the kind posed by the scholastic philosophers – for example, concerning the ontology of formal structures or the effort to devise a theoretical model for discussing an object, that is, the idea of informing a system that enables one to identify the rules of the game.

In the 'conclusion' of *The Aesthetics of Thomas Aquinas*, Eco discusses the similarities that connect scholastic to structuralist thought. He sees the idea of a *system of systems* as an ambition typical of the two philosophical constructions:

> It is an idea which Structuralist aesthetics has taken over in order to explain the nature of composite operations which impose a formal relationship upon cultural data preceding the operation – complexes of ideas, networks of emotional stimuli, phonetic and lexemic series, suprasegmental levels, large syntagmatic strings which culture has previously endowed with their own particularity, and so on and so forth. And here too the preexisting levels become part of the new compound, and are modified thereby, without losing their original autonomy. (220)

There is, according to Eco, a specific difference between the two systems: whereas in structuralism a structure is a system made up of 'empty' values, values that are defined only by difference, Aquinas' structure is made up of 'full' elements, substantial forms (219). But the idea of arranging elements in different combinations is common to the two systems, and he sees in them the same operating *forma mentis*. Although Eco will disprove the pre-existence of the structuralist models, his interest in the structuralist method of analysis is well known, and he is adamant in affirming the utility of Aquinas' method and range of questions for today's theoretical debates: 'Reading Aquinas can have the following value: it can suggest methods of analysis which can be adopted today' (216).

Another important framework that Eco distinguishes in the medieval model is the idea of an order in the cosmic whole, which provides an unlimited chain of relations among things. Everything stands for something else, creating an unending spiral of references. In Joyce, this principle is reflected in the author's use of language, in which every sign is connected to another sign by similarity, logic, or a series of puns. Eco's diagram, reproduced here as figure 1, reflects this Joycean game.

The medieval thinkers had an encyclopaedic approach to the reality of the universe. They elaborated a series of encyclopaedias that served to catalogue every object or event in the universe. Joyce adopted the same logic of the inventory, in listing for pages the innumerable objects that constituted a particular scenario. The connection with Eco's work is evident here. The most direct example is his insistence on the notion of encyclopaedia as superseding the Greimassian notion of the dictionary. Other examples are his discussion of resemblance[5] and the use of lists and catalogues in his novels.

Of course, there is a crucial difference between Eco's and Joyce's encyclopaedic idea and that of the Middle Ages. Eco writes, 'If you take away the transcendent God from the symbolic world of the Middle Ages, you have the world of Joyce' (*The Aesthetics of Chaosmos*, p. 7). The absence of a metaphysical foundation for reality characterizes both Eco's and Joyce's categorizations of the world, and this absence is by no means new, but already evident in the work of Renaissance thinkers such as Nicholas of Cusa and Giordano Bruno. I will discuss the Renaissance influence on Eco and Joyce later; for now, what is important to notice is the common effort of medieval philosophy and the philosophy of modernity to reconstitute some kind of lost order, whether it consists of universals or of faculties of the intellect.

Eco draws further analogies with respect to aesthetic principles. He argues that the three categories individuated by Aquinas to define the beautiful, *integritas sive perfectio, proportio sive consonantia,* and *claritas,* are unsurprisingly similar to the three Joycean principles of 'wholeness,' 'harmony,' and 'radiance' (19–20). But most important for our analysis, since Eco's aesthetics is developed more in the direction of the interpretation of text, is an ulterior connection between Aquinas' and Eco's methodologies, which most directly concerns the Thomistic theory of knowledge.

In his illuminating essay 'Thomas Aquinas: Natural Semiotics and the Epistemological Process' Roberto Pellerey looks at Thomistic epistemology identifying precise links with contemporary semiotics, and borrows specifically from Eco's semiotic theory and communication schema, discussed in both *La struttura assente* (1968) and *A Theory of Semiotics* (1976).

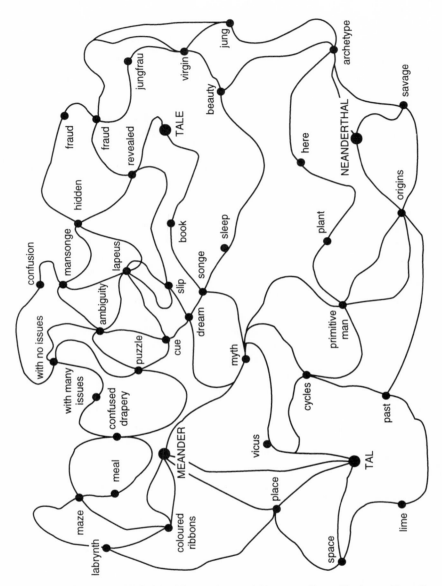

Figure 1. '*Finnegans Wake*,' in *The Aesthetics of Chaosmos.* From Umberto Eco, *Le forme del contenuto* (Milan: Bompiani, 1971), p. 105. © R.C.S. Libri SpA – Milano, Bompiani 1971. Reproduced by permission.

Both Aquinas and Eco would agree that cognitive abstraction must be based in sensible determination. Thomas Aquinas in particular identifies three types of cognitive abstraction: physical, mathematical, and metaphysical. The first represents an abstraction that prescinds from singular individuality and preserves sensible data; the second prescinds from sensible matter but preserves numeric aspects; and the third prescinds from concrete determinations and preserves the character of 'to be'.[6] Knowledge, therefore, depends on the observation of multiple singular cases. The difference between the two thinkers is that Aquinas would maintain that observation of multiple singular cases leads to an understanding of the universal nature, while for Eco it lies at the basis of a theory of abduction, which, far from allowing the intellect to comprehend the *quidditas*, the universal form, instead leads the intellect to the formulation of a hypothesis, which is then to be proved *true* by facts and which is subject to fallibility.

Aquinas sees *intelligere* as the *ultimam felicitatem*. Knowledge starts with the concrete object when this comes into contact with the human senses. The senses transform the information they receive into a complex sign, which is then transmitted to the intellect. These complex signs are called *phantasms*, or 'idola rei absentis,' and they are elaborated by fantasy and cogitative power. We can schematize the process:

Res → sensible species → bodily organ → sense → phantasm

The 'sensible species' is the impression the sense receives in the bodily organ; it therefore is the first sign received by the sense, which perfectly represents the *sensibles* that have generated it. The bodily organ then transmits the sensible species to the internal senses, first of all the *sensus communis*, which transforms the sensible species into a type of image representing things: the phantasm.

The schema that illustrates the first part of the epistemological process according to Aquinas calls to mind Eco's diagram of the 'informational' process:

Res → sensible species → bodily organ → sense → phantasm
sender → signal → channel → receiver → message or iconic sign

Eco's model describes a simple communicative situation that contemplates two machines at the opposite poles of the chain, because when two human beings are placed in those positions the situation becomes

more complicated. Eco therefore chooses to describe a technical process in which a signal is transmitted from one machine to another. This
simplified process allows him to build an exemplary *model*, a simple
structure of communication, which can be applied also to more complex situations. Only with such an instrument will it be possible to
'speak about *all* cultural phenomena under the communicative aspect'
(*La struttura assente*, p. 17).

In Eco's model, instead of the *res* that appears in Aquinas' diagram,
there is a *sender* or a *source of information*. This source is able to transmit
a *signal*, which, having gone through a *channel*, is captured by a receiv-
ing apparatus. The *receptor* then translates the signal into a given form,
which constitutes the *message* intended for the addressee. This process,
says Eco, is used in many mechanical devices, for example an alarm
system that can tell an engineer when the water level of a mountain
basin is dangerous, but it also constitutes the process used in radio
communication: 'The source of information is the broadcasting station,
which transmits the message. When a given combination of events to
communicate is identified, the sender conveys them to the transmitter
(the microphone), which converts them into physical signals that travel
along a channel (hertz waves), and they are then gathered by a transmitter that re-converts them into the *message* (articulate sounds) the
addressee will receive' (*La struttura assente*, p. 18).

So Aquinas' epistemological process, in which the senses receive information from things and then transform it into a complex sign that
is transmitted to the intellect, becomes Eco's model for the communication process. Once again, the difference is that for Aquinas the final
product of the process is the *quidditas*, the universal form, the *ratio
rerum*, which manifests itself in the form of *verbum*, whereas for Eco the
final product of the process is a message that is 'open' to numerous
interpretative choices and that is definitely a cultural phenomenon. In
any case, for the Eco of *La struttura assente* the main interest of semiology is in the study of the code: 'In the moment when it sets out to
define meaning, semiology runs the risk of ceasing to be itself, and
becomes logic, psychology or metaphysics' (35).

In spite of this fundamental difference, we can see how Aquinas'
methodology inspired Eco to convert the cognitive process he describes
into a theory of communication more appropriate for dealing with
current cultural phenomena.

The last point I would like to emphasize, one that, again, reflects the
influence of Aquinas on Eco, is the presence in Eco of a medieval
characteristic he identifies in Joyce: the taste for quotation at any cost.

Eco sees *Finnegans Wake*, even more than *Ulysses*, as 'an immense cata-logue of authoritative quotations' (*The Aesthetics of Chaosmos*, p. 11), and the same can be said of Eco's own fiction. All four of his novels form a chain of intertextual connections, and in this way they reflect what Eco sees as the medieval *modus operandi*. The beautiful phrase by Bernard of Chartres quoted in *The Aesthetics of Chaosmos* appears also in *The Name of the Rose*, and in the very way it represents Joyce's methodology it also represents Eco's own way of using the past. The phrase came to us thanks to its being quoted by John of Salisbury:

> Dicebat Bernardus Carnotensis nos esse quasi nanos gigantium humeris insidentes ut possimus plura eis et remotiora videre, non utique proprii visus acumine aut eminentia corporis, sed quia in altum subvehimur et extollimur magnitudine gigantes.

> Bernard of Chartres said that we are as dwarfs on the shoulders of giants, who can see farther and see more things than they, not only because we can use the sharpness of their sight and the height of their bodies, but because we are raised up high and can take advantage of their great size.
> (quoted in *The Aesthetics of Chaosmos*, p. 11; my translation)

What this means for Eco is that Joyce used quotations from the mas-ters of the past so that we could climb up on their shoulders and look farther ahead; Joyce uses Aquinas, for example, in that way. William of Baskerville in *The Name of the Rose* believes this method is what amplifies knowledge, and he quotes Bernard of Chartres. Chapter 5 contains a more systematic discussion of this subject; for now, it suffices to say that Eco, in his application of Aquinas' methodology and his use of quota-tions, proceeds exactly in this fashion, so that we can apply this sen-tence about Joyce's work to Eco's work as well: 'We will attempt to follow the process of the young artist who conserves and repudiates the mental forms that preside over the ordered cosmos proposed by medi-eval Christian tradition and who, still thinking as a medieval, dissolves the ordered Cosmos into the polyvalent form of the Chaosmos' (*The Aesthetics of Chaosmos*, p. 11).

## Analogy as Epistemological Tool: Nicholas of Cusa (1401–64)

The quotation that ends the previous section explains Joyce's passage from the idea of an ordered cosmos, which was dear to the Middle Ages, to the concept of Chaosmos, which Eco attributes to Joyce's encounter with the philosophy of Nicholas of Cusa and Giordano Bruno. In fact, there are some elements of medievalism in Nicholas of Cusa's thought that are fundamental to an understanding of both Joyce's and Eco's theory of analogy; moreover, Nicholas' philosophical synthesis reveals solutions and theoretical attitudes that would be appropriated by philosophy and science in the sixteenth and seventeenth Centuries.

The tradition of Neoplatonism was revived in fifteenth-century Italy by the circle of humanists around Marsilio Ficino in Florence. Excited by the discovery of an apparently ancient text, the *Corpus Hermeticum*, attributed to a mysterious Hermes Trismegistos, they thought they had found in it the confirmation of their theory that there are hidden truths beneath the scriptures and other hermetic texts. Many of them pursued this notion, sometimes to the point of heresy, as Christian dogma was frequently blended with traditional classical mythology, and the pervasiveness of their Absolute often brought them close to a pantheistic vision of nature.[7]

For these thinkers, a symbol was a sign of an impalpable quality, a divine message, that nobody could spell aloud. The Holy Scriptures spoke in a symbolic language, and the process of reading them was highly complicated, since they were in a position to say everything; as Eco writes in *The Limits of Interpretation*, 'Their meaning was the nebula of all possible archetypes' (11). This view had links to the medieval hermeneutic tradition belonging to the patristic and scholastic idea of interpretation, which frequently compared the inexhaustible depth of the scriptures to an *infinita sensuum sylva* (Jerome *Ep.* 64.2), an *oceanum mysteriosum Dei, ut sic loquar, labyrinthum* (Jerome *In Gen.* 9.1), or a *latissima sylva* (Origen *In Ez.* 4) (12).

Looking for a law that organizes signs in the world is discovering similarities among things, and only through its resemblance to what we see can we have a glimpse of what we cannot see; but whatever we may be able to say about reality, there will always be more to say and other problems to solve, on account of the inexhaustible character of metaphysical questions. According to Nicholas of Cusa, the *maximum* we can achieve is a *docta ignorantia*, and however hard we struggle, all we can accomplish is a consciousness of how little we know. Knowledge was for Nicholas a *mysterium tremendum* and a *mysterium fascinans*. 'Knowledge is not without a purpose,' he writes, 'its immediate object is our own ignorance.'[8] An enlightened ignorance is at least more illuminating than an irremediable ignorance.

Nicholas, who represents an interesting link between the Neoplatonism of the Middle Ages and that of the Renaissance, believed that every inquiry consisted in a 'relation of comparison.' The infinite is therefore difficult to understand, because it is above and beyond all comparison.

> Solomon, the Wise, affirmed that in all things there are difficulties which beggar explanation in words; and we have it from another, who was divinely inspired, that wisdom and the locality of the understanding lie hidden from the eyes of all the living. If this is so – and even the most profound Aristotle in his First Philosophy affirms it to be true of the things most evident to us in nature – then in presence of such difficulty we may be compared to owls trying to look at the sun.[9]

Owls trying to look at the sun: in our epistemological attempts we can perceive only a distorted image of the truth, because truth is beyond our grasp.[10] This is a mystical conception of the world, although different from the idea of brotherhood and sisterhood that St Francis of Assisi had applied to his vision of nature. But the mystical thinker needs to summon to his help logic – not Aristotelian logic, but the logic of mathematics. Nicholas, by logically demonstrating how the infinite line is a straight line and at the same time a triangle, a circle, and a sphere, by analogy demonstrates that the relationship of the Maximum (God) to all things is what the infinite line is to lines: 'When we use an image and try to reach analogically what is as yet unknown, there must be no doubt at all about the image; for it is only by way of postulates and things certain that we can arrive at the unknown'.[11]

Analogically also Nicholas compares the infinite circle to unity, since the circle is a perfect figure of unity and simplicity; and since 'the triangle is a circle,' the trinity is unity.[12] He uses paradoxes to demonstrate how contradictions are reconciled in the providence of God, and how negative theology can arrive at truths more adequate than the affirmations of positive theology. According to Nicholas, we may think of God as existent or as non-existent or as both existent and non-existent or as neither existent nor non-existent; in each case, we are presupposing the maximum of truth as the subject we are clumsily trying to characterize, and that maximum of truth is God.

Nicholas seems to be at the crossroads of two traditions: even while taking up the Neoplatonic notion of an unknowable universe, he declares that we can find a system, a code to help us read the world, and this code is mathematical logic. Paradoxically, in describing the world in quantitative terms, his hermetic model contributes to the development of scientific rationalism.[13] As Cassirer remarks, the world is for Nicholas the living temple and *codex* of God, and whoever reads in this book is holy; but his attitude to nature already looks towards Leonardo, Galileo, and Kepler.[14]

Cassirer grounds his implication, but it is possible to argue that the use of mathematics for mystical purposes was not new, and that the way in which Nicholas applied mathematics in order to arrive at truth differs greatly from modern scientific rationalism. It is sufficient to stress Nicholas' insistence on the utility of analogical thinking in demonstrating the infinity of God, in order to see how far his propositions are from those, for example, of Galileo (though they are probably closer to those of Leonardo).[15]

In chapter IX of the second book of *De docta ignorantia*, entitled 'The Soul or Form of the Universe,' Nicholas affirms that 'the form as it is in matter' is 'through that operation of the mind and by means of that movement, an image of the true ideal form; it is, in consequence, not the true form but is similar to it.'[16] Form has a desire to be actualized, and therefore descends and gives shape to matter; but since it is not its own being, it has a limited existence and cannot be absolute. Images are forms immersed in matter, and so can provoke in us only conjectures and not reveal the truth about anything, but they are similar to the ideal forms. *Docta ignorantia*, through a consideration of the plurality and diversity of things, can, paradoxically, perceive 'the unique absolutely simple essence of all things.'[17] Whereas in the Middle Ages an elaborate encyclopaedic grasp of beasts, herbs, and stones seems to assign meaning to every piece of furniture in the world, in Renaissance Neoplatonism an inexhaustibly meaningful symbolic form represents the ideal ungraspable form, because, as we learn from Hermes Trismegistos, infinite Unity is 'One and All,' or, better, 'All in One.'

How does Nicholas of Cusa's thought apply to Joyce's poetics? The acceptance of the *coincidentia oppositorum* that is at the heart of Nicholas' philosophy, according to Eco, enables Joyce to overcome the influence of Aquinas. What Joyce experiences is 'the opposition between a classical conception of form and the need for a more pliable and "open" structure of the work and of the world ... Joyce departs from the *Summa* to arrive at *Finnegans Wake*, from the ordered cosmos of scholasticism to the verbal image of an expanding universe' (*The Aesthetics of Chaosmos*, pp. 2–3).

With Nicholas, paradoxical thought makes one of its first appearances in the Renaissance, since his refusal of a rational way of understanding God requires a theology of human intuition, a mystical jump, that goes beyond the cause-and-effect explanation. For this reason, Nicholas is one of those thinkers who go against Foucault's theory of *ressemblance*. In *Les mots et les choses*, Foucault argues that there is a continuity between the epistemology of the Middle Ages and that of the Renaissance. This continuity is based on a particular mode of thought, accurately explored by Foucault: *analogical thinking*. For Foucault, the idea of *ressemblance*, similarity among things, played a fundamental role in Western epistemology, and to a great extent dominated the exegesis and interpretation of texts:

> C'est elle qui a organisé le jeu des symboles, permis la connaissance des choses visibles et invisibles, guidé l'art de les représenter. Le monde s'enroulait sur lui-même: la terre répétant le ciel, les visages se mirant dans les étoiles, et l'herbe enveloppant dans ses tiges les secrets qui servaient à l'homme. La peinture imitait l'espace. Et la représentation – qu'elle fût fête ou savoir – se donnait comme répétition: théâtre de la vie ou miroir du monde, c'était le titre de tout langage, sa manière de s'annoncer et de formuler son droit à parler.[18]

The four types of *ressemblance* identified by Foucault, *convenientia, aemulatio, analogie,* and *sympathie,* reveal how the world replicates itself, doubles itself, or creates a chain so that things can resemble themselves, but they also emphasize the notion of a mysterious world, which God has created for the benefit of human beings. As Paracelsus says, what God gave to human beings is hidden, buried like a treasure; but marks have been left, exterior and visible signs, signatures that can be deciphered if one is willing to explore God's project for humanity.

Nicholas of Cusa's thought runs counter to Foucault's assumption because it reveals that, at least in Italy during the flourishing of humanism, an epistemological change took place.[19] Even though the heraldic world of bestiaries and herbals had not fully lost its appeal, the natural sciences were becoming more mathematically oriented, and an emerging belief in the instability of the world was bringing a rejection of causalism: the reciprocal action of the various elements of the universe does not follow the linear sequence of cause to effect but a spiral-like logic of mutually sympathetic elements. If the universe is a network of similitudes and cosmic sympathies, then there are no privileged causal chains.

Eco exposes this epistemological change, brought about by writers such as Nicholas, in his book on Joyce, and attributes to Joyce the same passage from a universe dominated by order and similitude to a more open world dominated by symbolism. Similarly, though not to the same degree, it is possible to see a trajectory in Eco's own thought from the rigidity of canonical structuralism to the post-structuralism of the 'open work' (*l'opera aperta*). Through the study of philosophers such as Cusa, Eco redefines the medieval notion of encyclopaedia. The idea of a disruption of privileged causal chains eliminates the clear lines of separation that represented the medieval cosmos and institutes a universe of endless re-evocation (*renvoi*) in which the logic of semiotics rules: everything stands for something else.

Eco, of course, goes farther than Nicholas, since what was confused inspiration in the fifteenth-century Italian philosopher, becomes a unified system of knowledge in Eco's semiotics as early as 1975. The *Trattato di semiotica generale*, which was rewritten in English a year later as *A Theory of Semiotics*, is a highly remarkable attempt to go beyond the epistemological positions and idealist propositions of modern philosophy from Descartes to Kant, and to suggest, with Aquinas' help, a new approach to the phenomenon of signification. Although a complete alternative is not presented in this book, Eco establishes a fruitful separation between theoretical and practical semiotics and, in relation to a theory of codes, between *units of nature* and *units of experience*.

Deely criticizes the epistemological results arrived at in this work, seeing in it a failed attempt to distance semiotics from modern idealism, which he defines as 'the thesis that everything the mind knows is precisely what the mind knows of it, owes its basic constitution to the mind.'[20] Eco, he states, falls back into idealism when he decides to reject the classical notion of sign and to focus on sign-functions,[21] a more relational concept. Because a sign-function is a purely cultural link, the concept relates Eco's theory directly to idealism. If it is true that Eco is on shaky ground, what Deely fails to acknowledge is the fact that Eco's 'signal' is always presupposed to depart from a source, and that, although we may not have true knowledge of this source, we are compelled by *stimuli* to make inferences about it. Therefore, it is not, as Deely argues, that discourse attempts a definition independent from being, but that discourse attempts a definition of being, and although an expression does not designate an object ('the possibility of lying – says Eco – is the *proprium* of semiosis'), we as subjects can *know* something about facts or, perhaps more important, can at least recognize and study the possibility of being mistaken about them.

The concepts of conjecture and fallibility will be analysed later in this study, but it is relevant to acknowledge now that Nicholas of Cusa developed a notion of 'conjecture' that reminds us closely of Eco's theory of abduction. For Nicholas as for Eco, conjecture is at the basis of human epistemology. Ludovico Geymonat writes about this notion:

> In the reality of God and in the derivation of the world from the divine being, our mind will only be able to formulate 'conjectures:' not arbitrary, though, because they are based on the deep unity between our mind and God. The term conjecture indicates a non-knowledge, but a non-knowledge that, because it addresses the authentic object of knowledge, stimulates us to 'get closer' to it continually, but, nevertheless, the object remains always unreachable in its absolute essence.[22]

Although no mysticism is implied in Eco's concept of abduction, the notion of conjecture as a way of stimulating human knowledge in the right direction is similar in both Nicholas of Cusa and Eco. We will see later how Eco not only does away with the religious and metaphysical implications, but also theorizes a far more specific and individual use of abduction.

### Into the Renaissance: Giordano Bruno (1548–1600) and the Logic of Symbols

Eco clearly expresses the passage from the medieval idea of order to the Renaissance notion of symbol in his book on Joyce, specifically in the chapter 'Epiphany: From Scholasticism to Symbolism.' Eco's thesis is that Joyce, dissatisfied with Thomistic philosophy's aesthetic explanation and influenced by British writers such as Walter Pater, finds a different solution for his own aesthetics in developing the theory of *epiphany*.

According to this theory, reality does not reveal itself through its objective structure, but an object can become the symbol of an interior state in the artist: 'This is not an example of the revelation of a thing itself in its objective essence, *quidditas*, but the revelation of what the thing means to us in that moment. It is the value bestowed on the thing at that moment which actually *makes* the thing. The epiphany confers upon the thing a value which it did not have before encountering the gaze of the artist. In this respect the doctrine of epiphany and *radiance* is clearly in opposition to the Thomist idea of *claritas*' (*The Aesthetics of Chaosmos*, p. 27).

Whereas for Aquinas *claritas* was always linked to the object, for Joyce *radiance* is an entirely subjective matter; the object epiphanized becomes a pure symbol. This idea of epiphany, according to Eco, reached Joyce through Pater's *Studies in the History of the Renaissance*, which emphasized the incoherence and instability of the world and the durability of experience. But the idea of basing an epistemological hypothesis on inner sense had already been postulated by Giordano Bruno: 'First, since there is one, there are two, three, four; second, because one is not two, two is not three, three is not four. Third, because one and two are three, because one and three are four. To do this is to do everything; to say this is to say all; to imagine, signify and shape this makes all things objects to apprehend, to understand once apprehended, remembered when understood.'[23]

Thus writes Giordano Bruno in his treaty *De imaginum, signorum et idearum compositione*, published in 1591. According to Bruno, there is more light present in this than in all the sunlight that can be provided for our outer eyes: 'Because the eye sees other things, it does not see itself.'[24] In order to achieve knowledge of the world we should first know ourselves, and be able to 'discern our species' substance so that our eye could perceive itself, our mind unfold itself.' If only we could do this, everything would be simple and directly accessible to us; but unfortunately that is not in the nature of things, and our eye must be content to look at things as accidents of ourselves. In looking at all things in themselves, we will be able to perceive ourselves as in a mirror, for our intellect 'can not see itself and all things in themselves except in an outward appearance, likeness, image, shape or sign.'[25]

For Giordano Bruno, the intellect cannot analyse itself, and in looking at its reflection in the mirror of nature we can only guess how our cognition operates. His epistemology is based on the formula *veritas filia temporis*, and on the conviction that, whatever happens, 'truth' will finally be restored. The object perceived with the senses becomes secondary to the way in which the object appears to the one perceiving it. This emphasis on the subjective experience, which necessarily involves the philosopher's life itself, is somewhat similar to Joyce's theory of epiphany in its valorization of the 'internal sense' and its casting of the external event as the symbol of an interior moment.

As Eco suggests, even though Joyce's epiphany retains a connection with the Thomistic concept of *quidditas*, for Joyce the object is not revealed because it is verifiable, but because it becomes the symbol of the artist's interiority. Bruno developed nothing close to Joyce's aesthetics, but his distinction between *sensible* and *intelligible* love could, via Pater, have influenced Joyce's theory of perception.

What Joyce derived from Pater's book on the Renaissance was not just a way of overcoming medieval aesthetics but, more important, a sense of the dissolution of the ordered medieval cosmos. Once the definitions of cosmic reality given by Nicholas and Bruno had broken down the security of the finite universe, Joyce could not but embrace a vision of a 'polydimensional reality' (*The Aesthetics of Chaosmos*, p. 73), in which form can be seen from infinite perspectives, so that each thing reflects the cosmos in a singular manner. Nicholas' *coincidentia oppositorum* and Bruno's identity of contraries reveal a totality in which everything is polarized, in which a confused plurality precedes the perception of unity.

Towards the end of *The Aesthetics of Chaosmos*, Eco also emphasizes Bruno's theorization of the infinity of possible worlds, with its tendency towards cosmic metamorphosis and a semantic destabilization of the scholastic universe: 'Just as Bruno arrived at this vision of the world as a result of the discovery of Copernicus (and saw in it the fall of a static and limited conception of the cosmos), so the young Joyce, through Bruno, discovered the way to cast the stable and circumscribed universe of scholasticism into doubt' (73–4).

For Eco, multiple different tendencies converged in Joyce's poetics, creating the novels as resolutions in language of the new cosmic structure, and forming the conflict typical of the modern artist. Eco shares with Joyce this conflict and this representation of a new cosmic structure, but what distinguishes Eco is his rejection of the idea that through epiphany the object becomes pure symbol. In his aesthetics, Eco is closer to Aquinas' *claritas* than to Joyce's *radiance*; for him, the concept maintains a link to the object, and it is from this contradiction that semiotics is able to define an alternative path.

## From Logic to Wit: Emanuele Tesauro (1592–1675) and the Power of Metaphor

Eco's study of metaphor, in both *A Theory of Semiotics* (1976) and, even more, *Semiotics and the Philosophy of Language* (1984), gives him another powerful epistemological tool, since rhetorical figures, if used creatively, can change the way we approach the notion of content. This change is possible in that content is based not on a suspected similarity with the thing itself, but on a 'similarity' between semantic markers – what Eco calls a *semic identity*.[26] The idea further gives strength to the notion of semiosis and to 'the existence of a semantic global universe whose format is that of the Model Q.'

Eco's interest in metaphor as an instrument of cognition is what attracts his attention to a lengthy study of metaphor conducted in the seventeenth century by the Jesuit scholar Emanuele Tesauro.

Tesauro, an intellectual of aristocratic origins and the historical original of the Father Emanuele of *The Island of the Day Before*, chose to include the name of a new scientific instrument in the title of his book on rhetoric, *Il cannocchiale aristotelico* (The Aristotelian Telescope, 1653). The title is clearly paradoxical in its association of the ancient Greek philosopher with the new astronomical instrument.

Tesauro's purpose in writing a treatise on rhetoric was not simply to theorize the art of rhetorical speaking or writing, but also to show that the only possible way of producing the perfect text, which for him is a text that is 'arguto' (witty), is through the interpretations made feasible by the 'cannocchiale Aristotelico.' By looking through this instrument of knowledge, Aristotle's treatise on rhetoric, the ingenious human mind will be able to recognize 'wit' as the life principle of the whole cosmos, and will use it and learn from it in order to add its own witticisms to the whole made up by divine knowledge.

According to Tesauro, there are two ways of speaking: 'All the strength of every signifying Word ... consists in representing to the human mind the thing signified. But this representation can be produced, either with the naked and proper Word, which does not require any work from the ingenious mind: or with an ingenious signification, which both represents and delights. Whence two general differences in Oration are born: the first Proper and Grammatical: the second Rhetorical and Witty.'[27]

It is possible for humans to speak with *naked* and *proper* words, that is to say, with words that, in a particular language, already speak for things;[28] in such a case the ingenious mind does not need to struggle. But it is also possible to represent things through unusual words[29] or formulae; in this case, speech requires the employment of human 'ingegno.' In a sense, we abandon trite and ordinary means of expression in order to reach the elaborate utterance that adds something new to language.

Acute minds can produce new witticisms, which Tesauro calls the 'argutie humane'; these, he says, constitute the most admirable way of reasoning. Human witticisms are produced by metaphorical thinking, metaphor being 'the Great Mother of all Witticisms.' The true and non-

ordinary definition of metaphor is 'ROAMING WORD, QUICKLY SIG-
NIFYING AN OBJECT BY MEANS OF AN OTHER.'[30] But Tesauro does
not limit his idea of metaphor to a natural approach among things; for
the approach to be poetically successful, a *penetration* of the things
themselves is necessary. Different from the simile, which presents objects in successive order[31] (as Jakobson would say, *diachronically*), metaphor condenses the *obietti* in one word: 'Metaphor condenses them all
tightly in one Word: and almost in a miraculous way it allows you to
catch a glimpse of them one within the other. Whence greater is your
delight: in the same way as it is a more curious and pleasant thing to
admire many objects from a hidden perspective, than it would be if the
originals themselves were to pass successively before your eyes. Work
(as our Author says) not of a stupid, but of an ingenious mind.'[32]

The ingenious mind operates be means of metaphorical thinking,
metaphor being a creative and not a mimetic association. Metaphorical
thinking produces new truths. This concept interests Eco, as he re-
proaches contemporary theoreticians for having neglected the semiotic
importance of metaphor, which often escapes the linguistic realm to
appeal to visual, auditory, tactile, and olfactory experiences. For Eco,
metaphor is not simply a linguistic game, but a cognitive mechanism
that does not substitute for but increases knowledge (a concept that
Aristotle, and with him Tesauro, well understood). Even though
Tesauro's work is built out of a systematic research of analogies and
similarities in the same way as is the scholastic method, at the basis of
his reasoning lies the idea of a disproportion rather than the idea of a
harmonic order. In fact, the world is decomposed in a series of witty
metaphors capriciously arranged, which can be shifted and permutated
at will, in an imaginative game that is guided by wit. There is in *Il
cannocchiale aristotelico* a Rabelaisian and grotesque taste for a linguistic
fertility able to combine the most antithetical meanings.

We can say, therefore, that analogical fervour is dictated primarily by
the consciousness of opposition, and that universal sympathy is first of
all universal antipathy. Tesauro's search for a code, like that of his
contemporaries and his predecessors, is the search for a mediation, and
language becomes the link that connects different *things*. For this reason, metaphor for Tesauro is the primary means of knowing and signifying reality. As Mario Zanardi says, 'Metaphor, therefore, even before
being a modality (figure) or a disposition of the word and of the discourse to "say" one thing and to "signify" another one, is the realization
of the mobility and of the potential disposition of each being to be-

come an "other," even if it were only in the free play of an associative and commutative intelligence.'[33]

Metaphor shows a notion within a different notion (as, for example, when Aristotle says 'stubble' instead of 'old age'). In metaphor, remote ideas are linked together, so that the acute *ingegnum* becomes a sort of creator; but, as Zanardi recognizes, at the same time the baroque metaphor does not infuse mutability with reality, because what is dynamic is the imaginative force of the mind, wit, a movement of spiritual capabilities,[34] and not a metamorphosis of the real.

As he indicates in *Semiotica e filosofia del linguaggio*, Eco is interested in Tesauro because he sees in his book a disordered structuralist attempt at creating a system of contents organized encyclopaedically (169), where relations are established analogically, but the analogy is constituted by the contiguity of the *categorical index.*

One could object that what is striking in Tesauro's idea, clearly insisted upon in the title of the book, is the fact that it is not possible to rely on observation to get glimpses of the truth. The truth is not in the scientific knowledge promoted by Galileo's observation through the telescope; real knowledge is in words and signs, and the real telescope cannot but be the Aristotelian one. Only by interpreting Aristotle can the learned person find the categories according to which sophisticated images of the existent world can be built. By a rigorous reading of the inscripted reality, the wise person can organize and generate the reality of his or her speaking. Wit (*argutezza*) assumes an absolute value; it is interpretation of God and of the world, a cosmic language. Angels, nature, and God, when they reason with humans, express with verbal or symbolic witticisms their most abstruse and important secrets.[35] *Argutezza* becomes a principle of life and of universal communication.

Even though Eco seems conscious of the Neoplatonic influence in the metaphysics of Tesauro's theory, he appears to diminish the importance of the ontological relations that sustain Tesauro's structure (169),[36] because what interests him is the possibility entailed by Tesauro's *categorical index* of passing from one term to the other *ad infinitum.* He sees in it the model of unlimited semiosis, 'a hierarchical system ... of semi, a net of interpretants' (170). Tesauro's *categorical index* constitutes for him a real 'content system organized encyclopaedically' (169).

Tesauro is therefore another essential figure testifying how Eco's theory relies on earlier philosophy to search for the foundations of semiotics. I am not suggesting that theoreticians like Tesauro influenced the constitution of Eco's theory of interpretation, but that Eco found in writers like Tesauro historical precedents who adopted an open, encyclopaedic view of the universe.

As this study makes clear, not only do both the idea of openness and the ceaseless search for a code, which are characteristic of Eco's thought, play a part in the way he interprets these early writers and studies their effect on Joyce, but their interrelation also makes possible the original direction of Eco's theory of semiotics.

## The Evolution of Eco's Thought

Eco's study of Joyce is therefore extremely relevant, as it represents some of Eco's first reflections on literature and art.[37] Joyce's work will become a constant point of reference as an example of transition from a model of rational order, clearly represented by medieval scholasticism, to a sense of the chaos of the modern and postmodern experience, a transition experienced by Eco himself. Furthermore, here Eco touches the problem of the relation between words and objects. Although he knows that one can no longer have confidence in the Thomistic *quidditas*, in the abstract idea of reality that was typical of scholasticism, he is conscious that the semiotic enterprise is closer to the medieval attempt at finding a code than to the Renaissance philosophy of language. On the one hand, he acknowledges the metaphysical implications of a theory of signs, but on the other he chooses to focus on the code and on methods of interpretation.

Sometimes Eco perceives the rigidity of early medieval order, with its dictionary-type definitions, as a tool that is limited and limiting in any explaining of the contemporary communication system. Therefore, beginning with his criticism of the notion of structure proposed by structuralist philosophers, he introduces the idea of an 'open' structure, which takes advantage of the encyclopaedic model. The Renaissance idea of interpretation, with its freedom of association, is somehow closer to Eco's notion of semiosis than is the biunivocal correspondence of the Porphyrian tree, but at the same time semiosis is very far from the 'randomness' of Renaissance symbolism.

What I am trying to suggest is that medieval and early modern paradigms were important for Eco's ground-breaking theory, first expounded in *Opera aperta*, because they created the necessary tension that would allow him to argue the possibility of a textual interpretation that can be infinite but at the same time limited; he writes in *The Limits of Interpretation*, 'Thus many modern theories are unable to recognize that symbols are paradigmatically open to infinite meanings but syntagmatically, that is, textually, open only to the indefinite, but by no means infinite, interpretations allowed by the context' (21).

Eco is then able to go back and forth between the hermeneutic nature of the Renaissance paradigm and the more allegorical character of medieval theory. This balance reflects the idea that 'any act of interpretation is a dialectic between openness and form' (21).

In assimilating Renaissance hermeneutics to 'many contemporary theories' (20) – since both understand symbols as having any possible meaning owing to the contradictoriness of reality – Eco can appeal to the medieval search for a code in order to limit the emotivism of a more Romantic tendency. As he writes in *The Aesthetics of Thomas Aquinas*, 'Another positive factor is that contemporary thought, which has spent too long in discussions of the creativity of the human spirit, now feels the need to discuss the question of a fixed order of the psyche' (218).

Eco suggests that Aquinas' interest in the notion of form can serve to highlight problems in contemporary theories of interpretation. In *The Aesthetics*, he compares scholastic methodology to structuralism, not to suggest an ideological relation but to show similarities between them, such as the interest in the formal structure of the object to be investigated, the claim to interdisciplinarity, and the tendency to devise a theoretical model of the object (always with the risk of believing in the universality and ontological importance of these structures).

The study of scholasticism, says Eco, can highlight the dangers into which structuralism could run, but it can also provide 'examples of mental discipline in the solution of philosophical problems' (218).

For the same reasons, Eco also re-evaluates the importance of scholastic aesthetics, which stresses a cognitive approach to art.

> I can therefore suggest a number of reasons why the model provided by scholastic aesthetics is worth revisiting today. It offers us ways of explaining art in terms of intellect, as opposed to the emotivism of Romantic aesthetics. It offers us a more flexible conception of the relation between inventiveness in production and the rules of production, also the relation between materials and formal imperatives, and between the autonomy of aesthetic value and functional requirements. Scholastic aesthetics reminds us that art is connected with craft, and that there is an aesthetic aspect in production of every kind. It reminds us that aesthetic emotion depends upon complex operations of the intellect and involves systems of values, of ideologies, and thus of known cultural codes. (216)

Eco emphasizes the lesson from the past in the last chapter of his book on Aquinas, and he concludes with Bernard of Chartres' reflection that we are dwarfs on the shoulders of giants, thereby stressing the importance of humility in our looking back to the past.

What Eco learned from his study of medieval and Renaissance theories laid the foundation for his theory of modernity and postmodernity, as an analysis of his critical writings reveals.

# 3 Semiotics as a Solution: From a Theory of Aesthetics to the Study of Culture

## Pareyson and Aesthetic Theory

One of the most influential figures at the University of Turin during Eco's years as a student was Luigi Pareyson, an energetic professor of philosophy who had proposed the first comprehensive study of aesthetics after Benedetto Croce. Although I do not aim at an intellectual biography of Umberto Eco here, this episode in his life is fundamental, because it was Pareyson who aroused his interest in medieval aesthetics and who provoked his first reflections on the concept of 'form,' reflections that would occupy him intermittently in the years to come.

Pareyson's theory offered a way of overcoming Croce's late Romantic aesthetics, according to which art is the lyrical intuition of feeling and therefore neither moral nor cognitive. In a very Hegelian sense, any work of art was for Croce a creation of the absolute spirit and had little to do with matter. For that reason, the interpretation of a work of art was a re-creation: since its physicality was unimportant, its interpreters, simply, were absorbed by the spirit of the work and in it lost every sense of self.

To the idealistic Crocean theories, which had kept Italy at a distance from the new aesthetic research in other countries – from Bergson's to Dewey's – Pareyson opposed the idea of art as *form*, as organism in which the physicality and materiality of the object is reinforced. Matter is important, said Pareyson, because the material used by the artist offers a certain resistance, which manifests itself as obstacles and stimuli. The materials used as instruments are not only the marble or the wood employed by the sculptor, but also the rhetorical traditions employed by the poet. As Valery had pointed out, poetry is born in a struggle with the rules of metrics and of traditional language.

Furthermore, said Pareyson, art is not the product of an absolute spirit but a 'personal creation.' A person, having engaged in appropriate research and applied its results, creates the work in a dialogue with the material. The person becomes part of the form of the work of art as style, a particular way of forming. This was not mere formalism, because in Pareyson's view form is an organism endowed with an intelligent movement towards an aesthetic accomplishment ('forma formante').

A contradiction seems implicit: if the organic growth of the object follows nature's intentionality, the role of the artist appears marginal. But Pareyson solves the problem by postulating a dialogue between the artist and the organic form: human intentionality interferes with and enhances nature's formativity.

Pareyson's revolutionary concept of organic form, which the artist struggles to bring out of matter, brought renown to his aesthetics, and became known as the theory of formativity. Eco reviewed Pareyson's *Estetica* in *Lettere italiane* (July 1955), and his review later became an essay, included in *La definizione dell'arte* (1968), entitled 'L'estetica della formatività e il concetto di interpretazione' ('The Aesthetics of Formativity and the Concept of Interpretation').[1] After summarizing Pareyson's theory of formativity, Eco deals with two aspects of the philosopher's theory that he considers important for the evolution of aesthetics: the implicit doctrine of knowledge and the theory of interpretation that follows.

The metaphysics of figuration, writes Eco, implies a Figurator who created natural forms in a way that is not random but full of intention. Pareyson's metaphysical answer to the question of the foundation of knowledge does not satisfy the young Eco, who, thirty years later, would admit his own debt to Pareyson's ideas, but would specify that his version of Pareyson's aesthetics had been 'secularized.' In the early essay, Eco insists that it is possible to define the relation between the human being and the world through methodological hypotheses, by looking for its foundation in an interactive relation, 'the definition of which is nothing but the consecutive series of the partial, operative, hypothetical definitions that are attempted time after time' (*La definizione dell'arte*, p. 22). Modern aesthetics, according to Eco, cannot start from a priori definitions, but seeks to achieve a comprehensive phenomenology that takes into account aesthetic experience.

It is worth spending time on Eco's critique of Pareyson's theory because the theory very much influenced Eco's theory of interpretation, which, as we will see in chapter 4, is founded in the tension between a rigorous notion of form and the more flexible criterion of an unlimited network. Eco was able to work out a subtle connection between Pareyson's and Aquinas' theories of form.

In fact, it was Pareyson's contribution to the notion of interpretation that interested the young Eco. In Croce's philosophy, the interpreter disappeared, absorbed by the spirit of the work of art; for Pareyson, the interpreter was active, and his or her facing and discussion of the work manifested his or her own personality. Because the form is not 'closed' and defined but offers the possibility of infinite new perspectives ('una definitezza che racchiude un'infinità'),[2] the interpreter dynamically relives the process of formation and then reveals the work together with his or her own self. The interpreting personalities are infinite in number, so infinite in number will also be the possible interpretations. We see here in a nutshell the issues Eco will discuss later in *Opera aperta*. It was important for the young Eco to identify the possibility, in Pareyson's aesthetics, of justifying any critical approach; and to that possibility he adds the idea that, despite the infinite number of possible interpretations, the work of art remains, and its analysis must take its formal structures into consideration.

Under the influence of Pareyson's work, Eco decided to write his thesis on the aesthetics of Thomas Aquinas, and the work dramatically reveals that influence. In the first chapter, 'Aesthetics in Medieval Culture,' Eco returns to the traditional aesthetic theories of Baumgarten and Croce. It is clear to him that, if aesthetics is, as Baumgarten describes it, 'scientia cognitionis sensitivae, theoria liberalium artium, gnoseologia inferior, ars pulcre cogitandi, ars analogi rationis' (the science of sensitive knowledge, the theory of liberal arts, the epistemology of lower level things, the art of thinking aesthetically, the art of reasoning by analogy), then the medieval thinkers had no aesthetic theory. Nor did they have any kind of Crocean aesthetics, intended as a philosophical discussion of the 'lyrical intuition of feeling.' What they did have was 'a whole range of issues connected with beauty – its definition, its function, the ways of creating it and of enjoying it' (*The Aesthetics of Thomas Aquinas*, p. 2). Aquinas himself did not formulate a comprehensive aesthetic theory, but he treated beauty in connection with the good in many of his writings.

In the medieval treatises, the good and the beautiful are considered as one. The first to distinguish between them was John de La Rochelle, who concluded that 'beauty is the good when it pleases the apprehension, but good itself is what gives pleasure to the affections' (quoted

p. 43). One of Eco's most interesting contributions is the realization that beauty, for Augustine, for John de La Rochelle, and for Aquinas, is connected with *species* and thence with 'form.' Beauty, then, has to do with formal causes and ontological perfection.

What we testify to here is Eco's attempt to formulate a medieval theory of aesthetics in consonance with Pareyson's and its emphasis on form. Furthermore, the apprehension of beauty is defined as 'a kind of seeing or looking which is mediated by the senses but is of an intellectually cognitive order' (43). Accordingly, the theory of knowledge that emerges in connection with the objective conditions of beauty unsurprisingly emphasizes the concept of form dear to Pareyson. Often Aquinas uses the term form as meaning 'essence' or 'substance.'

> But what is it meant by 'substance'? The word signifies being (ens) thought of as something wholly complete, something endowed with a structure which can be analyzed, and which is an ontological unity. It means the existing *organism* in itself [emphasis added]. It is not something hidden beneath the structures, features, and properties of things; rather, it is the being itself of the structures, features, and properties, for these are simply modes of the being of substance. 'Substance' means the focal point of the organization, the selection, and the life of substance's own multiple aspects. It means the structural constitution of a concrete thing. (69)

In this way, Eco connects Aquinas' idea of form directly with Pareyson's idea of a growing organism endowed with structural properties. Beings are concrete realities and not simply manifestations of divine creativity. The ideas of proportion and harmony, which came to the medieval thinkers from antiquity through writers such as Boethius (*De institutione musica*), contribute to Aquinas' discussion of the beautiful. In the *Summa contra gentiles*, Aquinas states clearly that an agent requires matter in order to actualize his or her potential; matter is already full of potentiality, therefore, when the agent possesses a matter proportioned to his or her action. In a progressive movement, matters offers itself to form.

This idea of form as *act* and of the disposition of matter to receive form reminds us closely of the dialectic of artist and form ('forma formante') discussed by Pareyson. The necessary postulation of a Figurator in Aquinas' theory would again match with the metaphysical answer to the same question given by the Italian philosopher. But there is one difference in Aquinas: divine creations are beautiful, because the formal structure of a natural object is so complex that we can know it only with great difficulty; for that reason, human productions can be beautiful 'only in a superficial sense' (203).

Barely touched on in *The Aesthetics of Thomas Aquinas* is the question of interpretation, which will be the most important issue embraced by Eco in his subsequent works. The discussion of interpretation is limited to a short chapter on aesthetic judgment, in which Eco writes: 'Judgment involves joining and separating, and the marking out of properties, accidents, and contexts. It is only by way of this kind of knowledge that I can measure accidental against substantial *form*, substantial *form* against its matter, the object against its function, and so on' (197).

Eco attributes to Aquinas criteria of aesthetic judgment that he will later consider valid criteria for interpretation. The idea of separating and marking out the structural properties of the object makes for a contrast with Croce's theory of lyrical intuition of feeling, and promotes an aesthetics of interpretation based, like Pareyson's, on a patient, laborious research aimed at rehearsing the process of creation. That is why reading Aquinas can, according to Eco, suggest 'methods of analysis which can be adopted today' (216).

Later, Eco encountered structuralist theories, and in 1970 he added a conclusion to his work on Aquinas, in which he tried to draw parallels between scholasticism and structuralism. He realized that 'every system has a contradiction within itself' (xi) and that both movements ran into similar problems, as they both boasted a universal logic and claimed to be universal interdisciplinary discourses.

Eco's work on interpretation went in a different direction, the direction of the 'open work.' Already in 1959, in an essay entitled 'Note sui limiti dell'estetica' (Notes on the Limits of Aesthetic Theory, now in *La definizione dell'arte*), Eco had discussed how a 'scientific' study of a work of art cannot be sufficient to explain the multiple meanings of the object. There is 'something more,' which can be explained only in terms of the 'apertura' (opening) or 'ambiguity' of the work – 'meaning with this that the work of art constitutes a communicative fact that asks to be interpreted, and therefore integrated, completed by the intervention of the interpreter. This intervention varies according to individuals and historical situations, and is continually measured with reference to the unchanging parameter of the work as physical object'[3] (*La definizione dell'arte*, p. 48).

In the following passage, which contains the essence of Eco's subsequent discussions of interpretation and the role of the reader (see chapter 4), Pareyson gives the essence of his concepts of 'definitività' and 'apertura': 'There are in fact those who assert that the work of art is substantially incomplete, and that it therefore offers itself to the reader claiming his/her participation in the creative act of the author and his/her own amplification with the most diverse and original complements. And those who so believe do justice to the artist's intention, who often prefers the unfinished to the finished, sometimes in order to evoke, thanks to the indeterminacy of the incomplete, a mysterious ambiguity of meaning.'[4]

According to Eco, one can arrive at a degree of objective guarantee in the observation of the work of art when one is able to make its own desire, opinions, and tastes instruments for a verification of their relation to the formal structures that have generated them. From Kant on, aesthetics has tried to define the formal conditions for aesthetic judgment, but for Eco 'the maximum *scientificity* of aesthetics is not reached by establishing scientific rules of taste, but by defining the *non-scientificity* of the experience of taste and the margin that should be left to the personal factor'[5] (*La definizione dell'arte*, p. 61).

With these words, Eco set out on the path he would take towards his controversial *Opera aperta*, but his interest in aesthetic questions and theories of interpretation that could lead to a more objective study of works of art attracted him to the writings of Jakobson and the Russian formalists, and to what at the time was known as semiology (the writings of Barthes, Benveniste, Greimas, Lévi-Strauss, and Chomsky). His experiences culminated in three major works, *La struttura assente* (1968), *Le forme del contenuto* (1971), and *Il segno* (1973).

## From Semiology to Semiotics

Some characteristics of Eco's semiotics were discussed in chapter 2, where we noted the similarities between Eco's theory of communication and Aquinas' theory of knowledge. Aquinas was not of course the only influence on the young Eco. The numerous writings on semiology that appeared in the 1960s and 1970s could not but strike Eco as being tightly connected to his effort to elaborate a theory of communication that could serve as a model for analysing the complex instances of interaction in our culture.

When he was asked to contribute to a series of studies illustrating philosophical terms for the publishing company ISEDI, Eco wrote a small treatise on the concept of sign, *Il segno* (1973), in which he admirably assembled the findings of numerous studies on the subject, starting with Hjelmslev, Jakobson, Kristeva, Chomsky, Greimas, and Lévi-

Strauss and going back to Hobbes, Locke, Leibniz, and Peirce.

It is not my purpose to delve into Eco's intelligent compilation; one can consult the clear account given by Michael Caesar in *Umberto Eco: Philosophy, Semiotics, and the Work of Fiction* (1999). Much more useful here is discussing the identifiable links between Eco's theory of signs, from *La struttura assente* (1968) through *A Theory of Semiotics* (1976) to *Kant and the Platypus* (2000), and medieval semiotics from Aquinas to William of Ockham, and verifying their utility in terms of contemporary criticism.

The first debate Eco must acknowledge concerns the treatment of the three levels of a linguistic sign:

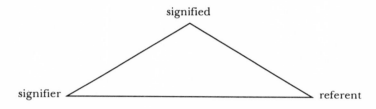

signified

signifier                                                                    referent

Aristotle had identified a tripartition of this minimal unity: *onoma* (written mark), *rema* (spoken sound), and *logos* (affection of the soul). In *Il segno*, Eco rewrites the triangle in terms of modern classifications (26):

> interpretant (Peirce)
> reference (Ogden-Richards)
> meaning (Frege)
> intension (Carnap)
> designatum (Morris, 1938)
> significatum (Morris, 1946)
> concept (Saussure)
> connotation, connotatum (Stuart Mill)
> mental image (Saussure, Peirce)
> content (Hjelmslev)
> state of conscience (Buyssens)

sign (Peirce)
symbol (Ogden-Richards)                                object (Frege, Peirce)
sign vehicle (Morris)                                         denotatum (Morris)
expression (Hjelmslev)                                      signified (Frege)
representamen (Peirce)                                     denotation (Russell)
seme (Buyssens)                                                 extension (Carnap)

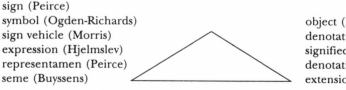

He recognized the persistence of the problem for the grammarians and linguists of antiquity, from Aristotle to the Stoics, and for medieval scholars. The central question was, 'Do words signify things directly or do they firstly signify concepts and only reach the level of *res* through the intermediary link of concepts?'[6] The answer for thinkers such as Boethius related to the second solution, and this view prevailed in medieval logic through the time of Thomas Aquinas. But the Oxford philosophers Roger Bacon and Duns Scotus argued in favour of the first solution.

In Aquinas' view, the linguistic sign produces a concept in both the mind of the speaker and the mind of the listener. Aquinas went so far as to say that a concept is not a linguistic sign unless the speaker has the will to manifest it to others. For other philosophers, things were signs and the universe a symbolic system through which God speaks to us. In *Il segno*, Eco quotes Alain de Lille (95), who in the twelfth century wrote:

Omnis mundi creatura
Quasi liber et pictura
Nobis est in speculum.
Nostrae vitae, nostrae mortis,
Nostri status, nostrae sortis,
Fidele signaculum.

Every creature in the universe
is reflected to us
as a book and an image.
Faithful sign
of our life, of our death,
of our condition, of our destiny. (my translation)

Eco compares this medieval view of the world as God's way of communicating to us with a tradition of aesthetics that from the Romantics to Heidegger was strictly associated with the philosophy of language. Although secularized, Baudelaire's view of nature as a symbolic forest is not dissimilar to Alain de Lille's. For Heidegger, the path is the same: 'It is not humans who create language to dominate things, but things, nature, or Being manifest themselves through language; language is the voice of Being; Truth is nothing but the unveiling of Being through language' (*Il segno*, p. 97). If we accept this, says Eco, there is no semiotics, but only hermeneutics.

With the help of Peirce, Eco is able to avoid this hermeneutic impasse by reshaping the triadic structure of the sign. He leaves at the base of the triangle the *representamen* and the *object*, but he gives the position of the *signified* or *reference* to the *interpretant*. This has important consequences for the whole of Eco's semiotics and theory of interpretation.

The concept of the *interpretant* still alludes to the earlier concept of the *signified*, because it is what the sign represents in the interpreter, what the sign signifies for the interpreter; but it has a different ontological status. This is because the *interpretant* is not a mode of expression of the object, but is in itself a sign, one of those signs that clarify another sign.[7] As Eco explains in *A Theory of Semiotics*:

> The most fruitful hypothesis would seem to be that of conceiving the *interpretant as another representation which is referred to the same 'object.'* In other words, in order to establish what the interpreter of a sign is, it is necessary to name it by means of another sign which in turn has another interpretant to be named by another sign and so on. At this point there begins a process of *unlimited semiosis*, which, paradoxical as it may be, is the only guarantee for the foundation of a semiotic system capable of checking itself entirely by its own means. Language would then be an auto-clarificatory system, or rather one which is clarified by successive systems of conventions that explain each other. (68–9)

The *signifier* is therefore replaced with a process of cultural substitution, a series of synonyms and paraphrases that can substitute for the sign. Consequently, signs are cultural units, and 'every attempt to establish what the referent of a sign is forces us to define the referent in terms of an abstract entity which moreover is only a cultural convention' (66)

This idea liberates semiotics from the metaphysics of the referent and makes of it a science of cultural phenomena, because communication is shown as a system of continuous permutations, and the sign as cultural unit is posed as its object. Similar is the position of the German philosopher Wittgenstein, whose writings on language much inspired Eco, for example this passage in *Philosophischen Untersuchungen*: 'The meaning of a word is what explains the explanation of meaning. That is: if you want to understand the use of the word "meaning," consider what is named "explanation of the meaning."' Wittgenstein's argument here is also anti-ontological: there is no meaning in an ontological sense, but only points of reference through which we can get to the meaning.[8] Meaning is not an entity existing between the word and the object, but the continuous substitution of signs.

Although this explanation seems to lead to a circularity without hope, it defines the normal functioning of communication, and for that reason needs to be studied and analysed. Attempts to schematize the laws of communication go back to the Middle Ages: the Porphyrian tree, for example, took into consideration the five 'predicabili' (gender, mode, difference, property, and accident), but this model was criticized by Boethius and Abelard for being constructed on difference. For Eco a bi-dimensional tree cannot represent the complex semantics of a culture. He takes, for example, the model created by Katz and Fodor:

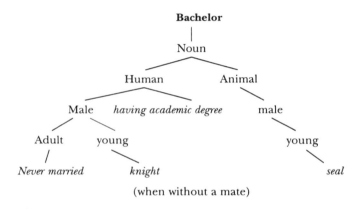

(when without a mate)

This model cannot reflect a process of unlimited semiosis, and it needs to be made more complex. Eco arrives at the so-called Model Q, which he takes from the American linguist M. Ross Quillian.[9] An application of that model results in the diagram reproduced as figure 2.

This brings us to the concept of 'encyclopaedia,' according to which multiple connections are possible, but in which, in a singular situation, certain properties of the sign are narcotized while others are emphasized. Paraphrasing Eco's words, a natural language is a system of signification that was thought up for the production of texts, and texts serve to emphasize or narcotize parts of the encyclopaedic information.

Patrizia Violi has made an intelligent study of Eco's model of encyclopaedia in her essay 'Individual and Communal Encyclopedias.'[10] According to Violi, this concept occupies a pivotal role in Eco's semiotic

PLANT: 1. Living structure which is not animal, frequently with leaves, getting its food
from air, water, earth.
2. Apparatus used for any process in industry.
3. Put (seed, plant, etc.) in earth for growth.

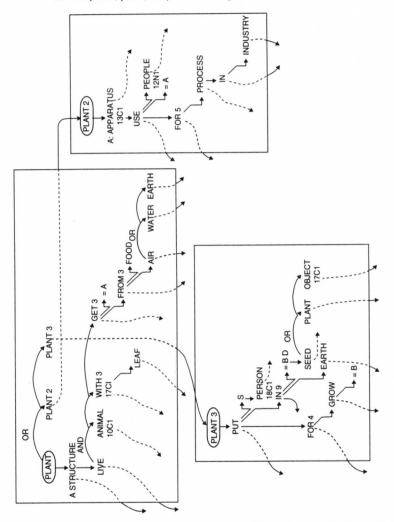

Figure 2. 'Model Q,' in *A Theory of Semiotics* (Bloomington: Indiana University Press, 1979), p. 123. From Marvin Minsky, ed., *Semantic Information Processing* (Cambridge: MIT Press, 1968). Reproduced by permission.

reflection, because on the one hand it makes possible a departure from the semiotic model that depends on the code and so moves towards 'a more dynamic and open vision of semiotics as an inferential process'[11] and on the other hand it opens up a static vision of interpretation towards the more dynamic concept of abduction.

Violi sees in Eco's theory a problematic notion of subjectivity, since the individual assumes an apparently passive role. This role results from the subject's coming to be 'constructed and defined by and within cultural semiosis':[12] the implication is that individual experiences are inscribed in the complexity of the inventories making up the common encyclopaedia. The subject does not create ex nihilo, but restructures and reinterprets what is already present in the encyclopaedic universe.

Violi identifies four types of encyclopaedias: the global encyclopaedia, the encyclopaedia as situated knowledge, the encyclopaedic competence, and the semantic competence. She is conscious that this division may appear problematic, but she suggests that her perspective is compatible with Eco's approach. In fact, what her discussion achieves is an interesting positioning of the subject in terms of the distinction between the empirical and the abstract subject, which is central in Eco's theory, particularly in connection with the role of the reader and the concept of interpretation.

It could be argued that Eco in part has already solved the dilemma of global versus local encyclopaedia through the concept of narcotization explained above. Nevertheless, Violi's study once again brings to light the grey area, the mysterious zone that exists in Eco's theory between the individual and the global encyclopaedia. If this area is not critically discussed in Eco's scholarly texts, it appears more indefinitely in his novels.

These, in essence, are the innovative ideas expressed by Eco in *A Theory of Semiotics*. In order to arrive at these conclusions, he looked back to the American semiotician C.S. Peirce and to the German philosopher Wittgenstein, but he was able to bring his findings farther thanks to his profound knowledge of medieval logic, in which the debate between semiotics and hermeneutics had already taken place.

The Middle Ages was a time of pan-semiotics like Eco's, in which everything was understood as sign. The well-known metaphor of the world as 'God's book' was used over and over again by medieval authors such as Pseudo-Dionysius, John Scotus Eriugena, Alain de Lille, and Thomas Aquinas. The conclusion of *The Name of the Rose* is that there are only signs and that the study of signs is the only way in which humans can try to understand the directions of the world. Since most medieval authors believed in the divine foundation of signs, William is definitely *ante litteram* when he exclaims:

> I have never doubted the truth of signs, Adso; they are the only things man has with which to orient himself in the world. What I did not understand was the relation among signs. I arrived at Jorge through an apocalyptic pattern that seemed to underlie all the crimes, and yet it was accidental. I arrived at Jorge seeking one criminal for all the crimes and we discovered that each crime was committed by a different person, or by no one. I arrived at Jorge pursuing the plan of a perverse and rational mind, and there was no plan, or, rather, Jorge himself was overcome by his own initial design and there began a sequence of causes, and concauses, and of causes contradicting one another, which proceeded on their own, creating relations that did not stem from any plan. Where is all my wisdom, then? I behaved stubbornly, pursuing a semblance of order, when I should have known well that there is no order in the universe. (*The Name of the Rose*, p. 492)

William's reflection goes beyond the medieval sense of universal order and represents well the mixture of medieval and contemporary philosophy that constitutes the postmodernism of *The Name of the Rose*. In fact, William quotes the famous Wittgensteinian image of the ladder immediately afterwards ('Er muoz gelîchesame die Leiter abewerfen, sô Er an ir ufgestigen ist').

Eco would return later to the ontological question of the sign, in one of his most recent books, *Kant and the Platypus*, and I will deal with it in the final chapter of this study. For now, what I would like to address is how the ideas of unlimited semiosis and of encyclopaedia can be retraced all the way to William of Ockham, not by chance the historical figure who inspired the character of William of Baskerville. Ockham, like Eco and Wittgenstein, believed that signs do not lead to the knowledge of *something*. In order to explain the knowledge process, by applying the famous concept of the razor he denied the existence of entities that cannot be experienced directly. This in contrast to Roger Bacon, who held that a concept was caused as *species impressa* by the object and therefore was an *image* of the object obtained by abstraction.[13] For Ockham, intuitive knowledge does not require the presence of the object; in fact, sometimes the object does not even exist, as in the case of the unicorn. For Bacon, on the contrary, it is the object that generates a 'species' (form, image, or simulacrum), which travels in every direction, and when it reaches the eyes it imprints itself and continues to travel along the optic nerves to the internal sense. Ockham does away with the *species*, since it is not on the basis of iconism that the intellect can develop a cognitive sign.

This critique of iconism is mirrored in Eco. When Eco was writing *A Theory of Semiotics*, of course, nobody believed in *species* travelling through the air and along the optical nerves, but what Eco does is challenge some naive notions regarding the iconic sign, such as those according to which the iconic sign has the same properties as the object, or is similar or analogous to the object, and is motivated by the object. He sees iconicity as a spiritual faculty that comprehends the forms of concepts. Iconic signs 'rely on the "same" perceptual "structure," or on the same system of relations' (*A Theory of Semiotics*, p. 193) of the objects, but they put together, on the basis of previous learning, a collection of phenomena or perceptual results. This, in fact, is William's chief problem, emphasized in the passage just quoted: the relation between signs, the ability of the human mind to connect them in meaningful ways.

Eco, then, constructs his semantics using the basic terms of scholastic philosophy, but with many correlations to the works of structuralist and post-structuralist thinkers – here once again is the tension that predominates in his way of theorizing. Although this oscillating balance has attracted some criticism, I argue that Eco has made of it a positive and innovative quality that has given energy and conciliatory power to his thought. By going back to Ockham and Aquinas, Eco is able to climb onto the backs of those giants and look farther than they. He can thereby offer a solution to the structuralist/semiotic debate concerning meaning and sign signification and give it an original spin.

Therein lies the innovation proposed in *A Theory of Semiotics*, which has been criticized as an obscure book. Its important concept of encyclopaedia has given force to Eco's theory of interpretation (see *Lector in fabula, Interpretation and Overinterpretation*, and *The Limits of Interpretation*). It has also rendered possible a whole new branch of semiotics: freeing it from the metaphysical, it has made of it the science of cultural phenomena.

**The Study of Mass Culture**

The theory of mass media was developed by Eco over many years, from the time before he came into contact with structuralist theories and consequently before he arrived at the formulation of his semiotic theory. The first stimulus for his interest in the world of new media was his experience at RAI (the Italian state-owned national television) as a young intellectual, right after his *laurea* from the University of Turin. Together with a small number of young graduates, including Folco Portinari, Furio Colombo, and Gianni Vattimo, Eco was hired to collaborate in cultural, political, and entertainment programs. Eco said of his internship, 'I did little, but I learned a lot.'[14] He attended the classes of a great journalist, Pier Emilio Gennarini, and Giuseppe Bozzini was teaching how to transmit live programs with spontaneity. Such experiences excited Eco's taste for analysis, and it was in these years (1961) that he published, among others, the essay 'The Phenomenology of Mike Bongiorno' in the *Pirelli* magazine (now in *Diario minimo*); it was the first analysis in Italy of a television character by a philosopher.

In *Il Verri*, Eco published a series of essays on the advent of the new media, which were later collected in *Diario minimo* (1963). It is clear in these essays that the lesson of the past is not forgotten, and that the contemporary media phenomenon is being intelligently and wittily related to the events of classical and medieval history. In the essay entitled 'Dove andremo a finire?' (Where Will We End Up?'), for example, Eco goes back to the Greek philosopher Heraclitus, who, when he died, left his obscure book in Artemis' temple, after saying: 'Why do you want to drag me everywhere, illiterate people? I have not written for you, but for those who can understand me. To me, one is worth a hundred-thousand, and the crowd nothing.'[15] Heraclitus lost, and his obscure book was opened to the hundred thousands, who can read it with the help of explanatory notes at the foot of every page. Heraclitus lost and the masses triumphed.

Eco's essay is constructed around the irony that mass civilization already existed in democratic ancient Greece, in which 'the Athenian man is happy to live as a face in the crowd,' and in which tabloid journalism is carried out by reporters such as Herodotus, Thucydides, and Xenophon. If this were not enough, public debates are held everywhere and teachers such as Plato dilute in lovely *digest* even the most dogmatic knowledge.

The comic quality of the essay is achieved by its juxtaposition of a picture of today's mass society, for which Eco quotes Zolla's *Eklisse dell'intellettuale*,[16] with the picture of Athenian society at the acme of its democratic expansion. The result is inevitably amusing; we cannot but laugh at Plato's mass eroticism, which is smuggled in as philosophy; at the cheap, Broadway-like sensationalistic quality of the Greek theatre of those times; and at the vision of Aristotle behind the scenes, a master of occult persuasion.

This is the technique that Eco adopts in many of the short essays written for publication in monthly or weekly magazines, which are devoted to a critique of society after the media revolution. Eco's clear object is to entertain his weekly or monthly readers, but his reflections on and criticism of different aspects of mass society are almost always a biting satire on the culture's thoughts and habits.

The most lively debates in the 1960s were those concerning the role of the arts and of the intellectual, in a world that had been changed by the advent of the media and by a continuous permutation of society, a world in which the masses more and more were dictating the cultural path. At an impasse between total acceptance of this recent phenomenon and total repudiation of it, Eco and his colleagues of the Gruppo 63 were trying to assume an active role in the decision regarding their fate. Eco wrote about the debate in *Apocalittici e integrati* (Apocalyptic and Integrated Intellectuals, 1964), in which he defined as 'apocalyptic' intellectuals those who regarded the tendencies of contemporary society as heralding the death of the human spirit, and as 'integrated' intellectuals those who accepted a specific technological progress as the natural development of an ever changing humanity. This dichotomy led him to an original discussion of the relations between literature and industry, which appeared to have become the pervasive totality of contemporary reality owing to its control of every aspect of society, including human relations and all types of production and consumption. The error of the apocalyptic intellectuals lies in the idea that mass culture is radically negative because it results from industrial sway, while the error of the integrated intellectuals lies in the idea that increase in industrial production is in itself 'good' and should not be subject to criticism.

Eco's solution is neither the denunciation of every aspect of mass culture nor an uncritical embracing of it in the manner of certain leftist proponents, but the establishment of a direction for research that would allow scientific analysis of the mass media, if for no other reason than to 'supply the elements of a constructive discussion that starts with an objective consciousness of the phenomena' (*Apocalittici e integrati*, p. 58). He proposes four lines of possible analysis: 1) study of the new languages and forms of the mass media; 2) critical research on the use that mass culture makes of 'high' culture; 3) aesthetic-psychological-sociological analysis of how the fruition attitude, or the attitude with which consumers consume or enjoy the product, can influence the value of the product; and 4) critical-sociological analysis of how stylistic devices can be used as simple rhetorical artifices that have nothing to do with the content of the product.

Whereas earlier critics such as Van Wyck Brooks and Dwight MacDonald had started their critique of mass culture with the canonical division into *high-*, *middle-*, and *lowbrow*, deprecating the way in which the so-called *midcult* used and trivialized avant-garde works, Eco insisted that, in order to come to an understanding of the contemporary phenomena, critics needed first of all to renew the concept of different cultural levels, because these do not correspond at all to class levels or levels of sophistication, and then to approach the products of the different levels, whether comic books or novels, songs or poems, television programs or paintings, with the same critical attitude.

Eco's proposed theory was very much influenced by the contemporary rise of structuralism and new theories of perception. In fact, his first key for the analysis of a work of art is to consider it as a *structure*. That does not mean that the work is self-sufficient, but that it coordinates a system of external references and is therefore a 'system of systems' (87). It proposes to us a message and asks us to decode it, but the code is not the language code because the signs are organized in a way the usual code did not foresee. The receiver therefore needs to discover the new code: 'The receiver penetrates, so to say, the message and converges into it the whole series of hypotheses that his particular psychological and intellectual disposition allows; lacking an external code to refer to completely, he or she elects as a hypothetical code the system of assumptions on which his or her sensibility and intelligence rely. The understanding of the work is born from this interaction' (98).

Eco is here introducing one of his first references to Peirce's theory of signs, in particular the idea of abductive reasoning, which will be discussed later. He is also reasserting the theory of analysis he had espoused in *Opera aperta*, the only difference being that in *Apocalittici e integrati* the elements of information theory are blended with those of communication theory. A new influence is also clear in *Apocalittici e integrati*, that of Roman Jakobson's *Essays in General Linguistics*, with which Eco had recently become familiar thanks to François Wahl, who had commissioned the translation of *Opera aperta* for Seuil. The new heroes of the era were the exponents of the new, reinvigorated European culture, such as the Frankfurt School, Prague's formalists, the structuralists, and Propp with his analysis of the fairy-tale. These were the authors most read by Eco and his colleagues in the Gruppo 63, and they were felt as a gust of fresh air in the closed and provincial atmosphere of Italian literary and cultural studies. It was in this context that Eco developed the idea of *openness* and wrote *Opera aperta*. In the next section, I will explain how the idea of openness resulted from Eco's new reading. His indebtedness to medieval philosophy, however, played a large role in its configuration.

### *Opera aperta* and Medieval Thought

The first essay of *Opera aperta*, 'The Poetics of the Open Work,' exposes the characteristics of *openness*, a concept with which Eco is much concerned, because he recognizes in it the main feature of the works of the avant-garde and because it establishes a completely new relation between the artist and the receiver of the artist's message.

> The poetics of the 'open' work tends, as Pousseur says, to promote in the interpreter 'acts of conscious freedom,' to pose him as active centre of a net of inexhaustible relations, among which he institutes his own form, without being determined by a *necessity* that prescribes the definitive modes of the organization of the enjoyed work; but one could object (going back to the larger meaning of the word 'openness' to which I referred) that any work of art, even if it is not delivered incomplete, asks for a free and inventive answer, if nothing else because it cannot be really understood if the interpreter does not reinvent it in an act of congeniality with the author himself. (*Opera aperta*, p. 35–6)[17]

To say that the interpreter participates freely in the reinvention of the work does not mean that the work is devoid of its own structure. On the contrary, even though the dynamic aspect of the open work renders it flexible and available for integration and complements, these are channelled a priori in the structural vitality that pertains to the work.

Eco contrasts the new avant-garde's open work with the medieval theory of allegorism and quotes Dante's *Thirteenth Epistle*, in which he describes four levels of text interpretation: the literal, the allegorical, the moral, and the anagogical. This theory, fundamental to medieval poetics, was by no means invented by Dante; others had already developed it, including St Paul and Thomas Aquinas. According to Eco, a work that is thus interpreted concedes to the reader a certain 'openness,' but an openness that is strictly contained by its rigid conditions.

Medieval works are therefore not 'open' in the sense that modern works are. Baroque works are more dynamic and offer the reader an inexhaustible variety of interpretations. Eco mentions *Finnegans Wake* as a modern work that represents the criteria of openness for its readers. For him, the work reflects the finite and at the same time unlimited presence of the Einsteinian cosmos.

Establishing the openness of avant-garde works had a sociological/ political value for Eco, especially at the time of the publication of his first book, because the open work would initiate an open debate and become the instrument of what Eco called a 'revolutionary pedagogy.' In the early 1960s, the common belief among the avant-garde was that the disruptive power of art would challenge the Italian political and economic system.[18] Eco's idea of openness seemed enthusiastically to affirm the role of the new artist. But soon it would become clear, especially in the pages of *Quindici*, that that was a naive credo and that the weaknesses of the Italian system were more deeply structural than had been thought. Disappointment with the events of the late 1960s – the dissolution of the student movement, the factory strikes and occupations, and the Milan bombing – marked the end of the avant-garde experience; intellectuals were forced to make a conscious political shift.

In *Opera aperta*, the idea of a dialogue between the artist and the masses still reflects the hopes of those intellectuals who saw in the avant-garde movement the possibility of a new communication and of a new relation with the reality of the industrial world. That is why Eco, a year after the publication of *Opera aperta*, felt compelled to write the essay 'Del modo di formare come impegno sulla realtà'[19] ('Form as Social Commitment'), in which he discusses the 'alienation' that seems to characterize modernity. Alienation, Eco says, cannot be eliminated, because humans perpetually alienate themselves in their work. But the positive side is that in the moment when we detach ourselves from the object, we go through a process similar to the Brechtian *Verfremdung*: once we recognize the object and understand it, we can use it and bend it to our pleasure. That is what avant-garde art proposes, an answer to today's industrial society that is balanced between acceptance of the alienated language in which the world expresses itself and the reversal of that language from within.

Medieval society is reflected in the works it produced, which represent a conception of the cosmos as a hierarchy of prefixed orders, a syllogistic science, and a logic of necessity. But the modern work is ever conscious of the dialectics of today's situation, and, 'in the moment in which it provides us with the instruments to understand and accept the situation that it describes, it tries to allow our discourse on itself' (*Opera aperta*, p. 290). This approach is typical of a culture that has an obscure relation with things and is attempting to rationalize and clarify the dialogue with things by conferring form on chaos. This form can reflect the disorder and dissociation of the world, but still finds peace in the transmission of an organized message: 'pendular oscillation, I said, between a system of probabilities that is by now institutionalized, and pure disorder: original organization of disorder' (121).

In *The Aesthetics of Thomas Aquinas*, Eco writes:

> Whenever a system of thought disintegrates, this never occurs just because an internal dialectical explosion, purely at the level of thought alone, produces contradictions within it, and causes it to be nullified in whatever supersedes it. Any system comes about as a response to specific social, political, and cultural questions, and to solicitations which are implicit in the relations of production and are mediated through the superstructure. Therefore, when a system breaks down, it does not do so just from within. It breaks down because of something *outside* it. (209–10)

In his 'Conclusion,' Eco refers to the historicity of philosophical systems such as Aquinas', saying that the breaking down of stylistic rules is strictly connected to social, political, and cultural questions. The same breakdown testified by medieval philosophy recurs in modernity, in which certain rules are defeated because they are no longer in harmony with the social and political questions resulting from the new modes of relations imposed by industry.

Reviewers of *Opera aperta* criticized the book's classifying as poetically or artistically successful only those works that would satisfy the requirements of the 'modern world'[20] and accused Eco of subtracting from Aquinas the epistemological criterion of the adaptation of the intellect to reality.

If Eco's indebtedness to St Thomas is obvious in *Opera aperta*, and if it is true that the Italian philosopher does attribute the fundamental characteristics of works of art to the state of reality, there appears to be something unchanging in the human intellect, which, no matter how conflicting reality may appear, always tends to a resolution, to a new type of organization, to a new order. Even in the serial composition of contemporary music, the composer, although he refuses the rules of the tonal system, introduces new forms of organization. This constant oscillation between order and disorder is what saves not only the author of the open work, but also the receiver, who has 'a tendency to resolve a crisis in rest, perturbation in peace, deviation in the return to a polarity defined by the musical habits of a civilization' (*Opera aperta*, p. 141).

Clearly the importance of external reality and human experience appear to be indisputable in Eco's approach ('we are forced, situation by situation, to call into question ... our acquired experience' (134)). In fact, Eco critiques *gestalt* psychology, which sees in perception a configuration of stimuli that is already objectively organized, and posits an isomorphism between the structures of the object and the structures of the subject. But Eco makes it also clear that the interaction between object and subject is at the basis of his theory, not in the sense that phenomenologists proposed, but more according to Piaget's criteria: the equilibrium in the interaction does not depend solely on the physical, because the subject actively compensates and constructs the 'reversible structures' (135) that are used in the perception of objects. Art is influenced by reality, but it is also capable of changing it. There is a resolution here between empiricism and the structuralism of the *Gestaltphenomenologie*, which frees the perceptive forms, opening them to the indefinite possibility of new structures.

Like Thomas Aquinas, Eco shows here something that has become an important mark of his way of proceeding: a tenacious effort at the composition/pacification of opposites. Even more than his system, what is masterly in Eco is his style, inspired, like Aquinas', by a sort of horror of contrasts that seem so radical as to appear insoluble, and by an expertise in analysing contrasts in such a way that their eventual peaceful composition seems completely obvious and necessary.

## From *Apocalittici e integrati* to *Il superuomo di massa*

The resolution that Eco was after in his subsequent book, *Apocalittici e integrati* (1964), is sought for in a theory of analysis that would allow the critic to study different kinds of cultural phenomena, and in particular, after the emergence of mass culture, a theory applicable both to the high literature of a Proust or a Joyce and to the larger range of mass cultural products like comic books and television programs.

The reaction of the critics confronting what Eco calls the *mysterium televisionis*, has been one either of morbid fascination or of complete rejection and the temptation to shut off the threatening device. The second kind of reaction has been demonstrated by Günther Anders, the apocalyptic critic who devoted hundreds of pages to describing the phenomenon of television without ever analysing the transmitted images with other than disgust. Anders' position reminds Eco of a similar critique, written centuries before, by St Bernard in his *Apologia ad Guillelmulum, Sancti Theodorici Romensis Abbati*, against Abbot Suger.

Suger wanted cathedrals to become immense stone books for the education of the masses: 'Pictura est laicorum literatura.' The pictures on the walls, the sculptures on the doors, and the images in tinted glass could all become instruments of communication whereby the faithful would learn about the history of the country, natural phenomena, and the divine mysteries. St Bernard's more rigid architectural program opposed this pedagogic plan and worried about its possible dark effects on the people.[21]

According to Eco, St Bernard's attitude, understandable given the medieval organic model of culture, should be brought before contemporary critics who are behaving in a similar way. Although today's situation is characterized more and more by the participation of the masses in cultural life, the models to be followed still are presented to them through means of communication dominated by the hegemonic class: 'From the star worship models of cinema to the protagonists of soap operas to the programs dedicated to women, mass culture mostly represents and proposes human situations that have no connection with the situations of the consumers, and nevertheless they become for them model situations' (*Apocalittici e integrati*, p. 20).[22]

The apocalyptic critic, therefore, who refuses to examine the instrument and its possibilities, does not help consumers thus exposed to the new type of messages. What is much more useful according to Eco is analysis of the structures of these messages, and such an analysis is what he proposes to undertake in the essays contained in *Apocalittici e integrati* and *Il superuomo di massa*.

Despite sociological differences, cultural issues seem to recur throughout history, which is why Eco can quickly juxtapose fourth-century Athens, twelfth-century Europe, and the twentieth-century West. The juxtaposition of cultures is itself a witty example of how Eco's historical mind can compare distant phenomena and apply its conclusions to an analysis of what appears to be a brand new and somewhat turbid subject.

Although what Eco defines as 'minimal messages' seem inconsequential objects (like Superman comics or the songs of Rita Pavone), together they constitute 'the most striking cultural phenomenon in the civilization in which we operate' (*Apocalittici e integrati*, p. 24) and are therefore worthy of consideration. Neglecting them would be acting like those learned doctors who considered a worthy science only the one that studied incorruptible realities, such as the celestial spheres or the *quidditates*. In fact, what is most important is not the dignity of the object but the dignity of the method, which should not be limited to a study of narrative structures, but extended to the analysis of the modalities of enjoyment.

One of the most interesting studies in *Apocalittici e integrati*, is Eco's sharp critique of the idea of 'superman,' as reflected not only in the comics/television superhero but also in many different popular novels and films. The idea of 'superman' is also the main object of *Il superuomo di massa*. Eco derives his interpretation from an essay by Antonio Gramsci entitled 'Popular Literature.'[23] According to Gramsci, the popular model of superman does not come from Nietzsche's Zarathustra, but from the feuilleton and the serial novels, such as those of Dumas and Sue.

Rodolphe, the romantic hero of *Les mystères de Paris* by Eugène Sue, is a prince, a benefactor, a judge, and a reformer, fundamentally a superman, who rectifies social injustices and therefore solves the intricacies of the plot according to the Aristotelian rules of beginning, tension, climax, solution, and catharsis. He is the hero who brings a dramatic situation to a conclusion but who also re-establishes the equilibrium and order of society, because after his intervention things will go on exactly as they have always gone on. This type of superhero acts on the one hand as the saviour of the humble and on the other hand as a laconic maintainer of the structure of society, a structure that is reflected in the structure of the narration itself.

Eco's analysis of Sue's novel is interesting not only for the acute identification of its narratological structures, but also for a controversial affirmation announced in the introduction of *Il superuomo di massa*, where Eco explains that what is fundamental in the study of literary works is the understanding of a dialectic between a 'semiology of narrative structure' and a 'sociology of literature':

> Every effort to define a signifying form without already investing it with a meaning is vain and illusory, in the same way as every absolute formalism is nothing but a masked content-ism. To isolate formal structures means to recognize them as *pertinent* in respect to a global hypothesis made in advance about the direction of the work; there is no analysis of pertinent signifying aspects that does not already imply an interpretation and therefore a filling-in of meaning.

In this case every structural analysis of a text is always the verification of psycho-sociological and ideological hypotheses, although latent. One might as well be conscious of this phenomenon, in order to reduce to a minimum ... this margin of inevitable subjectivity (or historicity). (28)[24]

Eco's position is clearly exposed here: despite the influence of structuralism in his theory, he reaffirms the need for a sociological context, which should not simply be used to establish what form of power was acting behind the author, but should constitute the basis of a beginning hypothesis concerning the structures of a text. But it is easy to make the opposite mistake, that of denying the existence of a set of general rules behind a game. The problem is to understand the circularity of the phenomenon: how the social influences the aesthetic, but also how the aesthetic throws new light on the social.

If there is a consolatory project at an ideological level, there must exist some narrative structures that promote it, working in parallel with the distribution criteria of the feuilleton. The recurring idea is, as Eco elaborates, the presence of a hero, endowed with special powers (which could be infrared vision or simply money), who incarnates the will to power of the common citizen. If in antiquity this power was identified with a semi-god and in the Middle Ages with a religious character endowed with the divine, the modern-world hero needs to become an archetype and a mirror of the social situation and to reiterate the narrative of power that readers want to see rehearsed again and again, with minimum mnemonic effort. Superman the comic-book hero therefore becomes a model of hetero-direction: the character forces the idea that, living in a particular social and economic situation in a community with a certain level of technological development, one is constantly told what one ought to desire and how one ought to obtain the objects of desire. The charismatic hero brings an authoritarian solution to the contradictions of society. Although he appears democratic and good-hearted, he alone decides what is good for the oppressed population.

The Count of Montecristo, as Gramsci had announced and as Eco restates, is probably the first popular hero to embody these characteristics, when half way through the book he exposes his ideas of individual superiority and his favouring of personal choice over law, with a sense of divine mission as his justification.

The Superman of the feuilleton realizes that the rich prevail over the poor, that power is founded on fraud; but he is not a prophet of social struggle, like Marx, and therefore he does not repair injustices by subverting the order of society. He simply opposes his own justice to a common justice, he destroys the evil, rewards the good, and re-establishes the lost harmony. In this sense, the democratic popular novel is not revolutionary; it is charitable; it consoles its readers with the image of a fairy-tale justice; but nevertheless it exposes problems and, if it does not offer acceptable solutions, it delineates realistic analyses. (106)[25]

Although Eco severely criticizes both the narrative structures and the sociological impact of the popular novel, he credits it with a certain positive value in its addressing of the public interest and its transmission of information. But Eco goes farther, in that his analyses of some popular novels (like those by Eugène Sue, Alexandre Dumas, and Luigi Natoli) constitute exemplary studies in popular culture and aim at giving the reader an example of the method with which to approach other works. Although these analyses have been blamed for a lack of rigour, being not in tune with more textually oriented structuralist analyses, Eco explicitly denounces what he considers a mistake on the part of literary criticism: the neglecting of sociological ties. This mistake also goes along with denying the existence of structural and narratological devices, which are inevitably used even by less sophisticated authors.[26]

In the history of ideas, *Apocalittici e integrati* and *Il superuomo di massa* represent society confronting a new situation and a need to understand mass communications. The works stimulated numerous articles in magazines and newspapers and a new academic interest in the works of popular culture, which interest led to the formation of the first department of semiotics at the University of Bologna.

## Counterculture and Cultural Studies

Interest in 'cultural phenomena' has played a dominant role in Eco's writings.

In *Sette anni di desiderio* (1983), Eco includes a section entitled 'Power and Counter-powers' ('Potere e contropoteri,' 217–31), in which the focus is on two concepts that can hardly be discussed separately: culture and power. In the essay 'Is There a Counter-culture?' Eco attempts a definition of the word 'culture.' After analysing various samples from widely used dictionaries, he develops his own definition, or, better, definitions: the aesthetic, the moral, and the anthropological. *Culture 1* usually connotes a realm opposite to that of science, politics, or economics, and privileges the formation of aesthetic taste. It distinguishes a condition of critical *otium* that is not accessible to everybody, owing to limitations of class and natural capacity. *Culture 2* is the possession of knowledge in all its aspects. A bank director or a financier can be considered a person of culture in this sense, but the term still names a characteristic of those in power. The knowledge it emphasizes is theoretical, so a mechanic would not be considered a person of culture. *Culture 3* is the combination of 'institutions, myths, rites, laws, beliefs, codified daily behaviours, value systems, and material techniques elaborated by a human group' (*Sette anni*, p. 222). This definition has a more neutral value than the other two, as it implies no positive or negative judgment of a culture but simply acknowledges its existence. In order to survive, a culture must be able to recognize and criticize itself. The critical capacity, according to Eco, leads to a fourth definition of culture, which is 'a critical recognition of emerging alternative cultures' (227). This is what can be referred to as 'counterculture,' because it prepares society for a change in the social or scientific or aesthetic paradigm and is the only cultural manifestation that a dominant culture is not able to recognize and accept. The role of the intellectual in such a situation is that of critical 'spokesperson' of great cultural transformations: the intellectual transforms and at the same time is critically conscious of the value of the transformation. The intellectual who participates actively in social or political changes cannot, according to Eco, avoid discussing the concept of power.

In dealing with this concept, Eco cannot but start with Foucault's notion, which he admits is the most thought-provoking notion of power today. Two characteristics of Foucault's definition interest Eco: 'First of all, power is not only repression and interdiction, but also discourse formation and knowledge production; second, ... power is not one massive whole, not a unilateral process between one commanding entity and its subjects' ('La lingua, il potere, la forza,' 1979 *Sette anni*, p. 217).

Power is the multiplicity of relations of strength, a game of oppositions and contrasts that affects everybody everywhere. According to this notion, an opposition of strength that simply attacks a so-called authority is a form of political infantilism: power is much more subtle and, because it can avail itself of capillary consent, it can easily heal a small wound. Much more effective, therefore, is a subtle but massive resistance that gives birth to a disintegration of consensus.

The risk that Eco identifies in Foucault's theory is that this type of resistance can become identified with a slow reform movement, which is a casual effect of a composition of forces that have been latent for a long time. The subject would lose a direct effect on the flow of history, as revolutions would be dependent on much larger forces. The subject would be lost in a universe without a centre, 'where everything is periphery and there is no "heart" of anything' (195).

After questioning Foucault's notion and Barthes' intervention regarding the power of language on the occasion of his appointment to the Collège de France, Eco leaves the discussion open both in terms of the subject's power and in terms of the function of literature as counterculture. He prefers to attack the concept by turning his attention to a vast series of situations in which the notion of power is played out. He writes, for example, on the transparency of television, on the role of soccer and the World Cup, on the power of *Playboy*, on museums, on advertising, on the function of comic books and striptease. One interesting example of a micro-situation in which the concept of power is played out concerns the accessibility of libraries. In his intervention at the twenty-fifth anniversary of the Milan public library, Eco ironically lists nineteen rules for the good functioning of the perfect library. These are, in fact, limitations imposed on readers by the library administrators – for example, limited hours, confusing catalogues, the absence of copy-machines, long delivery times, and other constraints that make it impossible for readers to have access to information and to enjoy the experience of research.

In a poignant moment, Eco here takes a strong position against the typical organization of Italian libraries (although he mentions no country in particular), directing harsh criticism at librarians' often excessive protectiveness of books, which interferes with the right of consultation conferred by Unesco on any member of the community without distinction of race, sex, religion, nationality, or cultural level.

This is only one example of Eco's tirades against the establishment, which are prompted not only by his passionate desire to bring about change, but also by his profound knowledge of the Italian situation. His biting satires against many of these micro-situations often have had a direct effect both on public opinion (thanks to his celebrity, his weekly or biweekly pieces are widely read in Italy) and on certain institutions.[27] His observations regarding customs or technological innovations are always sharp, although his method of analysis seems to vary.

One could say, in fact, that his semiotic method is more rigorous when the object of analysis is a delimited text. This is a type of criticism that writers such as Simon During have made against semiotics – the incapacity of semiotics to extend its criticism beyond the text. During has attacked semiotics for limiting its attention to the signifier while many life situations are mostly a matter of content.[28]

The writings collected in the three *Diari minimi* (1963, 1992, and 1999), *Il costume di casa* (1973), *Dalla periferia dell'impero* (1977), *Sette anni di desiderio* (1983), and *Sugli specchi e altri saggi* (1985) are clear examples of how unfair this criticism is. It is true that it would be difficult to apply the rigorous semiotic method that Eco elaborates in *A Theory of Semiotics* (1976) to situations such as cigarette-smoking, and Eco is conscious of that. He recognizes that most of the time the object is more powerful than our rules; our method, therefore, must be flexible enough to comply with the demands exerted by the object. In *A Theory of Semiotics*, he writes: 'We must then propose an apparently simplified *research model.* Finally we must constantly contradict this model, isolating all the phenomena which do not fit in with it and which force it to restructure itself and to broaden its range. In this way we shall perhaps succeed in tracing (however provisionally) the limits of future semiotic research and of suggesting a unified method of approach to phenomena which apparently are very different from each other, and as yet irreducible' (7–8).

The model of analysis that Eco offers for the study of cultural processes is very much simplified and is based on a distinction between the process of communication and the process of signification. Eco writes that, although the two approaches follow different methodological paths, 'it is impossible to establish a semiotics of communication without a semiotics of signification' (9). Peircian semiotics allows Eco a broader range of analysis, owing to the idea of semiosis; and because Peirce's notion of sign is not limited to the qualities of being 'intentionally emitted' and 'artificially produced' (15), it is not reduced to a theory of communication acts. The code is still of exceptional importance, but not in terms of the sender: the code becomes more important in terms of the reception by the interpreter, as we will see in the next chapter.

The idea of unlimited semiosis means that the set of possible interpretants of a sign is not limited to its semantic markers, but can be tied to a whole set of 'cultural units,' entities, Eco emphasizes, that are 'physically, materially, materialistically testable' (72).

Thus is the passage from the text to 'cultural situations' made possible, and Eco's short pieces, his 'bustine di Minerva,' which seem simple *divertissements*, constitute practical examples of how it can be done. It is worth giving these writings some consideration (see chapter 6). To Eco's amazement, they have attracted serious interest on the part of many readers and have been considered important in a range of contexts. It is disappointing, then, that During, in his collection of essays on cultural studies, mentions the valid experimentation of a Lefebvre or a De Certeau but neglects to mention Eco's important work on the subject.

# 4 The Aesthetics of Reception and the Reflection on the Reader: From the Labyrinth to the Southern Seas

But Redemption from what, old Rocambole? You knew better than to try to be a protagonist! You have been punished, and with your own arts. You mocked the creators of illusion, and now – as you see – you write using the alibi of a machine, telling yourself you are a spectator, because you read yourself on the screen as if the words belonged to another, but you have fallen into the trap: you, too, are trying to leave footprints on the sands of time. You have dared to change the text of the romance of the world, and the romance of the world has taken you instead into its coils and involved you in its plot, a plot not of your making.

(*Foucault's Pendulum*, p. 506)

Once upon a time there was ... a Reader!

In the 1970s and 1980s, in response to the dominant criteria established by formalism and the New Criticism, a debate was created by new schools of theory that called into question the role of the reader of texts and the implications of the reading process. Against the idea of impersonality, which, according to the formalists, ought to be cultivated by the critical theorist while interpreting a text, reader response criticism refocused on the text/reader relation, bringing to light the impossibility of aseptic neutrality on the part of the critic.

After years of discussion and sometimes self-regarding argument, the debate seemed to have been essentially interrupted or resolved with the adoption of conciliatory positions that see the argument as idle for critical purposes. Nonetheless, what is at stake is not simply a theoretical dilemma, but a pragmatic activity that re-presents itself every time we attempt an act of critical reading. Therefore, it is not idle to ask, What remains to us of that created figure, the reader, who was collocated inside and outside, in front of and beyond the literary text? Are any conclusions to be drawn, besides a healthy complication of the matter?

These questions, themselves fundamental, call forth a deeper question that is even more fundamental: What is the function of theory in literary studies, and, more specifically, in interpretation? While theory is a regulating principle preceding the study of literary works, its application to a particular text can be resisted by the text itself, and its regulations may often prove unsuitable for critical purposes. Because theory necessarily adopts a point of view, it cannot possibly accomplish a general and universally agreed-upon account of interpretation. But that should not discourage critics from trying to invoke an order, no matter how precarious that order may be. Order is what allows intelligibility, even though it undeniably establishes a hierarchy in the disposition of things and in the scale of being.

To return to our problematic reader, during the last two decades many critics occupying a spot in the cluttered critical scene formulated a theory of 'audience.' The theoretical and ideological positions varied among the mock reader (Gibson) and the implied reader (Iser), the ideal reader (Culler) and the actual reader (Jauss), the encoded reader (Brooke-Rose) and the super-reader (Riffaterre), the literent (Holland) and the narratee (Prince), the interpretative community (Fish) and the model reader (Eco) to the point that the univocal figure of the reader became multiplied in a variety of ghosts that were carefully distinguished from the empirical reader.

Elizabeth Freund, in *The Return of the Reader* (1987), attempts to reconstruct the old debate, intelligently analysing the various positions and emphasizing the 'promiscuous instability of literary meaning, and with it the vagaries of interpretation this instability gives rise to.'[1] According to Freund, as language is always in some degree unstable and 'different,' readers are always subject to misinterpretations. Freund asks Paul de Man's question: 'How are literary studies ever to get started when every proposed method seems based on a misreading and a misconceived preconception about the nature of literary language?' Notwithstanding her declared 'sympathy' for deconstructionist theories, Freund admits that literary studies do get started and, at the end of her book, suggests a reading based on a dialogue between the text and the interpreter.

Invoking Hartman, she reasserts a meticulous respect for the text and invokes the responsibility of the respondent: 'Dialogue itself is at stake,'[2] where dialogue is defined as a trope for reading that opposes any type of monological discourse, both the text's and the reader's.

Freund's conclusion seems to bring to an end the debate on how to read reading, by equally distributing the power between the two interlocutors, the text and the reader. But her conciliatory position, closely examined, does not appear completely impartial, in the sense that, when we invoke the responsibility of the respondent and advocate a respect for the text, it is the text that assumes primary importance.

The second problem with her conclusion pertains to that property of the text that allows it to answer the critic's questions. Once the author renounces the responsibility for answering these questions, the interpreter seems to be left with only one conversant to help him or her solve problems of understanding, to help uncover the figure in the carpet, to flash out the image hidden in the stereogram. What happens then to what surrounds the text? Furthermore, it is here, in the idea of a dialogue, that the question begins and by no means ends: Is it possible to explain further how this dialogue between the text and the interpreter takes place?

'Le récit est un piège': narrative is a deliberate trap, and not a clear and lucid explanation of its deceits. An illustrious author of the sixteenth century, Gian Battista de Contugi, whom Louis Marin defines as a second Machiavelli, wrote a treatise entitled *Of Traps, of Their Composition and of Their Use*, in which he describes three types of traps. The first type, the trap of imagination, is based on the principle of the attraction of the same to the same and on the pleasure that imitation creates, the pleasure of resemblance. The second type, the trap of appetite, presents something as an object of desire caused by hunger or thirst or sex. The third type, the trap of force, is one in which a machine, disguised, is placed along the route of the person or animal to be caught, so that this person or animal eventually falls into it; this trap works through dissimulation.

Louis Marin has used these images well to explain that the literary text is full of tricks that are there to misguide the reader; sometimes they point to a mysterious something that is not altogether there. The twentieth-century reader, especially the professional one, who has been trained in reading skills by decades of modernist art, cannot help but be attentive to these mechanisms of the text, which Marin identifies as rhetorical techniques, argumentative operations, and dialogic strategies. These aim at persuading and manipulating readers, at reducing them to silence or making them believe that the matter dealt with is rich and the field elaborate.[3]

Henry James in 'The Figure in the Carpet' gives a renowned example of a reader, whose name we never learn, who becomes obsessed by his desire to solve a mystery behind a group of texts. Provoked not by the texts themselves but by their empirical and malicious author, who criticizes him for not being able to understand the treasure buried in his books, the little something that makes them all cohere and live, the string the pearls are strung on, our reader spends years brooding over the texts and wasting his energy in useless attempts to discover the embroidered image.

His friend, who comes to full realization during a trip to India, dies without having had time to write his critical article on the subject. One by one all the characters in possession of the secret die and take the treasure with them to their tombs, thereby leaving our literary critic a victim of 'an unappeased desire,'[4] full of revenge against a group of conspirators.

How is the reader then, once provoked, supposed to save himself or herself from the text's snares and pitfalls, and is he or she doomed to become the victim of the desires that language is able to arouse? How can one respect and distrust a text? And, finally, is a reader just an interpreter, or somehow forced to become a creator?

As a smart and alert reader himself, Umberto Eco has devoted most of his literary and critical writings to the problems of interpretation, explicitly focusing on the role of the reader not just of literature but of history and of life itself. His productions offer passionate reflection on the theoretical and pragmatic act of reading, and show how interpretation is at stake in scientific studies and in the construction of knowledge.

When I became interested in Eco's writings, I was unaware of the variety and magnitude of his theoretical achievements. In his writings, the fascination and charisma of the critic/novelist are united with an amplitude of knowledge in a tangled knot that allows us to walk infinitely in his narrative woods. To read a novel is, for Eco, to enter a different world, to explore new possibilities, and somehow to re-create for ourselves a new domain. Whether Eco's world is a medieval abbey, the domain of the cabbala, an unreachable island, or a land of monsters, the reader cannot help but move within it as the main character of that possible universe, which develops inside and outside the mind as a most beautiful construction.

Through an examination of Umberto Eco's critical writings and, even more important, of his novels, I will try to explicate how Eco's theories can offer a different approach to reading, and I will individuate the role of his reader, not simply in the way Eco explicitly describes it, but also as it is defined by his narratives.   .

It is my contention that the reader of Eco's novels, differently from the reader described in his theory, fosters the conception of a layered interpretation, in which the text is rewritten various times by different interpreters with different shades, but that while these readers/creators struggle to rewrite their story, they are seized again and again by the threads of the plot, recaptured in the unfolding of the story, which 'they have not decided' (*Foucault's Pendulum*, p. 535). Each interpretation leaves traces in the sand, but the tale of the world ensnares us in its plot of meaning, in the deciphering of which we cannot limit ourselves. It seems to be the human plague always to try to renew it, to re-create the figure disguised in the embroidery, and, in critical terms, to shape its hermeneutics in a structure. This is a limitation that medieval scholars well understood, according to Eco, and their example should serve to moderate the interpretative excesses of a culture that has lost contact with the real.

## Eco's Theoretical Writings on Interpretation and the Role of the Reader

### The Early Years

In 1962, Umberto Eco published his first book, *Opera aperta*, in which he set forth the problem that a work of art both postulates a free interpretative intervention on the part of the reader and exhibits structural characteristics that stimulate and regulate the order of interpretation. He was unconsciously referring to the pragmatics of text, to the activity that brings the addressee to fill in the gaps, to connect what is in the text with the intertextuality from which the text originates, but his main intent was to establish what in the text stimulates and regulates interpretative freedom.[5]

Claude Lévi-Strauss criticized Eco's book in an interview in 1965:

There is a remarkable book ..., *The Open Work*, which defends a formula that I cannot accept. What makes a work a work is not the fact that it is open but the fact that it is closed. A work is an object endowed with precise properties, which the analysis has to define ... When Jakobson and myself tried to make a structural analysis of a sonnet by Baudelaire, we certainly did not approach it as an open work, in which we could find everything that has been filled in by the following epochs, but as an object which, once it has been created, had the stiffness, so to speak, of a crystal: therefore our function was only to bring into evidence its properties.

Eco reports this criticism in the introduction to his *Lector in fabula*, in order to comment on Lévi-Strauss' reading of his book.

When Eco says that a work is open, he does not mean that it contains everything that we can put in it, but that a text asks for the cooperation of its reader: the text wants the reader to make a series of interpretative choices, which, if not infinite, are certainly indefinite, in number, and in any case more than one. Why then not talk about 'openness,' he asks. This idea of a 'lector' who cooperates in the formation of meaning in narrative texts is fundamental in Eco's work, and it is the literary outcome of his Peircian semiotics as theory of knowledge. As human understanding is never clear and direct, for the reason that our knowledge is always mediated by our senses, to enlarge its lore the human being must formulate a number of conjectures or *abductions* based on physical perceptions. These conjectures, even though they are part of the reading process, at the same time involve a creative ability that allows the reader to make new connections and produce new meaning.

For Eco, therefore, the reader is both the receiver and the generator of knowledge. That is why the mechanics of understanding and the theory of language assume central importance in his works, which are centred on the concept of the 'sign.'

Giovanni Manetti, in *Theories of the Sign in Classical Antiquity* (1987), traces the origins of our conception of the sign in the divination practices and medical research of antiquity. The sign is a symptom, something that stands for something else; in the mind of the ancients, it is a divine indication providing human beings with a clue for interpretation. In this sense, the role of the interpreter is clear: to translate the secret message of the divinity. The story becomes more complicated when humans take upon themselves the faculty of creating signs.

To give a theoretical foundation to the science of the sign, semiotics, Eco writes *La struttura assente* (1968) and *A Theory of Semiotics* (1975), which switch the attention from the nature of texts to the nature of semiotic conventions, that is, to the structure of codes and to the more general structure of communicative processes.

*La struttura assente* is a pedagogical work based on the lecture notes of a course on visual semiology in the Department of Architecture of the University of Florence, but it contains a section added later (which gives the title to the whole book) that attacks structuralism as ontology and discusses its dissolution as hastened by the work of Derrida and Foucault. These two thinkers, together with Lacan, are also criticized in their methodology, and Eco discusses the possibility of complementing a hermeneutical interrogation with a structural definition. *A Theory of Semiotics*, however, although developing the same problems, is presented as a completely different work, not designed to take part in a debate but written as a treatise on semiotics that grants to the new theory the dignity of a discipline.

Later on, with *Semiotics and the Philosophy of Language* (1984), Eco traces a 'genealogy' of the sign in the philosophy of language in order to answer questions such as these: Can one approach different phenomena as if they were all problems of signification? Is there a unified approach able to account for all these semiotic phenomena? And last, is this approach a scientific one? Eco's reply is that the approach is not a scientific but a philosophical one.

In the first essay, entitled 'Signs,' Eco tries to characterize the concept of sign and to redefine it in terms of historical semantics. To that end, he looks at different linguistic theories and points out their problems. He looks at Hjelmslev's theory of the *figurae*, defined as content articulations in linguistic signifiers: for Hjelmslev, the linguistic sign is a detectable unit in the process of communication, and not a unit in the system of signification; the sign, or sign-function, appears as a net of aggregations and disintegrations constantly open to further combinations. Eco's critique of Hjelmslev's model is that it does not account for other non-linguistic signs that are not analysable into *figurae*, for example the cloud that announces the storm or the portrait of Mona Lisa. Eco also discusses Buyssens' theory of the *sème*, according to which the semantic unit is not the sign but the sentence, a view in line with his interest in communication as a concrete act.

Another kind of linguistic theory, which Eco sees as developing from Leibniz to Saussure to Derrida, understands the sign as difference: 'The sign can be known only through the signifier, and the signified emerges only through an act of substitution of the signifier' (*Semiotica e filosofia del linguaggio*, p. 18). The problem, according to Eco, is that the presence of one element is necessary for the absence of the other; furthermore, this theory has dangerous philosophical implications.

For Eco, the semiotic chain is not simply a chain of signifiers, and he argues that Freud and Lacan, in the chain of signifiers, in fact read words as complete sign-functions, and that the mechanisms of displacement and condensation, the Freudian slips, play on content *figurae*. He goes on to assert that the signifying chain produces texts that carry with them the recollection of intertextuality. He disagrees with the suggestion of Barthes, Derrida, and Kristeva according to which signification can be found exclusively in the text: signs pre-exist the text and contain the potential construction of different texts.

Going back in time, he traces the history of the sign starting with Plato and Aristotle (according to whom a sign is an affection of the soul) and then moves to the Stoics (according to whom a sign is 'something immediately evident which leads to some conclusions about the existence of something not immediately evident' (*Semiotica e filosofia*, p. 29)). Augustine, for Eco, is the one who brought together the theory of signs and the theory of language: we are moving from a dictionary model (Aristotle's principle of biconditional equivalence) to an encyclopaedic model. Eco's theory of the sign is based on Peirce's logic and defines a sign as a structured content space, a block of contextual instructions and expectations. The exploration of these eventualities produces an inspection of the content space in order to foresee which result will be more probable according to the contextual elements that precede and follow (35).

The encyclopaedic model assumes that the interpretation of content takes place only by means of interpretants, in a process of unlimited semiosis, and works for both categorematic and syncategorematic terms. A sign is a virtual text. An encyclopaedic model is defined as a type of labyrinthine knowledge, a labyrinth of the third type, a net, a meander, Eco's Model Q, and is also considered a work in progress, in which the contributions of thinkers such as Greimas, Fillmore, Bierwisch, Lakoff, Putnam, and Johnson have played an essential role.

Strangely enough, at the end of the chapter Eco appears to be worried about the possible implications of this type of view, and is able to affirm that dictionary-like representations can be used as tools: while the encyclopaedia is a semantic concept, the dictionary is a pragmatic device. As he moves to criticize the godless drift of deconstruction,[6] he appears to waver between the defence of his concept of openness and the need to stop the infinite play of deconstructionist practices.

As we will see reflected also in his other theoretical works, here Eco is struggling with his principal dilemma, his attempt to establish an *open-*

*ness* of the text that at the same time is 'codifiable' in a system. He is consciously asserting that, although not a 'structuralist,' he is concerned with structure, but with the structure of openness.

## *The Reader and the Concept of Interpretation*

The problem of interpretation, of its freedom and its aberrations, can be said to be always at stake in Eco's writings, but in the years 1976–8 he wrote a series of essays on the mechanics of the interpretation of texts, which are reunited in an organic way in *Lector in fabula* (1979).[7] The connection seems to be offered by concern with the interpretation of what Eco defines as a 'difficult' text, a short story by Alphonse Allais, 'Un drame bien parisien' (see Appendix A).

In *Lector in fabula*, the reader is collocated inside the text instead of simply behind it – a way of limiting and controlling the reader. Nevertheless, the reader, as a narrative function, is placed in charge of making inferences and assumptions and therefore is not a passive figure separate from the text but an active ingredient of the narration. Eco underlines throughout his writings that this so-defined reader is not the empirical reader, but a function inside the text that he calls his 'Model Reader.'

According to Eco, a text in itself is incomplete until it is actualized by its addressee; it is full of things not said, of blank spaces and interstices to be filled, because its author foresaw that they had to be filled by the addressee. A text is a lazy mechanism that lives on what Eco calls the *surplus value* of the meaning introduced by the reader: it wants to leave to the reader the interpretative enterprise, even though it usually wants to be interpreted univocally. It needs somebody to help it work. Unfortunately, the competence of the addressee is not necessarily that of the author, but what saves interpretation is the existence of linguistic and extra-linguistic forms that reinforce and sustain the effort of the reader.

A text therefore postulates the cooperation of the reader as its own condition of *actualization,* and to generate a text means to create a strategy. An author has to refer to a series of competences that confer meaning on the expressions he uses, and he has to assume that the competences to which he refers are the same as those to which his reader refers. Therefore 'he will foresee a Model Reader able to cooperate in the textual *actualization* as he, the author, thought' (*Lector in fabula*, p. 55), and able to act *interpretatively* as the author moved *generatively.* The means are the choice of language, the choice of a lexical apparatus, the choice of a style, an encyclopaedic choice, a geographic restriction, and other similar devices. In this sense, the author on the one hand foresees and on the other hand institutes the competence of the Model Reader.

The Model Reader is a textual strategy, a system of instructions designed by and within the text. In order to give a pragmatic example of how this works in text analysis, Eco chooses Allais' story 'Un Drame bien parisien.' The story is, according to Eco, a metatext, because its real interest is not in the story itself but in the comment that is made about the reader.

Along these lines, Eco defines as a 'closed text' a text in which the author shrewdly fixes the Model Reader, and as an 'open text' a text in which the author decides up to what point to control the cooperation of the reader, where it needs to be awakened, where it should be directed, and where it can be transformed into free interpretative adventure.

He argues that Allais' story is neither a 'closed' nor an 'open' text but situated right in the middle: it seduces the Model Reader by making him or her see possible 'heavens of cooperation' and then punishes him or her for overdoing it. Following the fabula of the story, the reader is frustrated and tries to invent extrachapters in order to rationalize the situation, but the only rationalization that Eco as a reader seems to find is that the reader is the victim of the text, even when he recognizes that the purpose of the text is that of punishing the invasive acts of the reader.

Eco considers 'Un Drame bien parisien' a very good example of persuasive discourse, as it makes clear the modalities of the *make believe* and of the *make do*. When the empirical reader reads the text for the first time, he or she assumes responsibility for the formulating of false inferences, but this type of reader is postulated by the text as an already constitutive element. As Eco perfectly says, Why should the Templar and the Pirogue scream with surprise? The only one that should be surprised is the empirical reader, who had cultivated expectations not satisfied by the text.

No matter what kind of interpretation of the story we produce, the text will take us to the same point, the point where we feel its ironic laughter. Even when we understand that the text is about contradiction and incoherence (the text starts with an oxymoron right in the title), the narrator strikes us with the apparent coherence of its denouement, a happy ending for the story of the couple. In the end the reader is puzzled, but has discovered that the world of his or her expectations is inaccessible to the world of the fabula (it is like playing two different games); but then at the same time the fabula reappropriates these inaccessible worlds, leaving the reader to suspect that the two worlds could come into contact.

There is a difference between the free use of a text taken as an imaginative stimulus and the interpretation of an *open text.* According to Eco, on the border between these two is Barthes' possibility of a pleasure text: one has to decide whether the text is used for pleasure or whether 'a text considers as constitutive of its own strategy the stimulation of its freest possible use' (59).

In *The Limits of Interpretation,* Eco notes that the classical debate aims at finding in a text either '(a) what the author intended to say or (b) what the text says independently of the intentions of the author.' In the second case, one can ask 'whether what is found is (i) what the text says by virtue of its textual coherence and of an original underlying signification system or (ii) what the addressees found in it by virtue of their own systems of expectations' (50–1).[8] In other terms, one can see a text as generated according to certain rules without assuming that the author followed them intentionally, or one can 'adopt a hermeneutic viewpoint leaving unprejudiced whether the interpretation must find what the author meant or what Being says through language – in the second case leaving unprejudiced whether the voice of Being is influenced by the drives of the addressee or not' (51).

Eco interestingly refers to the methods of interpretation of the Middle Ages and of the Renaissance, saying that the medieval interpreters would look in a text for a plurality of meanings though always maintaining the idea of an identity principle (no contradictory interpretation is possible), whereas the Renaissance symbolists would look for meanings following the idea of the *coincidentia oppositorum,* the ideal text being that which allows the most contradictory readings. This is interesting because the adoption of the Renaissance model opens up the problem of whether to look in a text for the meanings planned by the author or for the meanings the author ignored, and in this case, whether those meanings are part of the *intentio operis* or not. According to Eco, an interpretation, no matter how enriching and illuminating, has to be compared with the text and with the *intentio operis.* Nevertheless, he says, the practices of deconstruction privilege the initiative of the reader and 'reduce the text to an ambiguous bunch of still unshaped possibilities, thus transforming texts into mere stimuli for the interpretative drift' (52). We can see clearly here how the preference for the medieval model plays an essential role and is at the basis of his theory of interpretation.

As previously suggested, this is one of the most controversial aspects of Eco's theory. The paradox that seems in many aspects insoluble is this: How can we speak of the reader's freedom when the reader invariably must come to terms with the intention of the work?

Even though Eco provides a critical answer to this question, since the freedom of the reader is to move himself or herself inside the world of the text, there is a problem, because this concept seems to clash with the idea of intertextuality proposed in *Semiotics and the Philosophy of Language* (1984): What are the limits of the text? How important is the function of intertextuality, and how is it defined by the text?

It is a profound contradiction, but a fruitful one, because it is exactly from the contrast created by intertextual limits that the creative act of the reader can be launched and contained. As seen in chapter 2, the process of *unlimited semiosis* does have, if not limits, at least certain horizons that attract the interpreter, but at the same time demarcate a certain field of operation. The scholastic principle of identity is just one of the lines that define it. Multiple checks against the boundaries of the text save us from the likely insurgent reaction of 'reality,' both inside and outside the text.

Theoretically, Eco distinguishes between the *use* and the *interpretation* of a text: in the first case, the empirical readers use the text for any kind of purpose they ascribe to themselves; in the second case, the empirical readers try to become the Model Reader advocated by the text.

In other words, one is free to enjoy the role of the paranoid reader, over-interrogating the text or suspecting every single word choice, but this should not be considered interpretation. Eco plays that role when he speculates on why Dumas, in *The Three Musketeers*, situates rue Servandoni in the Paris of 1625, when the street was dedicated to the eighteenth-century architect only much later.[9] This is a competence that the text is not requiring, even though the historical and geographical research can be of the maximum enjoyment. The text requires a certain encyclopaedia, which does not include the knowledge of when rue Servandoni was thus named.

In trying to interpret a text, empirical readers become the Model Reader, and they succeed when they agree to move in the world designed by the Model Author. It is impossible to quantify the exact amount of information the encyclopaedia contains, but its thickness depends on the text considered. A text such as *Finnegans Wake* requires from the Model Reader an infinite amount of knowledge, probably even greater than that of the empirical author, James Joyce, as it encourages the reader to make connections and references even when the empirical author did not intend them. In that sense, *Finnegans Wake* is Eco's favourite example of an 'open' text.

The objection we can make to this notion is that the limits between the Model Reader and the user of a text can sometimes be hardly traceable. Even though Eco devotes a large part of his most recent publications to clarifying this problem, with numerous interpretative examples, this dichotomizing the employment of the text, allowing the possibility and validity of both behaviours, seems to deprive the reader of a part of it once the choice is made.

Another problem with Eco's limited 'openness' has been pointed out by Peter Bondanella in his recent book *Umberto Eco and the Open Text* (1997) and by Peter Carravetta in his essay 'Hermeneutic Aspects of Eco's Later Works.'[10] Bondanella sees in *Foucault's Pendulum* (1989) a strong criticism of deconstructionist theories, since in that work Eco gives a demonstration of how deleterious the effects of unlimited interpretation can be, not only for individual life, but for history as well. The paradox Bondanella defines is that Eco, as a semiotician, should not try to drive the reader to a more limited interpretation of the signs, almost to the point of advocating, at the end of the book, a state in which things stand for nothing but themselves,[11] where there is no need for semiotics. It is the state that Eco had previously criticized as the disposition of Hegel's Anima Bella, the non-alienated pure conscience that lives unhappy in its nostalgic emptiness.

Although Bondanella definitely has a point concerning the conclusion of *Foucault's Pendulum*, it is also true that Eco warns us not against interpretation but against overinterpretation. This term does not exaggerate, given that the characters in the book completely reinvent and rewrite history according to their made-up Plan, which they think they are reading in a short and partly erased message. Eco shows the immediate dangers of such a practice, since the same characters, whose desire to recreate the history of the world exceeds their intellectual curiosity, are killed by their Plan.

Eco does not condemn the much more reasonable interpretation of Lia, the Mother, who brings the protagonist back to earth, even though at that point it is too late. Eco invites us to think about how easily we overinterpret, while most of the time meaning is closer to the most immediate and commonsensical explanation.

Carravetta's point is similar, in that he sees Eco's later writings (starting with the early 1980s) as becoming more 'ethical, rhetorical, and boundary-conscious. In one word, hermeneutical.'[12] But once again, considering only this aspect of Eco's interests and theory prevents us from comprehending the larger scope.

*Foucault's Pendulum* was published while Eco was working on critical essays on interpretation, which would be collected and published a few years later under the title *The Limits of Interpretation* (1990). He was also invited to participate in the Tanner Lectures at Cambridge University, where an interesting debate on interpretation took place with Jonathan Culler, Richard Rorty, and Christine Brooke-Rose. The interventions were published in the collection *Interpretation and Overinterpretation* (1992).

In *The Limits of Interpretation*, Eco gives an example of his theory by recounting a story by John Wilkins (1641), which is worth including here:

> How strange a thing this Art of Writing did seem at its first Invention, we may guess by the late discovered Americans, who were amazed to see Men converse with Books, and could scarce make themselves to believe that a Paper could speak ...
>
> There is a pretty Relation to this Purpose, concerning an Indian Slave: who being sent by his Master with a Basket of Figs and a Letter, did by the Way eat up a great Part of his Carriage, conveying the Remainder unto the Person to whom it was directed; who when he had read the Letter, and not finding the Quantity of Figs answerable to what was spoken of, he accuses the Slave of eating them, telling him what the Letter said against him. But the Indian (notwithstanding this Proof) did confidently abjure the Fact, cursing the Paper, as being a false and lying Witness.
>
> After this, being sent again with the like Carriage, and a Letter expressing the just number of Figs, that were to be delivered, he did again, according to his former Practice, devour a great Part of them by the Way; but before he meddled with any, (to prevent all following Accusations) he first took the Letter, and hid that under a great Stone, assuring himself, that if it did not see him eating the Figs, it could never tell of him; but being now more strongly accused than before, he confesses the fault, admiring the Divinity of the Paper, and for the future does promise his best fidelity in every employment. (1)

For Eco, Wilkins seems to differ greatly from other contemporary theorists, who believed that every text is a machine that produces an indefinite deferral and a potentially infinite range of possible interpretations. Wilkins represents an exception, since he is looking for a certain stability of meaning. Eco argues that the letter the Slave regarded as divine would not fail to provoke the same reaction even if it were read in a completely different context, which would be, Where are the figs? With this example, Eco wants to demonstrate that sentences can have a 'literal meaning,' even though he knows that this point is controversial, and says that no reader-oriented criticism can deny that a fig is a kind of fruit. Any interpretation would have to take that into account.

The Peircian idea of *unlimited semiosis* is not based on the principle of universal analogy and sympathy according to which every item in the universe is linked to every other element by means of similitudes and resemblances. This is what defines the *hermetic drift.* Although, at a superficial glance, there appear to be similarities between the two, the fundamental principle of Peirce's semiotics is that by knowing a sign we know *something more,* and not simply *something else.* To know more does not mean to know everything, but only what is relevant according to a given *universe of discourse.* Eco also compares unlimited semiosis with deconstruction and affirms that deconstruction, which abandons the text to its essential drift, is mostly a philosophical practice that challenges the metaphysics of presence: Derrida wants to show 'the power of language and its ability to say more than it literally pretends to say' (33). But even though semiosis is unlimited, there is something that transcends the individuality of the interpreter, and that is the transcendent idea of community. A community guarantees, if not an objective meaning, an *intersubjective* meaning, a common core of ideas.

One chapter of the same book is dedicated to the role of the reader,[13] and in it Eco distinguishes between two types of Model Reader: a naive one, who understands the literal meaning of the text, and a critical one, who appreciates *how* the text communicates meaning. In a mystery tale, for example, the naive Model Reader is eager to fall into the traps of the Model Author, whereas the critical Model Reader also enjoys the brilliant narrative strategy. A critical reading looks for the 'strategy that produces infinite ways to get a text semantically right' (56), but even a critical reading is always conjectural and therefore the logic of interpretation is the Peircian logic of abduction. To make a conjecture about a text means to find its Law, the 'secret code.' Even though it is impossible to say which reading of a text is best, it is possible to say which readings of it are wrong, and which approaches 'reach more deeply into the structure of the text than others' (60). Infinite conjecture does not mean any possible conjecture: there is a way we can prove that a given *abduction* is an acceptable one, and that is by checking it against the text as a whole. There is an internal textual coherence that controls the otherwise uncontrollable drift of the reader.

A text for Eco is a 'syntactic-semantic-pragmatic artifice' (*Lector in fabula*, p. 67), a system of 'knots' or 'joints.' This definition, together with his theory of the Model Reader, probably goes beyond a textual semiotics such as the analysis proposed by Barthes with *Sarrazine* (1970), by Greimas with *Deux amis* (1976), and, at a different level, by Petöfi with *Le petit prince* (1975). For Eco, the notion of textual level is embarrassing, because in its linear manifestation a text does not present levels, and in any case it remains a theoretical notion, a 'metatextual schema.' In the concrete process of interpretation, all the levels and sub-levels can be reached through 'hops,' like the movements of the knight in a chess game. How many times, Eco wonders, does an author make a decision only at the moment of lexical realization, when he or she chooses one word instead of another?

In order to actualize the discursive structures, the reader needs certain competences, which can be grouped as follows: (i) lexical competence or knowledge of a basic dictionary (if the text says 'princess,' we understand that we are presented with a human being with implied physical characteristics); (ii) coreferential ability, or the capacity to refer to a previously nominated character (if, after the princess is presented, there is a sentence such as 'she was very beautiful,' the reader will not find it difficult to establish that the subject 'she' refers to the princess); (iii) ability to identify contextual selections; (iv) ability to recognize ready-made expressions (such as 'once upon a time'), rhetorical and stylistic hypercodifications; (v) ability to recognize inferences from typical 'frames' (such as knowing what a supermarket or a cocktail party is like); (vi) ability to recognize inferences from intertextual 'frames' (such as the comic fight between husband and wife and other topoi of classical rhetoric); and, finally, ability to recognize ideological hypercodifications (ideological competence).

The reader approaches the text with all this implied knowledge, but when reading the text, he or she actualizes only those properties the text needs actualized, while other properties remain *narcotized* (for example, if the author presents Raoul as a gentleman, we assume that Raoul is a man with two legs, two eyes, two lungs, and a pancreas, but the reader is not required always to remember all these qualities, which will therefore remain narcotized unless they are specifically required by the text). In order to decide which properties should be narcotized and which should be magnified, according to Eco, we must formulate a first hypothesis about the text, which he calls the *topic* (he uses the English term).

The *topic* is a metatextual instrument, and in order to individuate it, we need to find a certain regularity of textual behaviour. For example, in *Little Red Riding Hood*, the topic would be 'the meeting of a little girl with a wolf in the wood.' The topic, unlike the *fabula*, is an abduction scheme proposed by the reader and is a limitation imposed on the text (see, for example, how in 'Les Templiers' by Alphonse Allais the topic is not the Templars but remembering the name of the narrator's companion). The Model Reader is oriented to the reconstruction of the topic sometimes by the title (which can be misleading), often by key words that are sometimes abundant and sometimes strategically distributed, and often by a certain type of *dispositio*. It is a pragmatic phenomenon that depends on the reader's initiative (who essentially wonder, 'What is the author talking about?' which translated means, Maybe he/she is talking about this).

Another concept fundamental in Eco's analysis is the notion of *isotopy*, which Greimas had defined as 'a system of redundant semantic categories that render the uniform reading of a story possible.'[14] Eco observes that, since Greimas and his disciples have spoken of different types of *isotopies* (phonetic, prosodic, stylistic, rhetorical, syntactical, narrative, and so on), the term has become 'an "umbrella-term" that covers different semiotic phenomena generically definable as the *consistency of a reading process*' (*Lector in fabula*, p. 93), which a text establishes when it is subdued to rules of interpretative consistency. Although it covers different phenomena, the term *isotopy* refers to the constancy of a certain reading process of a text. What is clear is that 'the individuation of a topic is a cooperative (pragmatic) movement that addresses the reader to individuate *isotopies* as semantic properties of a text' (101).

The final fundamental notion Eco suggests in his treatment of the interpretation of a text is that of *fabula*, for the understanding of which he refers to the distinction drawn by the Russian formalists between *fabula* and *plot*. Whereas the *fabula* is the fundamental scheme of the narration, the logic of the actions, and the syntax of the characters – in other words, the course of events in a chronological order – the *plot* is the story as it is told, as it appears, with temporal dislocations and jumps forwards and backwards – in other words, the first synthesis attempted by the reader.

At this point, we are still at the narrative level. In order to pass from the narrative to the actantial level, and to pass from the macropropositions of the fabula to predictions concerning the course of events, it is necessary to perform ulterior 'reduction operations,' and in order to do this the reader must *exit the text*, that is, elaborate inferences recurring in common or intertextual *frames*. To activate this kind of 'frame' means to resort to a *topos*. These efforts on the part of the reader Eco calls 'inferential walks,' a term that reflects the nonchalant gesture of the reader, who evades the tyranny of the text in order to go and look for possible results in the common repertoire. It works in terms similar to these: If the *fabula* says '*x* performs an action,' the reader will hazard 'and because every time *x* performs that action there is the result *y*, then *x*'s action will have the result *y*' (117–18). In the case of Allais' story 'Un Drame bien parisien,' when Raoul raises his hand the reader assumes he is going to beat his wife Marguerite, according to the comic convention. Of course, sometimes the expectations of the reader will not be satisfied, but they are still to be taken into account since they are awakened by the text.

In this sense, we can speak of possible worlds, or worlds created by the expectations of the reader. A possible world is not an empty set, but a full set or, so to speak, a *furnished* set. Even though the notion is borrowed from formal logic, it is applicable to the semiotics of a narrative text as a 'structural representation of concrete semantic *actualizations*' (125).

In *The Limits of Interpretation*, Eco draws a clear-cut distinction between *semantic* interpretation and *critical* interpretation or, in different terms, between *semiosic* and *semiotic* interpretation. He explains the importance of this distinction:

> Semantic interpretation is the result of a process by which an addressee, facing a Linear Text Manifestation, fills it up with a given meaning. Every response-oriented approach deals first of all with this type of interpretation, which is a natural semiosic phenomenon.
>
> Critical interpretation is, on the contrary, a metalinguistic activity – a semiotic approach – which aims at describing and explaining for which formal reasons a given text produces a given response (and in this sense it can also assume the form of an aesthetic analysis). (54)

According to Eco, the text intention is not displayed by the Linear Text Manifestation, but it is possible to see it as a result of a *conjecture* on the part of the reader: 'The initiative of the Reader basically consists in making a conjecture about the text intention. A text is a device conceived in order to produce its Model Reader' (58). Of course, more than one conjecture can be possible: there are texts that allow a Model Reader to make infinite conjectures. The empirical reader is entitled to make conjectures of the kind a Model Reader would make.

Eco formulated and repeated this assumption in many of his books and articles, and it has generated a lively debate on the possibilities and dangers of interpretation and overinterpretation. The philosopher Richard Rorty, for example, has attacked Eco's idea on the ground that it implies the presupposition that a text has a 'nature,' while Rorty sustains that we must abandon the belief that it is possible to know What the Text Is Really Like, and focus only on the various useful purposes a text can have. He prizes those texts that 'will help you to change your purposes, and thus to change your life.'[15]

Eco's reply to Rorty's criticism reasserts the importance of the text as a parameter for its acceptable interpretations and of the role of the critic as the discoverer and elaborator of the theoretical devices behind the enchantment and fascination of a literary work. The interpreter's critical awareness does not reduce the pleasure of a text; on the contrary, it can only enhance it. Rorty emphasizes the importance of the *use* of a text, and Eco does not deny this possibility. A line can be drawn between the *use* and the *interpretation* of a text: while both can be valuable sources of fruitful questions, we cannot undervalue the significance of literary studies as a discipline.

To Eco, theoretical questions are central, and, as Jonathan Culler suggests, they should urge us to cultivate 'a state of wonder at the play of texts and interpretation.'[16]

In recent years, Eco has reflected further on the question of interpretation and on the resistance offered by the text and reality to our will to decipher hidden meanings (see, for example, *Kant e l'ornitorinco*, 1997); but his point of departure remains the same, a pact between Model Author and Model Reader, a cooperation based on mutual respect. The text noticeably prevails in the relation, but this is true only when we as readers choose to approach it. It is then that we assume a certain 'role,' which is that of testing our hypothetical inferences. Confronting the risk of fallibilism, our interpretation can be accepted or rejected by the consensus of the community, which is what privileges one interpretation over another (Kepler's instead of Tycho Brahe's), because in the end what counts is the testing of the interpretation against the whole system, the paradigm that supports it.[17]

### 'Who's Guilty?': The Doomed Reader in *The Name of the Rose*

> It appears that the Oulipo group recently built a matrix of all possible detective stories and found that a book still needs to be written in which the murderer is the reader.
>
> Moral: obsessive ideas exist, never personal (books speak with one another), and a real detective investigation has to prove that we are the guilty ones.
>
> (Eco, 'Postille a Il nome della rosa,' in Il nome della rosa, p. 533)[18]

In 1983, Umberto Eco published his 'Postscript' to *The Name of the Rose* (1980), in which he meant to explicate the process of composition that led to the production of *The Name of the Rose*. Using the term 'production' does not seem out of place here, as the novel was carefully and painstakingly planned, with an image of the Model Reader well present at the time of writing.

Eco admits that he wrote thinking of his reader, but he also stresses that he was creating the reader at the same time. He argues that he did not write to please readers and thus make the book marketable, but that it was inevitable that his formula for creating a novel would attract a great number of readers: a medieval setting, a detective story, and two charismatic characters (Adso for his innocence and purity, William for his intellectual curiosity and his 'Sherlock Holmes' style).

Can we blame Eco for it? Many commentators have criticized *The Name of the Rose* for having been organized according to the laws of the market and for being devoid of *engagement*, suggesting that it contained nothing revolutionary or ideologically contentious.[19] The book has been considered pure entertainment for the 'frequentors of modern scriptoria' ('Postille,' p. 171).

The question is, what kind of reader did Eco want to create? It is probably true that many medieval experts found the book a sophisticated amusement, and it is probably likewise true that more 'naive' readers (in the sense of Eco's definition) skipped the historically descriptive pages, but none of these empirical readers corresponds to the shrewder Model Reader created by the text.

Eco says explicitly that his object was to draw the reader into the trap and bring him or her to damnation by signing a pact with the devil. In fact, not by chance, one of the models for the book was *Doctor Faustus*. The plan is therefore to fascinate readers, to show them the art of research and investigation, to absorb them in the world created by medieval manuscripts, so that once they are in it they will not be able to leave it, and their passion thus aroused for interpreting signs will remain with them ever after. Research, at least for Eco, also implies entertainment.

That does not mean, as has been suggested,[20] that the reader of the text is called upon to 'agree' with the values of the Model Author or of the empirical author. Although Eco sets the readers up, so that they play his game and become a prey of the text, it is possible for readers to refuse to play that role. That would also explain why Roger Rollin's experiment on *The Name of the Rose*, reported in his essay '*The Name of the Rose* as Popular Culture,' showed different responses to the various questions asked. Rollin, trying to imitate Holland's reader-response project in his psychological testing of a group of readers of the novel, created a questionnaire on *The Name of the Rose*, in which he asked a limited group of people to answer a series of questions on their reading.[21]

The problem of the readers who fall into the trap of the book is that they will necessarily become guilty of overinterpretation following the model of William of Baskerville,[22] but they will do so with the humility of the reasonable researcher, knowing that this search can be fallible.

In *The Name of the Rose*, fallibility, in accordance with Eco's Peircian philosophy, is considered a condition for knowledge itself. One famous example in the book is the episode in which William of Baskerville analyses the story of the abbot's horse, Brunellus. William makes an abduction, on the basis of a number of signs, which turns out to be the right one. He chooses the most elegant and economical explanation and also specifies, 'The others believed me wise because I won, but they didn't know the many instances in which I have been foolish because I lost' (305).

Even though the mystery of the abbey eventually is revealed and the guilty conspirator discovered, there is a sense of defeat at the end of the book, since William's conjecture about the Book of Revelation turns out to be incorrect and he is not able to supersede the authority of Bernardo Gui, the dark figure of the Inquisitor.

The main point of the discussion between Bernardo, representing the Inquisition, and Michele da Cesena, representing the Franciscans, which takes place in the last two 'Days' of the narration, consists in the interpretation of the Sacred Scriptures, and an attempt to resolve the controversy over the poverty of Christ. The Church had a political reason for assuming a strong position on the matter, and for refusing mercy to those who would doubt its doctrine. Medieval heretical sects were not unbelievers, but believers in a different interpretation of the scriptures, which conflicted with that of those in authority. When Adso asks the abbot who decides the level and context of interpretation, Abbone bluntly states that authority is the most reliable commentator, 'otherwise how to interpret the multiple signs that the world sets before our sinner's eyes?' (448).

The scriptures are for William an 'open' text, but authority becomes the one who 'closes' it. This is where Eco has the medieval theory of signs clash with a version of Peircian unlimited semiosis. It is clear, therefore, that the novel criticizes a single-hearted, authoritative interpretation, and the work portrays the consequences of such an interpretation in the bloody tortures, interrogations, condemnations, and martyrdoms perpetrated by the Church in those years.

It is true that William's conjecture about the Book of Revelation (the abduction according to which the sequence of murders followed the order of the trumpets of the Apocalypse) is incorrect,[23] since his 'metabetting,' his bet that the possible world he outlined was the same as the real one, will prove wrong, but the validity of his reasoning remains as a precious value, and we sympathize with him.

Only in this sense can *The Name of the Rose* play the role of Abbé Vallet[24] for the reader, as his book did for Eco, becoming a model and a stimulus for a certain type of research or investigation: 'But videmus nunc per speculum et in aenigmate, and truth, instead of directly, manifests itself in little stretches (ah, so illegible) in the error of the world, so that we need to spell its faithful little signs, also there where they appear obscure and almost interlaced with an intention completely bent to evil' (19).

The fact that we should distrust the book and carefully consider its suggestion is made very clear in the introduction, in which the Model Author declares that he found a book written by Abbé Vallet in 1842, who translated from Latin into French the medieval manuscript of Adso of Melk: 'Of course, a manuscript,' and of course, a lost manuscript, as a temporary companion subtracts it from the Model Author, who for its reconstruction has to rely on his own notes and on some citations found in *On the Use of Mirrors in the Game of Chess* by Milo Temesvar.[25]

Not only does Eco overprotect himself, filtering his voice through a number of rewritings and translations, but he also situates his reader in the most uncertain position for valuing authenticity. In a sense, Eco is mocking this ability of the reader, as we all know that there is no manuscript; but he is also doubting his own ability to re-create a lost world and is concerned with verisimilitude, likeliness, and historical accuracy. His model is, 'of course,' Manzoni's *The Betrothed*.

The idea of the manuscript also serves him as a justification for his neglect of actuality. He writes in the introduction to *The Name of the Rose*: 'I transcribe my text with no concern for timeliness. In the years when I discovered the Abbé Vallet volume, there was a widespread conviction that one should write only out of a commitment to the present, in order to change the world. Now, after ten years or more, the man of letters (restored to his loftiest dignity) can happily write out of pure love of writing' (5). The author's expression of relief at dealing with a story so far removed, so deeply in the past, that it has no reference to our time, is naturally an ironic affirmation.

'For this is a tale of books, not of everyday worries ...' (5). This type of comment is what Eco considered the most useful trope for the writing of his book: a preterition, a figure of speech in which one claims to disregard something because everybody knows about it, and even while saying so, talks about it. *The Name of the Rose is* about daily miseries, and in fact is concentrated in ten days, and one is actually struck by how contemporary certain quotations from medieval texts sound.[26]

The Model Reader created is a reader who admires the challenge of interpretation, the search for truth, the witticism of the human mind; who has a passion for accumulating knowledge (the function of the library), but who is also melancholically conscious of its frailty and, nevertheless, will cry sincerely when confronting the burning of the library. It is one who, like Adso, will start with a few incinerated fragments and will endeavour for years to reconstitute a minor library, made of citations.

But while Adso longs for his ineffable union with God and darkness, and finishes his story with a melancholic *ubi sunt*, the reader closes the book with the sense that, although everything passes, somebody will keep rewriting and reinterpreting the stories. The reader is doomed to the attempt to reconstruct the past, to getting lost in the rhyzomic labyrinth of the mind.

### 'It's the Reader's Fault': *Foucault's Pendulum*

If with *The Name of the Rose* Eco tries to capture readers in his trap, signing their pacts with the devil, in *Foucault's Pendulum* the reader becomes the guilty conspirator.

Like the first novel, *Foucault's Pendulum* contains a certain amount of detailed historical elaboration and numerous references to old texts of occult philosophy regarding the Templars and the Rosicrucians, and once again it contains a detective plot and begins with a murder.

The poor Casaubon, a blending of Adso and William, is thrown into the middle of a mystery, which requires a detective figure, the chief of police De Angelis (with an appropriately angelic name, since he will have to form a contrast with the diabolicals). Together with his friends of the publishing company Garamond, Belbo, and Diotallevi, Casaubon becomes a victim, not of his adversaries but of his inquisitive mind,[27] and struggles to interpret a mysterious piece of paper the writing on which has been partially erased, and which is thought to be somehow connected with the suppressed Order of the Templars. The three friends grow more convinced of the existence of an ingenious Plan, and start constructing an entire story around each word of the message, until they give birth to a universal Plan that implies their dominion of the world: 'I do not know if what I remember, with such anomalous clarity, is what happened or is only what I wished had happened, but it was definitely on that evening that the Plan first stirred in our minds, stirred as a desire to give shape to shapelessness, to transform into fantasized reality that fantasy that others wanted to be real' (*Foucault's Pendulum*, p. 337).

On the night of 23 June 1984, when Casaubon is only thirty-three, the age of Christ, he is witness to the ritual of a sect in which his friend Belbo and Belbo's girlfriend Lorenza are killed for refusing to give information about the made-up Plan, a plan that was never there in the first place, but the creation of which has tragic consequences. At the end of the book, Casaubon quietly awaits his own death at the hands of the diabolicals.

Casaubon, the major instigator, becomes the reader who exceeds the rules of 'reasonability' and must pay with his own life. Whereas in the beginning he tries to follow the model of the philosopher who is his namesake[28] and cautions his friend Belbo in his interpretative attempts, later he indulges more and more in them until he becomes the major inspirer and creator of the Plan.

The three friends believe that in their interpretation 'tout se tient,' every piece of the puzzle seems to fit, but their logic is based on false reasoning, analogical thinking, the idea that everything has mysterious connections with everything else. This type of thinking, according to Eco, encourages paranoid interpretation, an uncontrollable drive to shift from meaning to meaning, to the point where every connection is possible, supposing one has the right string of signifiers or numbers.

> It was also the day I began to let myself be lulled by feelings of resemblance: the notion that everything might be mysteriously related to everything else. (p. 164)

> The world was full of marvelous correspondences, subtle resemblances; the only way to penetrate them – and to be penetrated by them – was through dreams, oracles, magic, which allow us to act on nature and her forces, moving like with like. (pp 184–5)

The aura of Renaissance hermeticism purposely contrasts with the Italian atmosphere of the 1970s and the dramatic political events of the era (red terrorism and Moro's assassination). In the memories narrated by Belbo, we even go back to episodes belonging to the postwar Resistance movement.

The characters live in this world of political delusion, in which everybody, for different reasons, has his or her own regrets. Belbo feels he has missed the two historic opportunities of the century: he is too young during the Resistance movement (and in the little action he experiences he proves to be a coward) and too old for the 1968 student revolution. He expresses his rage and disenchanted melancholy to poor Casaubon, who had been in Brazil for the previous few years.

> And then you gave it all up. We, with our penitential pilgrimages to Buchenwald, refused to write advertising copy for Coca-Cola because we were anti-fascist ... But you, to avenge yourselves on the bourgeoisie you hadn't managed to overthrow, sold them videotapes and fanzines, brainwashed them with Zen and the art of motorcycle maintenance. You've made us buy, at a discount, your copies of the thoughts of Chairman Mao, and used the money to purchase fireworks for the celebration of the new creativity. Shamelessly. While we spent our lives being ashamed. You tricked

us, you didn't represent purity; it was only adolescent acne. You made us feel like worms because we lacked the courage to face the Bolivian militia, and you started shooting a few poor bastards in the back while they were walking down the street. Ten years ago, we had to lie to get you out of jail; you lied to send your friends *to* jail. That's why I like this machine [the computer Abulafia]: it's stupid, it doesn't believe, it doesn't make me believe, it just does what I tell it. Stupid me and stupid machine. An honest relationship. (pp. 236–7)

Casaubon, by contrast, regrets having started his university experience two years after the 1968 revolution, when the fire had already been appeased; even though he joins the protest marches, he chooses to graduate with a philosophy dissertation on the Templars.

In this way, the present mixes with the past, and, although an interpretative game, the past is brought back to life; a whole tradition, gnosticism, and a medieval order, the Templars, are revived. The whole underlying story of *Foucault's Pendulum* is linked to the clamorous historical hoax of the *Protocols of the Elders of Zion*, the story of which Eco recounts more clearly in *Six Walks in the Narrative Woods* (164–72).[29]

This historical phenomenon transformed fiction into a nightmare, and Eco invites us to think of the effects of fiction on life: sometimes the results can be innocent and pleasant, but at other times interpretation can dangerously change reality.

The reflection on the complex relation between the reader and the story, fiction and reality can constitute a form of therapy against any slumber of the reason that generates monsters.

In any case we should not stop reading fiction works, because in the best of cases it is in them that we look for a formula which gives meaning to our life. After all, throughout our life, we look for a story of origin that tells us why we were born and why we have lived. Sometimes we look for a cosmic story, the story of the universe, sometimes for our personal story (which we tell the confessor or the psychoanalyst) ... Sometimes we hope to make our personal story coincide with that of the universe. (*Six Walks in the Fictional Woods*, p. 173)

The reader enters the experience of reading with a warning: interpreting is fundamental, but the criterion of constant suspicion, which reads a secret into every written or spoken word, can lead along a dangerous path.

While Belbo and Casaubon write the end of their story, Lia, Casaubon's girlfriend, gives her interpretation of the mysterious message, which is more matter-of-fact, economical, and pragmatic: the message is nothing but a merchant's laundry list. But at this point, it is too late to survive the truth, and Belbo will hang tied to Foucault's Pendulum, designing with its movement the tree of the Sephirot.

The ten Sephirot[30] give the titles to the ten chapters of the book, and synthetize the story of every universe; they are the ten points of manifestation and outpouring of the divine in the world (*Foucault's Pendulum*, p. 597). Giving to his book the form of the *Sepher Yezirah*, Eco is teasing the reader in implying that it is constructed like the Jewish text, in which numbers and letters are inextricably associated, every letter suggesting a number, and every group of letters having a numerical signification as vital as its literal meaning. The doctrine of the Sephirot is treated in the Zohar, and it represents absolute truth, while the *Sepher Yezirah* provides the means by which we may seize, appropriate, and make use of it.

The suggestion that *Foucault's Pendulum* can be read as the *Sepher Yezirah* is of course ironic, but it somehow reflects Eco's wish: like Hugh Vereker in James' 'The Figure in the Carpet,' he indicates the existence of a secret design and invites the reader to explore it. His book is a carpet with a figure of its own, not necessarily the figure the reader is looking for. The risk the reader runs is looking for truth, trying to reconstitute a text that is necessarily mendacious. 'Not bad, not bad at all,' Diotallevi said. 'To arrive at the truth through the painstaking reconstruction of a false text' (p. 459).

Belbo even sets his computer, nicknamed Abulafia,[31] to generate random collocations for use in his paranoid interpretation, a very postmodern 'cognitive mapping' that aspires to reflect the complex net of information amid which we live. But even the computer, when Casaubon tries to obtain access to Belbo's files, simplifies the elaborate lucubration of its user. 'Do you have the password?' Abulafia asks. Casaubon does not have it and is forced to think and to try various possible combinations: maybe one of the ten Sephirot; maybe a reference to the world news, like 'Mombasa'; maybe the name of God, Jahveh, in all the possible combinations of its six letters; maybe Sophia, or the name of Belbo's lover ... Nothing works, because the answer to the simple question 'Do you have the password?' is a simple No, the economical and pragmatic explanation that violates Abulafia's secret.

The files Casaubon retrieves reflect a succession of past moments and constitute little boxes inside the bigger Chinese boxes out of which the book is constructed. As Eco suggests in his Norton Lectures, when a book mentions explicit time periods, the time line needs to be examined in order to understand how the *fabula* and the *plot* are formed. Figure 3 shows a time line that uses the data given in the text.

*Foucault's Pendulum* is constituted by a game of Chinese boxes. The first one, the biggest, which includes the rest of the narration, is hinted at in the second section of the first chapter and is closed in the last chapter. Everything in it takes place while Casaubon is waiting for the arrival of the Diabolicals in Belbo's country-house. The second box contains all the events that take place during the night of St. John, the night between June 23 and 24, in 1983, when Casaubon is in the Conservatoire in Paris witnessing the ritual performed by the 'Diabolicals' on Belbo and Lorenza. This box also contains the final part of the narration with Casaubon's flight from Paris and his refuge in Belbo's country house.

Inside these bigger boxes, there is a smaller one, which starts in chapter 2 and is situated in time two days before, 21 June, when the narrator remembers reading the computer files in Belbo's office before flying to Paris. This box is closed at the end of chapter 7.

The fourth box is the one that contains the narrator's memories, and it proceeds quite chronologically (the time line is interrupted only here and there by Belbo's memories and by his computer files) from 1968 to 1983, covering a period of fifteen years. But the space of the narrative is not equally distributed among these years. For example, chapters 5 and 6, the core of the book, deal with eight years (from 1975 to 1983), while the last part of the book, from chapter 7 to chapter 10, tells of only one year, 1983. The narration therefore fastens in the centre of the text and pauses in its final part, to focus on the details of a few days.

The grid shown in figure 3 is constructed according to the space/time coordinates of the plot and follows the model Eco used for his analysis of Nerval's *Sylvie* in his Norton Lectures and in his 'Rereading of *Sylvie*' in his edition of the text. It helps us visualize the rhythm of the narration, and, as Eco insists, it by no means diminishes the pleasure of reading the text. The grid is constructed outside the text, but when readers go back to their reading, they will be recaptured by the pace of the narration. Rhythm and atmosphere are created by the relation of the *fabula* to the *plot*, 'and it is this relation that governs the

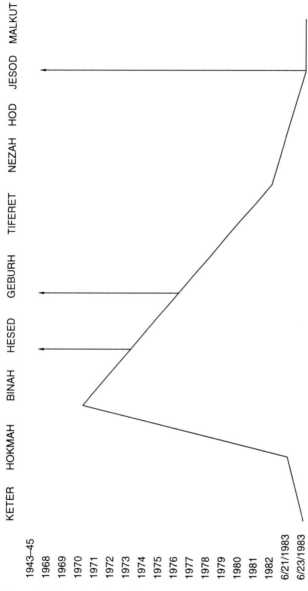

Figure 3. The time line of *Foucault's Pendulum*

lexical choices themselves at the level of discourse' (*Six Walks in the Narrative Woods*, p. 53).

We must recognize that Eco warns us in *La struttura assente* against allowing theoretical explanations to become poetics. That is, Eco, while writing his novels, was not exactly following his semiotic practice.

> Any of us would be surprised if, after listening to a lecture by Piaget on how we perceive objects, we met a painter who intended to paint 'à la Piaget.' We would reply that, if Piaget's theories are true, they define any possible perceptive experience and that therefore also Raphael was painting 'à la Piaget.' Namely, we should never make of a theoretical explanation a model for practical operations. We should not make aesthetics poetics; we should not make the metaphysics of Being become a driving system for vehicles (even though our vehicles and our driving are but epiphanies of Being). (265)[32]

About *The Name of the Rose*, Eco also said: 'I never suspected that my novel was so consistent with my research in semiotics, because I told my story by accepting a split personality, and I did not (consciously) try to put in my novel the theories I had developed in my scholarly writings. I will admit, though, that even the most schizophrenic personality cannot be as split as that. A good reader can understand the relationships between my various books better than I can.'[33]

We can say, therefore, that even if Eco did not construct his novels according to his semiotic theory, this theory must have (at least unconsciously) influenced his decisions and choices, at both the structural and the lexical level.

Brian McHale, in *Constructing Postmodernism*, carefully points out the postmodernism of *Foucault's Pendulum*, and his theory nicely complicates the issue of interpretation.

High modernist texts such as *Ulysses*, he says, functioned as instruction manuals for reading 'modernistically,' that is, paranoiacally. In a sense, they created modernist readers. Later, the New Criticism and similar practices[34] legitimized modernist reading practices, so that we have come to take paranoid reading for granted. What postmodernist texts do is to anticipate paranoid reading-habits on the part of readers, and 'to incorporate representations of (fictional) paranoid interpretations (conspiracy theories) or paranoid reading practices, or ... thematize paranoia itself, thereby reflecting on and anticipating, and perhaps preempting, actual readers' paranoid readings.'[35] Both *The Name of the Rose* and *Foucault's Pendulum* (and we could add *The Island of the Day*

*Before*) are part of this genre, which according to McHale includes books such as Robbe-Grillet's *La jalousie*, Nabokov's *Pale Fire*, Pynchon's *The Crying of Lot 49* and *Gravity's Rainbow*, and DeLillo's *Running Dog*, *The Names*, and *Libra*.

Eco's message, though, is different from that of the other authors mentioned. In the end, *Foucault's Pendulum* criticizes paranoid readings and therefore, as McHale asserts, opposes the master-narrative of postmodernism, according to which postmodern poetics fosters world-making and -unmaking. McHale concludes that Eco's differing narrative 'issues an endorsement of *this* world.'[36]

What is more striking in Eco's book, I believe, is that while it is true the text applauds an 'economic' interpretation that is more connected with *this* world, it is also true that the narrator and the Model Author himself are fascinated by the world of overinterpretation, which merges with creation. The image of the pendulum is thus a perfect metaphor for this oscillation between interpretation and overinterpretation. Even though the warning is there and in the end Casaubon simply enjoys looking at the hill, the fascination with the mystery of the world and of understanding seems hard to resist.

> Why doesn't understanding give me peace? Why love Fate if Fate kills you just as dead as Providence or the Plot of the Archons? (640)

> It isn't enough to have understood, if others refuse and continue to interrogate. (641)

Even though Casaubon knows that there is no Templars' Map, and, implicitly, that there is no postmodern cognitive map, the Diabolicals (read Interpreters) refuse to admit it and will continue to interrogate the universe searching for an answer, until they realize themselves that the search is never-ending.

*Foucault's Pendulum* is not simply an endorsement of *this* world, but a melancholic meta-reflection on postmodern understanding.

## Postmodernism and Baroque in *The Island of the Day Before*: The Multiplied Reader

> We are such stuff
> As dreams are made of, and our little life
> Is rounded with a sleep.
>
> (Shakespeare, *The Tempest*, 1613)

Roberto delle Grive, a baroque Robinson Crusoe, has been ship-wrecked in a deserted ship, the *Daphne*. He is limited in space, since he cannot pass the boundaries of the ship, and his consciousness floats in and out of himself, following the movement of the waves. Tired, hurt, and even drunk, Roberto looks at himself living, inscribing himself in the scenario he is observing, without being able to trace the difference between reality and his own imagination. The bright antipodal light of the sun is too strong for his eyes, which in the assault of Casale were hurt by the same arrow that killed his father; he therefore wonders in the night and looks at the landscape only in the dim light of dawn, with half-closed eyes. His adventure is like a dream, in which he sees himself acting, from outside, as though seated in a theatre.

He is, one would say, a man of his time, for whom the psychic, paradoxically, is as exterior as the physical. Appearance is his condition, and memory his truth. He lives like a monad, completely isolated in a world that is structured like his imagination, which takes shape only in his letters, in his communication. Looking towards the unreachable island, he believes he sees something, which is immediately connected to something else, far away in time and space, through his method of comparing, of finding resemblances between things and thoughts that apparently look different. In this way, his mind wanders through disparate events, historical connections, cultural descriptions, and philosophical concepts, while he remains the centre of his interpretations and abductions. He waits; he dreams, and he waits for the end of the dream.

In order to deal with his own consciousness, he needs an alter ego, and he has a powerful, lifelong one, his imaginary brother Ferrante; but for a while he also has Father Caspar, the Intruder in the ship, intruder, of course, from Roberto's perspective, as the Jesuit was there before him. With Ferrante, Roberto has a relationship of confrontation, since when he was a child, the only son of a loving father, he had to find somebody to compete with, somebody able to show him his own ego. Once he glimpses him in the mirror and sees him as a Spanish soldier, the enemy he is facing at the assault of Casale. For the baroque subject, there is no advance in knowledge without conflict, as is testified by the agonistic character of baroque figurativity.

The final confrontation is, of course, death, in which Ferrante will be implicated in Roberto's imagination in an externalization of the conflict, but Roberto knows from the beginning that he has no escape and will die, and he has learned to cope with death since he contracted the plague and was instructed by the words of the Pyrronian Saint-Savin. The baroque confrontation with death is a representing of one's own end, a splitting of one's self, and a looking at one's own life and death; it is a slow construction in Roberto's mind, a theatrical performance, a way of retaining what he knows he is going to lose. In the words of Saint-Savin, 'Often men, rather than admit they are the authors of their fate, see this fate as a romance narrated by a fanciful and scoundrel author' (*The Island*, p. 82); and later, 'It is necessary to meditate early, and often, on the art of dying, to succeed later in doing it properly just once' (132).

## Seeing *and interpreting nature*

Eco said repeatedly in various interviews that, after *The Name of the Rose* and *Foucault's Pendulum*, he wanted to write a book about nature, and he did. What better opportunity to describe nature than setting the novel in a ship anchored a few miles from a deserted island in a mysterious geographical position in the Southern Hemisphere? In fact, we must fish for natural description in the book, since we are looking at the landscape through the eyes of the narrator, who is looking through the eyes of Roberto, who is a highly unreliable source.

The first 'natural' description is actually the portrayal of the artificial paradise that lies in the depths of the *Daphne*, itself made of natural wood (as is often emphasized). Roberto finds himself in a garden, full of the most incredible species of plants, trees, flowers, and fruit: it appears to Roberto (or to the narrator trying to understand Roberto's feelings) like an Eden sprouting from the wood of the *Daphne* itself. It is an artificial paradise, where nature, affectedly, is disposed for scientific observation:

> Uncertain if he was wandering in a mechanical forest or in an earthly paradise hidden in the bowels of the earth, Roberto roamed in that Eden that provoked odorous deliriums.
>
> Later, when he tells all this to the Lady, he speaks of rustic frenzies, gardens of caprice, Protean bowers, cedars (cedars?) mad with lovely fury ... Or else he re-experiences it as a floating cavern rich in deceitful automata where, girded with horribly twisted cables, fanatic nasturtiums billow, wicked stolons of barbarous forest ... He will write of the opium of the senses, a whirl of putrid elements that, precipitating into impure extracts, led him to the antipodes of reason. (40)

What kind of nature are we talking about here? What is Eco's main character observing? In the time he spends alone in the ship, before the Intruder appears, Roberto lives in the dark and goes outside onto the ship's deck only during the night. He cannot stand the bright sunlight, multiplied by the reflections of the ocean, so he turns inward and builds with his imagination. It does not really matter whether the tropical paradise that is part of his story belongs to his observation or has been fabricated by his imagination; what is made clear is that in his accounts, the letters to the Lady, Roberto reconstructs his vision according to his baroque fancy (or perhaps, we should say, the narrator constructs Roberto's reconstruction according to what we think baroque fancy is). In any case, the resulting portrayal is more like Andrew Marvell's 'The Mower against Gardens' or John Donne's 'An Anatomy of the World' than like a 'modern' natural description. Scents, colours, and shapes benumb our seventeenth-century hero, who is confused by the artificiality of the natural arrangement; to him, it resembles a work imagined by a painter, who wanted to violate nature's laws in order to invent 'convincenti inverosimiglianze' (convincing improbabilities).

Eco is clearly playing with the idea that the Baroque, like the postmodern, perfectly represents a mixture of the artificial and the natural. Whereas for the medieval subject the observation of nature was unmediated by artificial devices (such as glasses, for example, which are an invention of the late Middle Ages), for the modern subject an often absolute scepticism interferes with our perception of and faith in the real.

The reader goes back and forth between the light-toned description of the narrator and the effects produced by the vision in Roberto's mind, which seems somehow distinct, though itself the creation of the ironic narrator. 'Impacciatissimo Adamo,' Roberto does not have names for all these new creatures,[37] and the appellations he contrives seem ridiculous: 'It was like calling a goose a swan' (41). The inadequacy of language becomes apparent every time Roberto is confronted with unusual objects; the suggestion is that reality is more than we can name and that signifiers are deficient before nature's marvels.

Writing a book about nature seems paradoxical: in the moment nature is written about, we are already in the world of art. Where is nature in Eco's book? What does Roberto see and not see? What does the narrator, who is merely reading (or pretending to read) a manuscript, present? Or do we have, more directly, Eco's vision during his trip to the Solomon Islands? It is difficult to separate the different voices/eyes.

Eco seems to relish the description of Roberto's vision at dawn, on the deck of the ship, looking away from the sun towards the west: 'It immediately appeared to him as a jagged turquoise outline, which in a few minutes' time was divided into two horizontal strips: a brush of greenery and pale palm trees already blazing below the dark area of the mountains, over which the clouds of night obstinately continued to reign. But slowly these clouds, still coal-black in the center, were shredding at the edges in a medley of white and pink' (64). We think we have found a description for its own sake, but what matters to Roberto is not so much the soothing beauty of the landscape, but the philosophical explanation of his interpretation of the vision. It is worth quoting another passage in order to convey the delicacy of Eco's description, when he graphically visualizes the landscape, somewhat slackening the reins of his intellectual writing. (Not that these descriptions are not *concettose*, but they are very distant, for example, from the *dialoghi sui massimi sistemi* that we will have later.)

> It was as if the sun, rather than confront them, was ingeniously trying to emerge from inside them, though the light unraveled at their borders as they grew dense with fog, rebelling against their liquefaction in the sky in order that it become the faithful mirror of the sea, now wondrously wan, dazzled by sparkling patches, as if shoals of fish passed, each fitted with an inner lamp. Soon, however, the clouds succumbed to the lure of the light, and yielded, abandoning themselves above the peaks, while on one side they adhered to the slopes, condensing and settling like cream, soft where it trickled down, more compact at the summit, forming a glacier, and on the other side making snow at the top, a single lava of ice exploding in the air in the shape of a mushroom, an exquisite eruption in a land of Cockaigne. (64)

Here we have a wonderful depiction of a rising sun piercing through the remaining clouds of night, with sparks of light and mountains spuming with whipped cream, and a glimpse of an enchanted marine landscape. But it is as if the narrator were teasing the reader, showing that it would be easy to write a romance, but that the intent of the book is more philosophical. The landscape, in fact, is immediately intellectualized: Roberto asks himself whether he is dreaming, since what is happening to him occurred only in the romances of his childhood, but his eyes are aching, and pain is the evidence that he is *seeing*. For him, what is important is that in his vision he can prove the theory of the Canonico di Digne: nature is made of minuscule atoms that, like a storm, bombard human eyes. Vision is simply the encounter of this dust of matter with the eye. Unfortunately, distant objects cannot send perfect *simulacra*, as Epicurus thought; we can derive only *segnacoli, indizi*, signs that allow us to conjecture a vision.

For Eco, vision is an abduction, our interpretation of reality, but by it we are left with one certainty:

> Among the many certainties whose lack he complained of, one alone is present, and it is that all things appear to us as they appear to us, and it is impossible for them to appear otherwise.
>
> Whereby, seeing and being sure he was seeing, Roberto had the unique sureness on which senses and reason can rely: the certainty that he was seeing something; and this something was the sole form of being of which he could speak, for it was nothing but the greater theater of the visible arranged in the basin of Space. Which conclusion tells us much about that bizarre century. (65–6)

And about our century as well. For Roberto, this confirmation is enough to justify his shipwreck. Not much different from the theories of language and reality of John Wilkins, concerned with his basket of figs, Roberto's ideas and the theory of 'that bizarre century' are not far from Eco's Peircian pragmaticism.

*The Island of the Day Before* is a book about knowledge and interpretation, about how human beings perceive reality, and Roberto, a man of the seventeenth century, of the late Renaissance, who is open and 'almost' devoid of scholastic prejudices, and who looks at the reality of a new world with a clear mind, is Eco's ideal instrument for scouring the regions of the human intellect.

In Peircian pragmaticism, experience teaches everything, where experience is defined in the Baconian (Francis Bacon) sense as something that is 'open to verification and reëxamination.'[38] This, according to Peirce, does not mean that we have only to 'make some crude experiments, to draw up briefs of the results in certain blank forms ... and that thus in a few years physical science [will] be finished up – what an idea!';[39] on the contrary, the best kind of experience is an interior illumination that belongs to our logical ability, a formula called the *guiding principle* of inference. The object of our art of reasoning is to discover, from the consideration of something we already know, something we do not know: 'A being the facts stated in the premises and *B* being that concluded, the question is, whether these facts are really so related that if *A* were *B* would generally be. If so, the inference is valid; if not, not.'

When our mind accepts the premises, we feel an impulse also to accept the conclusions. Of course, even though we are logical animals, we are not perfectly so, and our inferences can often be biased, but what determines us to draw one inference rather than another from given premises is a habit of the mind. Our inference can be regarded as 'permanent' only if it affects every individual: 'The method must be such that the ultimate conclusion of every man shall be the same. Such is the method of science.'[40] The fundamental hypothesis is that there are Real things, 'whose characters are entirely independent of our opinions about them; those Reals affect our senses according to regular laws, and, though our sensations are as different as our relations to the objects, yet, by taking advantage of the laws of perception, we can ascertain by reasoning how things really and truly are; and any man, if he have sufficient experience and he reason enough about it, will be led to the one True conclusion.'[41]

This seems to be Roberto's reaction to an immediate truth, when he first looks at the unusual content of the *Daphne*. His instantaneous inference will be at the basis of all his future learning, and we will see how skilful he becomes with his abductions later in his adventure. He discerns very well that human conclusions are *fallible*, but he also perceives that the first step, in Peircian terms, towards *finding out* is to acknowledge that 'you do not satisfactorily know already.'[42] In order to advance, knowledge must escape the blight of 'cocksureness,' and, conscious of *fallibility*, human beings must combine a strong faith in the reality of knowledge with an intense desire to find things out. Only with these premises can learning grow.

When they are in contact with objects unfamiliar to them, like Roberto in the heart of the ship, human beings both run the risk of getting lost and have a chance to look at reality with a clearer mind. As Peirce suggests: 'Let a man venture into an unfamiliar field, or where his results are not continually checked by experience, and all history shows that the most masculine intellect will ofttimes lose his orientation and waste his efforts in directions which bring him no nearer to his goal, or even carry him entirely astray. He is like a ship in the open seas, with noone on board who understands the rules of navigation.'[43]

Roberto runs the risk of losing his contacts with reality and experience, and while he lives alone in the isolated ship, his mind closes in on itself and refuses almost completely to look and see; he avoids the light of the day and barely perceives the landscape surrounding him in the darkness. His reality becomes the world he describes in his letters, one of the infinite possible worlds of imagination. But when the Intruder starts to trespass on the boundaries of his kingdom, Roberto slowly regains his contact with reality.

In the beginning, he looks at the landscape surrounding the ship with a pair of seventeenth-century sunglasses. Later, and partly owing to his experimental swimming, the dark glasses disappear to leave room for the metaphysical dialogues with Father Caspar. When Father Caspar disappears into the depths of the ocean, his learning also blinded by his previous solitary meditations, Roberto's intellect once again closes in on itself and projects the reality of his thoughts into his romance, a fantastic voyage of his imagination that ends in a link with his halluci-nated reality.

It is clear in the novel that Roberto always needs an *Other* in order to try himself, an enemy, an adversary; when he does not have a physical one, he must invent an imaginary one. He starts as a child, when he creates the ghost of Ferrante, his supposed natural brother. Through-out his life, whenever he lacks a point of reference, Roberto gives life to his personal ghost until, towards the end of the novel, Ferrante be-comes a character in the book Roberto is writing. When he dies as a character and is condemned to an eternal consummation, Roberto dies too. It is as if for him life without confrontation, physical or imaginary, could not be. This metaphor reflects Eco's theory of the resistance of Being, which he explores in *Kant and the Platypus* (2000), and to which we will return in chapter 7.

Roberto decides to risk his life in an effort to attain the island, be-cause, if he does not reach it, he will not know what to narrate to himself ('non avrebbe più saputo che cosa raccontarsi,' 460), but his attempt fails, and he disappears into the abyss.

*The Multiplied Reader*

Once again, the main character of Eco's story is a reader, an inter-preter, only this time he is a baroque reader, who perceives the world through his baroque imagination and understanding. The narrator of the story has found the letters Roberto has written to his Lady between July and August 1643, and comments at the end of the book on writing out of a palimpsest:

If from this story I wanted to produce a novel, I would demonstrate once again that it is impossible to write except by making a palimpsest of a rediscovered manuscript – without ever succeeding in eluding the Anxiety of Influence. Nor could I elude the childish curiosity of the reader, who would want to know if Roberto really wrote the pages on which I have dwelt far too long. In all honesty, I would have to reply that it is not impossible that somebody else wrote them, someone who wanted only to pretend to tell the truth. And thus I would lose all the effect of the novel: where, yes, you pretend to tell true things, but you must not admit seriously that you are pretending.

I would not even know how to come up with a final event whereby these letters fell into the hands of him who presumably gave them to me, extracting them from a miscellany of other defaced and faded manuscripts. 'The author is unknown,' I would, however, expect him to say. 'The writing is graceful, but as you see, it is discolored, and the pages are colored with water-stains. As for the contents, from the little I have seen, they are mannered exercises. You know how they wrote in that century – People with no soul.' (512–13)

The style of the narration imitates baroque writing, enriched as it is with numerous metaphors and similes. The letters supposedly written by Roberto, reported during the course of the narrative, are striking for the artificiality of their style, to the point that even the narrator doubts them and struggles to translate them: 'I say he wrote this first missive later, and before writing it, he had a look around; and in subsequent letters he will relate what he saw. But those, too, raise the question of how to treat the diary of a man with poor vision, who roams during the night, relying on his weak eyes' (6).

We have here an unreliable source, which the narrator is trying to interpret, both at the lexical level and at the level of authorial intention. We find ourselves as readers, therefore, interpreting the interpretation of an interpretation. Roberto describes, but also invents; he is trying to write a story, a romance, and the narrator is doing the same. The reader is therefore completely displaced in a myriad unreliable points of view, in the manner of baroque texts such as *Don Quixote*, which Michel Foucault describes in *The Order of Things*: '*Don Quixote* is the first modern work of literature, because in it we see the cruel reason of identities and differences make endless sport of signs and similitudes; because in it language breaks off its old kinship with things and enters into that lonely sovereignty from which it will reappear, in its separated state, only as literature; because it marks the point where resemblance enters an age which is, from the point of view of resemblance, one of madness and imagination.'[44]

As innocent as Adso at the beginning of the story, Roberto later learns the rules of scepticism from the witty Saint-Savin, who considers the first quality of the honest person to be scorn for religion, and who also teaches him how fiction is constructed.

In a bigger world, in which the two hemispheres have opposite laws, and in a society that has learned to deal with simulation and dissimulation, humans are encouraged to use their wit as the new instrument of knowledge. A man of his time, Roberto uses his wit and almost impersonates the readers of his writings, reacting to his love letters as if they were directed to himself. He appropriates the style Saint-Savin has taught him, which is in vogue during his era.

In this way, *The Island of the Day Before* becomes a baroque universe: 'Roberto learned to see the universal as a fragile tissue of enigmas, beyond which there was no longer an Author; or if there was, He seemed lost in the remaking of Himself from too many perspectives' (146). The baroque universe, like Eco's book, is a world without a centre, or, if there is one, it is the self of the reader, who is invited to find his or her own perspective in the myriad points of view. In the same way, this world struggles to find the *Punto Fijo*, while its facets multiply in a variety of explanations and paradoxes.

In his desperate attempt to map the *Daphne*, Roberto is trying to map his knowledge and his imagination, an attempt appropriate to the baroque mind and similar to that of the postmodern subject (we hear ad nauseam talk about cognitive mapping or, more recently, the mapping of the DNA in the Genome Project). But, unlike the Renaissance humanist, baroque and postmodern subjects look for a centre they cannot find, because cognitive changes have transformed the vision of the world.

With this book, Eco is developing ideas he had touched on in *Opera aperta* (1962), and which his colleague Omar Calabrese had developed more recently in his *Neo-Baroque: A Sign of the Times* (1987). In *Opera aperta*, Eco had written:

[In the Baroque form] what is denied is the static and unequivocal definition of the classic Renaissance form, of the space developed around a central axis, delimited by symmetrical lines and closed angles, connected in the center, so to suggest more an idea of 'essential' eternity than of movement. The Baroque form is, on the other hand, dynamic; it tends to an indeterminacy effect ... and it suggests a progressive dilatation of the space; the search for movement and for illusionist effects determines the fact that Baroque plastic masses never allow a privileged, frontal, definite vision, but they induce the observer to move continuously to see the work under always new aspects, as if it were in continuous metamorphosis. If Baroque spirituality is seen as the first clear manifestation of modern culture and sensibility, it is because here, for the first time, humans evade the habit of the canonic ... and find themselves, in art as much as in science, in front of a world in movement which demands from them acts of invention. (31)[45]

Calabrese, writing about mannerism in Eco's novels, sees *The Name of the Rose* as the prototype of the neo-baroque aesthetic, because it is a 'fresco of semantic, narrative, and figurative invariables in which everything is quotation, and where the presence of the author survives in the combination and insertion of systems of variables adapted to the different types of model reader envisaged by the novel.'[46] The cultural phenomena of our time, according to Calabrese, 'are distinguished by a specific internal "form" that recalls the baroque.'[47] Eco wrote in the foreword to Calabrese's book that he shared Calabrese's ideas concerning the neo-baroque, which must have encouraged him to write a postmodern baroque novel.

*The Island of the Day Before* is definitely the most multifaceted of Eco's novels, and it makes great demands of the reader, especially because it seems to require an immense *encyclopaedic* knowledge: from literature to science, from magic to social practices of the time, from navigation to geography, from rhetoric to political theory and history. Furthermore, as Calabrese points out, it envisages different types of model readers, so that empirical readers can easily lose their selves in the variety of perspectives offered.

Roberto himself finds it hard to identify his own self, and becomes a multiplicity of selves looking at himself: he sees himself looking at another himself sitting in front of himself (451). His image is always a reflection in the mirror; his novel in the novel is a creation of many different worlds, in which many Robertos do different things. The island of the day before itself represents another world in which Roberto's story could have taken place in a not far present perfect, where his desire for larger spaces could have been satisfied.

Becoming the author of the story of his own world, Roberto also becomes its reader, and he can participate in the circumstances of his characters as much as we as readers do, to the point that he forgets he is writing/reading and believes that everything has really happened, until his fiction merges with his life, which is also fiction.

### Baudolino, Reader/Writer

Eco's fourth novel, *Baudolino* (2000), will be more thoroughly examined later in this study, but since the issue of interpretation plays an important role in this work, it is appropriate briefly to discuss a few points here.

Baudolino, the main character of the book and, once again, a medieval hero, is an avid reader. We learn from the novel that, when he is at the court of Frederick the Great, he reads as many books as he can, and later in Paris, thanks to his friend Abdul's uncle, he is able to obtain access to the library of the Abbey of St Victor, one of the richest libraries of the time (the same library which Pantagruel entered). There he spends long morning hours reading about distant lands, fantastic regions of the world, and monstrous individuals. At the same time, because of his passion for narrating, Baudolino retells these stories to his friends and to Niketas without differentiating between fantasy and reality. Like Don Quixote, Baudolino lives his first adventures as a reader.

As Eco has explained in *Sulla letteratura* (2002), Don Quixote's library is a library from which one exits, as opposed to the Borgesian library, from which one does not exit. Don Quixote thinks he has found the truth in books; he is therefore convinced that by imitating books he can find his way in reality. Borges' library, by contrast, is the universe, and there is no need to leave it.[48]

After reading about monsters, Baudolino sets out to meet them, or at least he says he does, but we as readers know that he might be a liar (because he paradoxically says so), and we are aware that we should be sceptical of his 'stories.' Baudolino often refers to historical facts that are assumed to be true, but in fact he is compiling from books of different origins, so it becomes difficult to distinguish which are true and which are fictitious. It is possible, therefore, that readers will consider as fictitious stories that others have considered as true. In a way, Baudolino is a little like the omniscient being in Thomas Pavel's *Fictional Worlds* (1986), also mentioned by Eco in *Sulla letteratura*, who is able to write an *opus maximum* containing true affirmations both on the real world and on possible worlds.

The effect of the experiment is that the reader is at a loss, especially because Baudolino seems to adapt quite well to both fantasy and reality;

despite the obvious irony, we do not notice the clashes that are so apparent in the adventures of Don Quixote. I would argue, therefore, that Eco's library is more like that of Borges than that of Cervantes, because ultimately Baudolino never escapes from the world of books. Universal culture becomes a playground for Eco, as it was for Borges and Joyce, the difference being that whereas Joyce plays with words and Borges with ideas, Eco plays with both.

As we will see in the following chapter, the game of intertextuality is one of postmodern writing's experimental aspects, but what is important to underline here is that, according to Eco, the real hero of the Library of Babel 'is not the Library itself, but its Reader, new Don Quixote, mobile, adventurous, untiringly inventive, alchemically combinatory, able to dominate the windmills that he/she causes to rotate ad infinitum' (*Sulla letteratura*, p. 127).[49]

It is clear from this survey of Eco's novels that they can be considered examples of what has been called postmodernity, even though the precise definition of that term remains a subject of debate. One characteristic the novels share is a reflection on language and on what it means to interpret in the 'postmodern' world; they are highly conscious of how they themselves can be interpreted.

Brian McHale, in *Constructing Postmodernism* (1992), examines a revealing feature of postmodern theory. He believes that since literary theorizing has become more and more difficult, instead of theory discussing narratives we now have narratives discussing theory: 'The narrative turn would seem to be one of the contemporary responses to the loss of metaphysical "grounding" or "foundations" for our theorizing. We are no longer confident that we can build intellectual structures upward from firm epistemological and ontological foundations.'[50] McHale sees this response as prompted by 'theorists' such as Richard Rorty, Fredric Jameson, and Jean-François Lyotard, who have induced us to think in terms of 'telling stories' rather than 'doing theory.' It is true that the contemporary way of writing historiography, philosophy, sociology, psychology, and even economics has been characterized by what Christopher Norris in *The Contest of Faculties* (1985) calls the 'narrative turn' of theory. But what is being suggested here is also that, owing to the absence of a 'grounding,' narrative becomes a means of building foundations, since storytelling contains its own self-legitimation. Critics such as Lyotard, for their part, warn against grand metanarratives, since no one can believe in them anymore. These critics have created an anxiety over narrating, a paralysing fear of not being seen to narrate.

Writers have found their way between these two positions so as to 'tolerate the anxiety,' as Barthelme described it,[51] without falling back on the innocent narrative of earlier times. In 'Postille a Il nome della rosa,' Eco sets forth his own definition of postmodernism:

> The postmodern answer to the modern consists in recognizing that the past, as it cannot be destroyed, because its destruction leads to silence, needs to be revisited; with irony, in a not innocent way. I think of the postmodern attitude as that of one who loves a very learned woman, and knows he cannot say 'I love you desperately,' because he knows that she knows (and she knows that he knows she knows) that these expressions have already been written by Barbara Cartland. Nevertheless there is a solution. He can say: 'As Barbara Cartland would say, I love you desperately.' At this point, having avoided false innocence, having clearly said that it is no more possible to speak in an innocent way, this person will have said to the woman what he wanted to say: that he loves her, but that he loves her in a time of lost innocence. (*Il nome della rosa*, p. 529)

Eco, in any case, is a rare example of the writer/theorist, the writer who discusses theory and the theorist who discusses writing (even though the two are different), and he demonstrates that this position is still a possible one. Being highly conscious of the absence of a metaphysical grounding for theory, Eco rejects the need for such a foundation and proceeds in his conjectural method of assessing knowledge. I would argue that this is what distinguishes him from other postmodern writers, and that this uniqueness is due to a particular training that has taught him to value the lesson from the past. The richness Eco found in medieval philosophy always puts his postmodern view in perspective, and acts as the intelligent boundary that decelerates his *fugues*.

For all the reasons indicated, Eco creates, both in his scholarly articles and in his novels, a Model Reader whose principal characteristic is the ability to shift perspective quickly. This figure is a good example of the postmodern reader, who through his own abductions tries to give a form to his knowledge, to trace down a map of it. Even though his abductions can be betrayed and shifted by the narration, this reader is able to change and start over again not from zero, but on the basis of accumulated experience.

Having to filter the story through many rewritings and translations, which are of the essence of postmodern writing, readers tend to drift as they follow the threads of their conjectures (like William with his theory of the Apocalypse; like Casaubon with his ideation of the Plan; like Roberto with the writing of his novel; like Baudolino with his rewriting of history), but they are invariably recaptured in the end by the rhyzome of the universe.

Eco once experimented with the writing of the first part of a novel entitled *The Pharaoh's Curse*, which he subsequently left to three other renowned Italian writers to finish (Giuseppe Pontiggia, Gianni Riotta, and Antonio Tabucchi). The book was published as a summer reading supplement to the Italian newspaper *Il corriere della sera*. The spirit of Eco is clearly discernible in it. The Model Reader of this short book, like the reader of Eco's major novels, is one who laughs at narrative witticism, combining his sense of humour with his search for truth. Eco seems to have adopted the principle of baroque wit without believing in the metaphysics of it, which writers like Tesauro had tried to establish.

The continuous rewriting of the story of the world, even in our epoch of lost innocence, offers this artful reader an intricate net of meanings that he or she is constantly trying to map, but that escape the attempt to ensnare them in a comprehensive net. The solution is not offered, and ultimately there is no belief in the existence of truth, but it is the human curse (not the Pharaoh's) to strive to reconstruct, like Roberto in his isolated ship, the form of the universe.

# 5 Intertextuality: The Middle Ages, Postmodernity, and the Use of Citation

Following the analysis of Eco's theory of reception, I would like to propose the study of a technique fundamental to understanding how the label 'postmodern' suits Eco's fiction: the technique of arranging the literary text as a network of quotations.

Although the word 'intertextuality' is of recent use in literary studies and is usually associated with postmodernity, its implications seem similar to those of earlier terms such as 'allusion,' 'tradition,' and 'influence.' But despite their longer history, even these ideas could not have developed until notions of originality and genius came to the foreground, around the mid-eighteenth century. Is it possible, then, to associate the concept of intertextuality with previous eras such as the Middle Ages? I will argue in this chapter that, although the contemporary word has taken on a special meaning, the question of how medieval texts refer to each other and to ancient writings is of particular significance for Eco's fictional writing and theoretical work.

If postmodernity is at the core of Eco's work, his theory and fiction are never free of the influence of the medieval model. Eco's intertextuality or postmodernity, therefore, is still based on the reconstituted medieval idea of the encyclopaedia. Not only does Eco take his intertextual quotations from medieval texts, he also derives the idea of the hypertext from both his postmodern contemporaries and those medieval writers who influenced him and who absorbed knowledge without regard for copyright. In fact, what Eco's fictional writing achieves is a succulent mixture of medieval compendia and postmodern principles of narrativity. The sequence of his first three novels seems almost ironically to acknowledge this: from the medieval story to the postmodern novel, and then to the missing link, the baroque travel narrative.

## Techniques of Citation in the Middle Ages

According to Bakhtin and Kristeva, every text is constructed as a mosaic of citations, and every text represents the absorption and transformation of another text. But in the Middle Ages, quotation has peculiar characteristics owing to the cultural belief in a transcendent unity. Not only are texts constituted as mosaics of citation, they are themselves unstable as they transmigrate into the work of one author after another, without regard for their identity or origin. Texts are plundered, expropriated, and reattributed with great fluidity and neglect of chronology: paradoxically, they construct 'a critical discourse that is founded on the notion of intertextuality as deviation from the norm of intellectual property and of the homogeneity of the single texts.'[1]

Eco described medieval techniques and principles of quotation in an intervention at a conference on the ideologies and practices of reuse in the High Middle Ages, which took place in Spoleto, Italy, in 1998. Eco's piece, which was published in the booklet 'Ideologie e pratiche del reimpiego nell'alto medioevo' by the Italian Study Centre on the High Middle Ages in 1999, is entitled 'Riflessioni sulle tecniche di citazione nel Medioevo' (Reflections on the Techniques of Citation in the Middle Ages).

Medieval writers tend not only to include numerous citations of other contemporary or classical authors in their texts, but also to present as faithful citations that have been more or less altered. Eco introduces a set of categories for *reimpiego* (second-hand use), offering the following diagram, based on the witty metaphor of second-hand clothes:

|  | prolonged use |
| --- | --- |
|  |  |
| SECOND-HAND USE | turn-up<br>mend<br>patchwork<br>*bricolage*<br>restoration |
|  |  |
|  | recycling or re-fusion |

Medieval writers employed the whole repertoire of techniques, mending and restoring texts to make them carry their ideas, and doing some patchwork on texts that stretched too far from the rules promoted by authority. Presenting themselves as the perpetuators of two traditions, the biblical and the classical, they invariably presented a text as original, no matter how much it had been mended, patched, restored, or recycled. Their peculiarity consisted in their needing to trace every affirmation of their own to an authority. Eco quotes various examples of the technique, from the writings of Beatus of Liebana to those of Pseudo-Dionysius, from the works of John Saracenus to those of Thomas Aquinas, who saw no problem in reinterpreting some assertions of Albertus Magnus and in pushing them to the point where they say the contrary of what the master originally said.

Whereas, beginning with the Renaissance, modernity strives to present second-hand ideas as new, the Middle Ages reuses texts to reinforce tradition. Thomas Aquinas undoubtedly says something new, but he does everything he can to present his ideas as repetitions of what the masters have already said: 'Being able to demonstrate that a thought was ancient was a sign of reliability' ('Ideologie e pratiche,' p. 475).

Eco praises medieval scholars for their modesty in making an effort to show that what they had discovered had already been discovered. This is the opposite of what happens in modernity: 'Our time, more and more insensitive to our historical debts, reuses or even reinvents some concepts without knowing they have already appeared, intending them as original' (480).

Eco criticizes the somewhat arrogant attitude of certain contemporary scholars and writers and confesses an admiration for and a conscious imitation of the medieval method that are fundamental to his entire work both as a critic and as a writer of fiction. For example, he maintains that in *Kant e l'ornitorinco* (*Kant and the Platypus*) he uses Kant in order to demonstrate that what he, Eco, is saying comes from the Enlightenment philosopher; but in fact, like the medieval writers, he makes Kant think things Kant could never have thought, such as the idea of the platypus, which was brought to Europe shortly after the philosopher's death. Eco concludes with a very interesting affirmation: 'In the end, I was covering myself with Kant's *auctoritas*. One is born a Medieval' (*Kant e l'ornitorinco*, p. 481) – explicitly, though jokingly, defining himself a born medieval scholar.

This concept is important for an understanding of Eco's use of intertextuality and of his postmodernity. Although Eco's novels present themselves and are recognized as works of Italian postmodernism, Eco describes his method as founded on medieval practice, which is characterized by a commitment to accurate study of the past and a patient rehearsing of its philosophy. As we shall see, the two are not mutually exclusive.

### Postmodern Quoting and Eco's Novels

Eco does a formidable job of both patchwork and bricolage in his novels. *The Name of the Rose*, for example, has been considered Eco's manifesto of postmodernity, but in an interview with the Italian newspaper *La repubblica*, Eco made this declaration regarding his best-selling novel: 'It is my ambition that nothing in my book be by me but only texts already written.' He described the novel as comparable to a reliquary 'produced with a medieval artisan's technology: disparate pieces, assembled together around the bones of a saint who is more than one thousand years old.'[2]

The intertextuality of *The Name of the Rose*, the 'textile of other texts, a whodunit of quotations, a book built by books,' is, yes, postmodern, but first of all it is the work of a medieval artist. Nevertheless, there is one major element that distinguishes postmodern from medieval intertextuality. Medieval writers were humble masters of *collage*, but postmodern authors add to this the irony of the creator who is conscious that what he says has already been said. As Eco explains in 'Postscript' to *The Name of the Rose*, his postmodernism, far from being a catch-all, implies an ironic rethinking of the already said that does not exclude heuristic possibilities. Citations, semiosic relations, and encyclopaedic features, especially when they connect past and present, are vehicles that allow associations to produce new meaning. We can, conclude, therefore, that if *The Name of the Rose* has the characteristics of a medieval artisan's virtuosity, the juxtaposition of past and present and the ironic reflection on what remains unchanged in the human soul render the book an exemplary masterpiece of postmodern fiction.

The character of William of Baskerville, for example, condenses multiple characteristics: despite his connection with Conan Doyle's Sherlock Holmes and other contemporary features, his teachings resemble the thoughts of various medieval authors. All this makes of him, as Giuseppe Zecchini says, 'everything that a single man should have included in order to become the authentic anticipator of the historical developments in Western thought.'[3] In a few episodes, William's theory is nothing but the contamination of Marsilius' thought with the ideas of William of Ockham and Roger Bacon.[4] Indeed, in the discussions regarding politics, Eco amply draws from Marsilius' *Defensor pacis*, Ockham's *Breviloquium*, and Bacon's *Opus majus*, but sometimes he goes so far as to make the different thinkers' ideas coincide, whereas in truth they would have disputed over quite a few issues. The fact that Eco reinterprets Marsilius and turns him into a 'democratic' thinker represents a manoeuvre that would not have been unfamiliar to Thomas Aquinas, but what makes Eco's gesture different is his being conscious that by reconciling the ideas of two different thinkers he is in fact creating something new, a peculiar character who represents the precursor of liberal-democratic modern thought. Thomas Aquinas would probably have regarded the reconciliation of two different lines of thought simply as a stronger restatement of what authority had already expressed, only in different words.

It is not by chance that one of the central themes of the novel is humour and laughter, which the venerable Jorge is prepared to use any means to eliminate from his universe. Of course, the medieval world was not devoid of supporters of laughter and the ironic smile, as William demonstrates with a whole array of authentic quotations of medieval reflections thereon. But William reacts more like a 'modern' when he declares that Aristotle 'sees the tendency to laughter as a force for good, which can also have an instructive value' (*The Name of the Rose*, p. 472) – the modern element being the view that laughter can lead to doubt and 'doubt is positive.' The idea that laughter can redeem from fear and lead to the questioning of authority would not have appealed to many medieval thinkers, however enlightened.

If the principle of potentially infinite repetition and reference was encouraged by the medieval mentality, the idea that conscious manipulation of antecedent texts might reveal concepts that would contradict *auctoritas* formed no part of that mentality. At most, such manipulation would have been expected to restate more forcefully concepts already present, and therefore could not have served as the powerful cognitive tool it becomes in Eco's work.

So despite his admiration for and imitation of the medieval technique, Eco's intertextuality is the fruit more of the influence of writers such as John Barth, Thomas Pynchon, and Donald Barthelme and of critics such as Julia Kristeva and Leslie Fiedler, mentioned by Eco in the 'Postscript,' than of the direct influence of medieval intertextual theory.

Another characteristic that distances Eco's intertextual practice from the medieval one is the way in which the reader is invited to collaborate in the construction of meaning attempted by the text, extracting 'out of a text what he perceives to be new among so much imitation or repetition; just as it is up to the reader to use the text as a dynamic intertext – or, if we wish, as a metaphoric bridge – between the past and the present, the old and the new.'[5]

The collaboration of the reader, which is called forth in all Eco's novels, connects the works more to the postmodernity of a Calvino than to the rehearsing of Aristotelianism practised by Thomas Aquinas. The dynamic intertextual relations created by Eco's texts, often constituted by explicit and recognizable quotations, force the reader to open other books and commence a kind of quest, leading to intellectual 'epiphany.' But the limits of this quest are imposed by the universe created by the author of the text we are reading. In this sense, another element of medieval influence plays in Eco's theory and fictional practice: the idea of the limits of interpretation. Eco points out in his introduction to *L'idea deforme. Interpretazioni esoteriche su Dante* ('The Misshapen Idea: Esoteric Interpretations of Dante'):

> With a sacred text one is not allowed many liberties, because there usually is an authority and a religious tradition which claims the keys to its interpretation. For example, medieval culture did nothing but encourage the effort of an interpretation infinite in time, and at the same time limited in its options. If something characterized the medieval theory of the four meanings it was that the meanings of the Scriptures (and for Dante also those of secular poetry) were four, but (i) these meanings had to be found following precise rules and (ii) these meanings, although hidden under the literal surface, were not at all secret; on the contrary – for those who could read the text correctly – they had to be overt.[6]

Eco defines texts as 'machines for generating interpretations.' He puts this definition into play in all of his novels; his plan is a witty and knowledgeable game played with the reader. At the same time, as he has argued in several essays on the theory of interpretation, our infinite semiosis revolves around the limits placed by the universe of the text, and the medieval theory of interpretation offers us a precious example of how infinite interpretation can be based on a limited number of rules.

*Foucault's Pendulum*, in itself an ensemble of intertextual links, is a vivid exploration of the dangers run by readers when they cross the line. Can quoting and interpreting quotations bring us to the creation of something new? The novel would almost seem to indicate so, if it were not for its ironic 'take' on the question of interpretation. As Linda Hutcheon puts it, *Foucault's Pendulum* is 'irony-clad,' constituted of 'ironized intertextuality,'[7] and in it not only Calvino, Borges, Poe, and

Del Giudice are overtly referred to, but also *Star Wars,* the film version of *Gone with the Wind,* and Pink Panther and Indiana Jones films. Even more than the main character Casaubon, the character Belbo maintains in his computer an array of passages that are full of intertextual references.

Irony, a typical element of postmodern narrative, plays with the readers' own paranoia and keeps at bay an overinterpreting mode that might tempt them. In that way, at the same time that the novel reunites a series of intertextual references, constituting a structured labyrinth of connected fragments, it compels readers to follow its own paths, which are infinite but not unlimited. The medieval principle of infinite but limited interpretation and the postmodern ironic 'take' on the issue of interpretation together form the peculiar balance represented by the swinging of the pendulum.

Eco's third postmodern collage, *The Island of the Day Before,* is also based on the principle of intertextuality and metanarrative, and once again it shows how the heuristic possibilities of this method can attract different categories of readers, since from Dante to Borges the values of the encyclopaedia – *docere, delectare, movere* – have not changed. As Capozzi has insightfully written:

> As Eco exploits parody, intertextuality, kitsch, pastiches, rhizomatic structures, palimpsests and citationism, he shows that knowledge is dynamic, cumulative, associative, and, most of all, interactive. From *The Rose* to *The Island* he resorts very cleverly to absorbing stories, familiar frames, or prefabricated images that can best depict his basic theories on cultural trends, interpretation, pragmatics of language, philosophy, and aesthetics. Furthermore, the rhizomatic or labyrinthine intertextuality at the foundations of his palimpsests – explained repeatedly by William to Adso in *The Rose* – is an excellent vehicle for demonstrating how something new can be derived by juxtaposing and embedding the old and the new, past and present.[8]

In *The Island,* references to baroque authors such as Tesauro, Marino, Galileo, Hobbes, and Locke and to seventeenth-century poetry are frequent, but these are mingled not only with echoes of eighteenth- and nineteenth-century novels such as *Robinson Crusoe, Treasure Island,* and *The Three Musketeers* but also with postmodern texts like Calvino's and Borges' novels and even with the products of Hollywood.

Nor is Eco's most recent novel, *Baudolino*, an exception. As Capozzi has pointed out, this postmodern encyclopaedic pastiche is full of intertextual claims and humour, in a perfect fusion of history and popular culture.[9] Besides identifying the Borgesian practice of dealing with apocryphal documents and of considering events real because they were mentioned in a book, Capozzi notes direct or indirect reference in *Baudolino* to many different authors and texts, including Dante, Rabelais, the poets of the *dolce stil nuovo*, Swift's *Gulliver's Travels*, *The Thousand and One Nights*, Sandokan's novels by Emilio Salgari, Ariosto, Tolkien, Luigi Malerba, Agatha Christie, and Calvino, and even films such as *Indiana Jones* and *Monty Python*.

This entertaining encyclopaedia invariably adds something new to our universe of learning, or to what Eco would call our encyclopaedic competence, and that is for Eco the value of reading books. As William of Baskerville would say, books speak about other books, and they connect us through time and space to multiple links and sometimes to forgotten knowledge. Reading and knowledge are for Eco, as for Borges, an interactive game that we rehearse every day just by living in our postmodern culture.

### Eco, Borges, Postmodernism, and Play

Borges' influence on Eco as both a critic and, even more, a writer becomes clear when one considers the short stories that inspired some of Eco's critical works (such as 'Abduction in Uqbar,' which bears the influence of 'Tlön, Uqbar, Orbis Tertius' and analyses *Six Problems for Don Isidro Parodi*) and his novels. *The Name of the Rose* has manifold connections to the story of the Library of Babel, and 'Death and the Compass' seems to be the stimulus for *Foucault's Pendulum*. Eco's intertextual discourse is overt here, and it is exactly this explicitness of reference that makes the game interesting. As Eco himself declares in *The Limits of Interpretation*, 'What is more interesting is when the quotation is explicit and recognizable, as happens in postmodern literature and art, which blatantly and ironically play on the intertextuality' (88).

The elements that Eco found appealing in Borges sometimes became principal elements of his own work. Eco could not be immune to the profoundly ironic 'take' of Borges' narratives, which magnificently suited his own personality and writing style. But another fundamental element is the tone of mystery in the stories, in which much is not said (any great and lasting book must be ambiguous, Borges says) and is left to the reader to decipher: the text is for Borges a mirror that makes the reader's features known. The collaboration of the reader became a feature of great importance in both Eco's theory and his novels.

In addition to this, Borges maintains that books and reality often mingle, and that it is difficult to discern which manipulates the other. For example, in 'Death and the Compass,' the main character, Lönnrot, who is himself a reader, thinks he is correctly interpreting reality by understanding the significance of a book, but in fact it is reality that has manipulated his reading and has deceitfully dragged him to his own execution. Similarly, in *Foucault's Pendulum* the main character, Casaubon, ends up mixing reality and language, and a text becomes responsible for his real death. Eco supports the idea that overinterpretation alters a whole system of relations, because modifying a part in the sequence shifts the labyrinthine structure of the entire encyclopaedia inside and outside the text.

Also important is Borges' provocative use of the principle of repetition, which, according to Eco, is a radical and postmodern aesthetic solution. In his short narrative entitled 'Pierre Menard, Author of the *Quixote*,' Borges tells of the astounding proposition of a French author, Pierre Menard, who in 1934 decides to write the *Quixote*. It is not that he is planning on writing another *Quixote* – which would have been easy – but the *Quixote* itself: he wants to reproduce, without copying, a few pages that would coincide with those of Miguel de Cervantes. By doing this, says Borges, Menard ends up enriching, 'by means of a new technique, the halting and rudimentary art of reading.'[10]

Menard's peculiar reading of Cervantes represents a parody of what constitutes twentieth-century reading, in the sense that the contemporary reader involuntarily rewrites the books of the past, and his or her readings are 'almost infinitely richer' than the original works. The postmodern writer, therefore, is constantly rewriting something that has already been narrated, but is always conscious of it. His or her mastery consists in detecting the strategy of variation that will be employed in working the story over, so that it will appear to be different. This technique produces what Eco has theorized as the double Model Reader, according to which, the reader is almost forced to evaluate the work as an aesthetic product and to enjoy the strategies that have made it function (*The Limits of Interpretation*, p. 92); the technique causes the disappearance of the naive reader. In postmodern aesthetic, what constitutes the value of a text is not its innovative genius but the pleasure of repetition.

It is possible to argue that the phenomenon of repetition and intertextual references is by no means new and is probably as old as literature; we have seen how, especially in the Middle Ages, authors borrowed from one another in many different ways. In fact, generations of medievalists have seen intertextual relations 'as a sign of creative sterility, of a poverty of literary imagination, as if authors conveniently drew from a literary tradition and from a body of stock conventions because they lacked the ability to create "original" themes and structures.'[11] Similar criticism has also been brought against postmodern aesthetics, which has been blamed for lacking innovative potential. The important distinction is that, if medieval aesthetics regarded intertextual borrowing positively because it valued participation in the cultural tradition more than idiosyncratic detachment from it, postmodern aesthetics values intertextuality because it produces irony and so forces readers to shift their level of enjoyment to the critical one.

Like Eco, Borges was a passionate reader of medieval literature and constantly drew from it in his writings. Both Eco and Borges seem in some cases to follow the example of the medieval fabliaux, in which repetition is important because it follows a cyclical conception of time. Eco in particular is extremely careful in his temporal and spatial division of his novels' plots, but Borges too speaks of the succession of crimes in his narratives as a cyclical, iterative process; in 'Death and the Compass,' for example, Lönnrot meditates on the problem of symmetrical and periodical death.

On the same level, the literary clichés adopted by the two authors often seem banal repetitions typical of a genre, in most cases that of the detective novel. 'Naturalmente, un manoscritto!' begins *The Name of the Rose*, and the opening both expresses the irony of an author conscious of the literary convention and reminds us of Thomas Mann's *Magic Mountain* ('Eine Frau, natürlich!'). The convention of the found manuscript has a long history in Italian literature as well, from Manzoni to Sciascia. Even more conventional is the beginning of chapter 1 of the same novel – 'Era una bella mattina di fine novembre' (It was a beautiful morning at the end of November) – of which some critics have written that only Snoopy could have allowed himself a similar start; but it is a purposeful act, reminding readers that the book will fall into a particular category and will not fail to meet their expectations. In fact, one of Eco's theses regarding works of mass culture is that one does not read them for the pleasure of finding something new, but for the tranquillity provided by the safety of repetition:

> The strong points of the narrative are not those in which something unexpected happens; those are the pretext-points. The strong points are those in which Wolfe repeats his habitual gesture ... The appeal of the book, the sense of rest, of psychological distension that it is able to confer, is given from the fact that, sunk in his chair or in his train seat, the reader finds again and again and point by point what he already knows, what he wants to know once again and for which he paid the book price ... A pleasure in which the distraction consists in refusing the unfolding of events, in escaping the tension of past-present-future in order to withdraw in a *moment*, a beloved moment, because it is recurring. (*Apocalittici e integrati*, pp. 249–50)[12]

As Eco writes of the film *Casablanca*, the exaggeration of banality allows for the suspicion of the sublime, an observation that summarizes very well the foundation of postmodern aesthetics. Eco's novels do not exactly follow this model and in fact go a step farther. If there is repetition, there is always implied a direct irony, based on the consciousness of the already said.

Rocco Capozzi, playing with Eco's concept of unlimited semiosis, has nicely defined his practice as 'unlimited intertextuality.'[13] Writing books about books, texts about texts, the author initiates the reader to the semiotic practice, teaching him or her how to read and to use signs. The worldwide success of Eco's novels is therefore not surprising: the dialogue he establishes with other texts stimulates the intellectual curiosity of courageous readers and does not leave them unsatisfied. The learned vulgarization of philosophical and historical concepts belonging to cultures of the past distinguishes Eco's work, and the simple medieval principle of *docere et delectare* is with him reaffirmed. While Borges' works with their often cryptic tone are almost guaranteed a restricted audience, Eco's novels are constituted by fragments cut out of a universal encyclopaedia, and consequently appeal to a universal audience.

Despite some important similarities, therefore, there are profound differences between the writings of Eco and those of Borges. While Eco, like Joyce, builds novels that are 'total' and infinitely rich, Borges produces skinny and cold short narratives that are rigorously and meticulously constructed. In this respect, Eco's novels are closer than Borges' to the medieval idea of the cosmic Book, a *compendium* that medieval writers thought would reflect the word of God, a vast encyclopaedia copied down and transmitted from writer to writer. Furthermore, although he believed it honourable to draw from older books, Borges thought it more honourable to owe nothing to his contemporaries. Eco's intertextual method, by contrast, makes no chronological distinction in its use of references and employs contemporary references even when the action takes place in the past. As I will suggest in the next section, in this respect Eco's theory and writing practice more closely resemble those of Italo Calvino, whose work has been a powerful inspiration for him.

### Calvino's 'Multiplicity' and Postmodern Fiction

Eco began the Norton Lectures at Harvard University in 1992 by referring to Italo Calvino, who had been invited to give the series eight years before. Unfortunately, Calvino died before delivering his five lectures, on 18 September 1985, and did not live to write the sixth. Eco mentions in his opening that, while he was writing *Lector in fabula* Calvino was working on *If on a Winter's Night a Traveller*, and that the two books were published almost contemporaneously; evidently, the two authors were concerned with the same issue, the role of the reader, in the same time period. But their interest in the role of the reader is not the only thing they have in common.

Although Eco mentions the publication of his book on the reader in the same year as Calvino's (1979), he does not mention the publication of his first novel, *The Name of the Rose*, in the fall of the following year. What do the two books, *The Traveller* and *The Name of the Rose*, have in common? They share an overtly similar technique: both have a thick plot constructed as a collage of texts, citations, narrative clichés, and various levels of style and writing. It does not matter whether or not the reader is able to identify all the quotations – the task would be an impossible one, except for a living encyclopaedia. What is important is that this accumulation of literary topoi, as Burkhardt Kroeber suggests,[14] stimulates in the reader an investigative search and a taste for research.

In the same fashion that many different works, medieval and other, come together in Eco's book, ten alleged novels come together in

Calvino's *Traveller* to form an eleventh novel, which is held together by the frame. Calvino explains in his fifth Norton Lecture that his purpose in writing this novel was to sample the multiplicity of narrative and to unite concentration with potential infinity.

Calvino expressed on other occasions his preference for short narratives, for fairy-tales and quick energetic adventures, and hence his admiration for Borges' stories; for him, the prose writer, like the poet, achieves success through a patient search for the 'mot juste,' the unique, dense, and concise expression that captures the lightning-swift trajectory of the mental circuits. It is difficult, he asserts, to maintain this kind of tension in very long works, whereas in Borges' writings one can find multiple moves and variety in a crystalline and synthetic literary style. *If on a Winter's Night a Traveller* is certainly a longer novel, but it is composed as a collection of fragments that contain the same nucleus but develop it differently.

Calvino mentions his own novel in his Norton Lecture entitled 'Multiplicity,' in which he analyses what he considers the most important characteristic of the literature of the twentieth century: its encyclopaedism. He says, 'Knowledge as multiplicity is the thread that connects the main works of both what is called modernism and what is called the *postmodern*, a thread which – besides all of its labels – I would like to see develop also in the next millennium.'[15]

He sees multiplicity in the most interesting products of twentieth-century literature, such as Thomas Mann's *Magic Mountain*, Musil's *The Man without Qualities*, Proust's *Recherche*, Georges Perec's *La vie mode d'emploi*, and Carlo Emilio Gadda's *Quer pasticciaccio brutto de via Merulana*. In a passage worth quoting in its entirety, Calvino refers to Eco's theory of the open work, though without explicitly paying tribute to him:

> What takes shape in the great novels of the twentieth century is the idea of an *open* encyclopaedia, an adjective that certainly contradicts the noun *encyclopaedia*, etymologically born of the pretence to exhaust the world's knowledge by enclosing it in a circle. Today it is not possible to think of a totality that is not potential, conjectural, multiple.
>
> Different from medieval literature, which aimed at works expressing the integration of human knowledge in an order and a form of stable condensation, like the *Divine Comedy*, where a multiform linguistic richness converges with the application of a systematic and unitary thought, the modern books we love most are born from the confluence and the clash of a

multiplicity of interpretative methods, ways of thinking, and styles of expression. Although the general design has already been meticulously planned, what is important is not its closing into a harmonic figure, but the centrifugal force that issues from it, the plurality of languages as a guarantee of a non-partial truth. That is proved by the two major writers of our century, who look back to the Middle Ages, T.S. Eliot and James Joyce, both scholars of Dante, both with a strong theological consciousness (although with different purposes). T.S. Eliot dissolves the theological project in the lightness of irony and in vertiginous verbal enchantment. Joyce, who has every intention of building a systematic and encyclopaedic work, interpretable on different levels according to medieval hermeneutics (in fact, he devised tables of correspondences between the chapters of *Ulysses* and the parts of the human body, arts, colours, symbols), essentially accomplishes mainly an encyclopaedia of styles, chapter by chapter in *Ulysses*, or in the converging of polyphonic multiplicity in the verbal texture of *Finnegans Wake*.[16]

It is significant that Calvino refers here to Joyce as an example of a writer with both an encyclopaedic and a 'medieval-like' project. What is important is that for Calvino the fragmentation in style ultimately needs to give way to apparent wholeness in the finished work. In *The Traveller*, he provides a practical example: a number of fragments alternate with the frame, in the manner of the *Decameron* or *The Thousand and One Nights*; despite the fragmentation, the book offers continuity in time.

Partly on that account, Calvino admired the work of Georges Perec, whose *La vie mode d'emploi* he describes in the same Norton Lecture. Perec saw narrative as a puzzle, a whole composed of bits and pieces. The pieces by themselves mean nothing, but put together they become readable. The difficulty in putting together the puzzle consists not in the technique of the painter or the subject of the picture, but in the way it is cut; the well-defined objects, the details, and the borders are easy, but the sky or the sand or the prairie is famously difficult. Furthermore, the space is organized so that there are false elements, pieces that fit together perfectly but that in fact belong to the opposite side of the picture.[17] All this reveals that the puzzle, like the narrative, is a sophisticated game in which the author has previously thought out each intuition and each move of the player/reader. In order to explain to his reader the 'use' of life, Perec must give himself a container and a few rigid rules; only by doing so can he escape the arbitrariness of existence; and his rules, instead of limiting his narrative freedom, stimulate it. As Calvino puts it very well, the elements that make Perec's novel 'the last true event in the history of the novel' are

> The enormous but at the same time contained project, the novelty of the literary configuration, the compendium of a narrative tradition and the encyclopaedic summa of the different forms of knowledge that give shape to an image of the world, the sense of today which is also made of the accumulation of the past and the vertigo of empty space, the continuous presence of both irony and anguish, in short, a way in which the pursuing of a structural project and the imponderable of poetry become one thing.[18]

The medieval idea of the summa of different forms of knowledge that constitute a whole is reflected in all of Eco's novels. The careful way in which the different pieces of the puzzle are cut by Eco shatters the reading experience, and at the same time holds it together according to their order. Readers go through these novels with an urge to find completion, entirety, and closure, a solution to discontinuity, but when the novel frustrates their expectations they realize they are on the wrong quest: literature, like reality, is a succession of fragments, and the book cannot give closure. That is why both Perec's book, with its ninety-nine chapters, and Calvino's novel, with its eleven chapters plus a twelfth that has more the function of an epigraph, leave a small opening to the idea of incompleteness. The endings of Eco's novels likewise leave the reader with an open quest.

The stream of quotations reflects the fragmentation of life, and a writing ready to deviate is what makes the reader indulge in digressions and increase the time that separates him or her from the conclusion, in an attempt to escape it. But why would the reader try to escape closure? Calvino asks, and his answer is that it is because closure represents death.[19] He quotes Primo Levi, reviewer of the Italian edition of Laurence Sterne's *Tristram Shandy*, who wrote: 'All means, all weapons are good to save oneself from death and time. If the straight line is the shortest between two fatal and inevitable points, digressions will prolong it: and if these digressions become so complex, entangled, tortuous, so fast as to make one lose one's track, hopefully death will never find us, time will lose us, and we can remain concealed in the changing hiding-places.'[20]

Although Calvino favours the straight line, he recognizes that texts multiply their space through the books of a real or an imaginary library, in the same way that life's space digresses owing to the most heterogeneous elements. Carlo Emilio Gadda, whom Calvino mentions in his Norton Lectures, also inserts these heterogeneous elements in his novels, creating infinite relations between things, not simply to reflect the real but to transform it: to know, for him, is 'to insert something into the real; it is, therefore, to deform the real.' As a writer of a form of encyclopaedic text and of detective novels, Eco must not have been indifferent to Gadda's way of writing fiction, but Gadda's frenetic deforming of both the real and the self do not match Eco's more controlled and ironic style.

What these writers have in common, from Calvino to Borges to Gadda to Eco, is the idea that the accumulation of fragments will, in different ways, stimulate an investigative search in the reader, who will become a Don Isidro Parodi, a detective who has no power to act on account of his physical condition (he is in jail), but who is able to solve his investigations in his solitary room just by 'reading' the stories that are narrated to him. This is the main project of postmodern literature: if it cannot say much that is new, it can at least make readers smarter by introducing them to irony, or parody (which the detective's name in Borges' stories clearly evokes), and by raising their aesthetic enjoyment to the level of criticism.

Eco's fiction reveals itself as a subtle blend of the medieval and the postmodern. Eco knows very well the invaluable lesson taught us by medieval authors, the lesson not only of their intellectual humility but also of their complex model of the world as an accumulation of more or less forgotten truths. In the medieval *compendium*, quotations help keep these precious truths alive; in our world of forgetful abundance, the closest we can get to searching for the truth is trying to connect lost bits of disparate information, hoping that one day they will make sense and give meaning to life. With different methodologies, postmodern authors do just that, either by making connecting moves that resemble the jumps of the horse on a chess-board and leave the mysterious links to the intelligence of the reader, or by guiding the reader across the chess-board with queenlike moves, from square to square, but still letting the reader choose the direction.

Eco's novels have all the complexity of the medieval cosmos, but their fragmentation offers the closest example readers can find to the lack of completion that dominates life. Although there appears to be a sense of closure and of apparent order, the links created are in fact as infinite as the readers' search for knowledge.

Capozzi is right, then, when he describes the heuristic function of Eco's intertextuality. It is up to the reader to discern and pursue the move into a new territory. Eco's technique does not work in the way Harold Bloom sets forth in *The Anxiety of Influence*, because the rehearsing of previous texts does not simply imply a metaphorical besting, if not killing, of the father (or mother). It is not an unconscious misreading of a previous text that characterizes postmodern fiction, although we of course still do that (not by chance, one of Eco's collections of short essays is entitled *Misreadings*). But as has been said, it is the ironic rereading and recombination of the puzzle that defines the postmodern, or even further, as Borges put it, the creation on the part of the author of his or her own precursors.

Oscar Wilde, characteristically unconventional and ahead of his time, once ironically remarked: 'It is only the unimaginative who ever invents. The true artist is known by the use he makes of what he annexes, and he annexes everything.'[21]

# 6 A Theory of Medieval Laughter: The Comic, Humour, and Wit

If we wanted to find a unifying theme to illuminate Eco's writings and personality, we would have to think of 'wit.' A 'serious' intellectual, Eco much resembles a medieval scholar who delights in language games and paradoxes. We find a passion for wit and laughter in almost all his writings, in which the seriousness of the argument is often illustrated by entertaining and witty examples. A Rabelaisian taste for the use of certain rhetorical devices characterizes Eco' style more than anything else in both his written and his oral presentation.

Eco writes in the preface to Giorgio Celli's *La scienza del comico* (The Science of the Comic, 1982) that in his sixties he is planning to write a book on the comic and is therefore grateful to all those who have treated the subject before – Aristotle, Bergson, Freud, 'and others.' He says that the comic is serious business and that, when one has understood it, one has solved the problem of the human being on earth. He also writes that he hopes to die before actually writing his masterpiece, so that others can write books and dissertations on the book he has never written.

Eco was killed on 5 July 1981 by Giorgio Celli on the third page of *Il resto del Carlino*, a major Italian newspaper. Why did Celli, a humorous scientist and Eco's colleague at the University of Bologna, decide 'literally' to kill Eco using one of the media Eco had theorized so well? Among intellectuals, Eco warns us, it is well known that the third page of an Italian newspaper lies, so Celli was paradoxically telling the truth: he had not killed Eco. He chose Eco as the target of his joke, of course, not just for his media expertise, but, much more, because he knew his appreciation and understanding of humour and jokes.

It is not my intention in this chapter to beat Eco to the writing of a treatise on the comic, but simply to emphasize an important and neglected side of his theory, one reason for his uniqueness and his fame, and to show its inspiration in his favourite medieval predecessors. One could argue that there is very little of the comic in the works of Thomas Aquinas or William of Ockham, but the wit with which they attack established doctrines and authorities has interesting reverberations in Eco's style.

William of Ockham's wit is manifested through the figure of William of Baskerville in *The Name of the Rose*. The eminent philosophical position of irony and laughter in the novel is emphasized when William comments, 'Perhaps the mission of those who love mankind is to make people laugh at the truth, to make truth laugh, because the only truth lies in learning to free ourselves from insane passion for the truth' (491).

This short remark summarizes Eco's attitude to cultural ideologies. The demystifying aspect of laughter works in him as an anti-fanatical and anti-dogmatic element of both psychological liberation and social affirmation. According to Thomas Stauder, Eco was reading Bakhtin's book on Rabelais while writing parts of *The Name of the Rose*. In an interview with Rosa Maria Pereda, Eco declared: 'I knew I had to invent a mysterious book for the background of my novel, but the fact that it was Aristotle's was coincidental. It was also coincidental that I was reading about the polemic on whether Jesus laughed, *that I was reading the text of Bakhtin on Rabelais*, that the "Coena Cipriani" fell into my hands' (emphasis added).[1]

Bakhtin's book is quoted in many parts of the novel, and there is even an ironic suggestion that a book by Rabelais is located in the famous library:

As a single entry there was a group of four titles, indicating that one volume contained several texts. I read:
  I.   ar. de dictis cuiusdam stulti
  II.  syr. libellus alchemicus aegypt.
  III. Expositio Magistri Alcofribae de coena beati Cypriani Cartaginensis Episcopi
  IV.  Liber acephalus de stupris virginum et meretricum amoribus
'What is that?' I asked.
'It is our book,' William whispered to me. 'This is why your dream reminded me of something. Now I am sure this is it.' (439)

Douglass Parker has suggested that we are dealing here with a part of François Rabelais' anagram, Alcofribas Nasier, used in the subtitle of the first book of 'Gargantua,' and in other parts of the work.[2]

Eco wrote about Bakhtin's book in an article entitled 'Corpo Dio' (body of God) in the magazine *L'Espresso* on the occasion of the publication by Einaudi of the Italian translation of the book. Eco's admiration for Bakhtin's work appears clearly in the article:

> One can say that Bakhtin is a giant because he overcomes with one leap the Russian formalists with whom he has always been associated: nor can he be labelled only as a semiotician. He is one, but, in the most glorious meaning of the term, he ties the study of linguistic systems to that of culture, he goes beyond formal linguistic research, and he offers new keys with which to interpret other languages, those of the body, of food, of the feast. Most of all, ... he makes a fundamental contribution to a philosophy, an aesthetics, a semiotics of the comic.[3]

Furthermore, one does not need Bakhtin to enjoy Rabelais' work:

> 'Gargantua and Pantagruel' needs no introduction. It is sufficient to look at it to find it gloriously modern, a post-historical vanguard, post-sixty-eight, post-seventy-seven, post 'autonomi' with ski masks; and the red brigades with their little pistols are ridiculous compared to the way this jolly friar, with his quill, strikes at the heart of centuries of culture, of morality, of politics, overthrows the Sorbonne, turns the world upside down and stages exclusion, exiles, rejected culture, the culture of the belly, of the bird, of the popular carnival; he reflects more of the Renaissance with his friars and scholars who piss, fart, stuff themselves with food and recite phallic litanies, than Michelangelo with his domes ... and with so much irreverence he gives us back dignity, at least for the body, but also for the soul. Because a soul that is capable of laughing is more human than those capable of crying, witness Aristotle, 'De anima,' third book: only the human being among living creatures is able to laugh.[4]

The importance of laughter in *The Name of the Rose* confirms this view, and one can see how the debate on whether Christ laughed caused numerous battles and deaths. In the Middle Ages, the Church maintained a monopoly on humour. The knowledge and use of it was limited to members of the Church, who could employ it in their sermons in the form of exempla in order to attract the interest of their listeners.

All the classic wit of ancient Rome remained intact in the archives of the Church for centuries, until Renaissance scholars worked on its resurgence.[5]

There was, nevertheless, another type of humour, different from the exempla, that was part of popular culture, a kind of jocular spirit, the carnivalesque laughter to which Bakhtin was referring, and it was present in both the written and the oral tradition – in, for example, the writings of Antonio Pucci (1312–75), Boccaccio (1313–75), Sacchetti (1335–1400), and Bracciolini (1380–1459).

Thomas Aquinas contributed a great deal to what Jacques Le Goff has called the 'réhabilitation du rire honnête,' a subtracting of laughter from the vicious circle in which theology had entrapped it. He distinguishes *eutrapelia*, the good disposition to happiness, from *bolomachia*, the excess that follows an immoral ruling. 'Savagery,' which Aquinas sees as the inability to have fun, is also a negative quality. Laughter retains a dignified, moderate attitude that allows for control of the desires and passions.[6]

There is a great deal of *bolomachia* in Eco's novel, for example in Adso's 'vision' and in the references to the 'Coena Cipriani,'[7] but what is taboo for the medieval Church is the other type of humour, the philosophical one, the one that can call into question centuries of metaphysics. This is well testified in Jorge's comment:

> 'But laughter is weakness, corruption, the foolishness of our flesh. It is the peasant's entertainment, the drunkard's license; even the church in her wisdom has granted the moment of feast, carnival, fair, this diurnal pollution that releases humors and distracts from other desires and other ambitions ... Still, laughter remains base, a defense for the simple, a mystery desecrated for the plebeians. The apostle also said as much: it is better to marry than to burn. Rather than rebel against God's established order, laugh and enjoy your foul parodies of order, at the end of the meal, after you have drained jugs and flasks. Elect the king of fools, lose yourselves in the liturgy of the ass and the pig, play at performing your saturnalia head down ... But here, here' – now Jorge struck the table with his finger, near the book William was holding open – 'here the function of laughter is reversed, it is elevated to art, the doors of the world of the learned are opened to it, it becomes the object of philosophy, and of perfidious theology.' (*The Name of the Rose*, p. 474)

Aristotle had already declared laughter proper to human beings, but like Jorge he had also declared that the comic mask is ugly and deformed. What would have happened if he had legitimized laughter? Jorge's answer is that the simple would have lost their fear of the devil, and society would have become corrupted. As Massimo Parodi has commented, 'It is necessary to fight against the monks who defend, without a smile, their world of signifieds, their library, their labyrinth, their disquieting world in which books/signifieds speak with one another.'[8] As long as cultural signifieds are protected and mystified with a serious intent, they remain intimidating for those who are excluded from possessing them, and remain locked up in their self-referentiality. It is only when the vulgar mind is able to smile at them that they become available and shared.

This is one of Eco's main objectives, which he has pursued since the beginning of his career: the ironic treatment and popularization of what was commonly referred to as 'high culture,' with the aim of destroying the psychological barriers that have kept 'unauthorized personnel' from enjoying a portion of the world. That is why Aristotle, in *The Name of the Rose*, is brought down to earth by means of a hypothetical book on laughter and comedy. In Jorge's mind, such a book would break down the barriers of the monks' library, and their *signified* would be open to public derision.

Eco's novel has been harshly criticized for placing before readers words, events, and historical facts with which most would not be familiar (as Raul Mordenti has pointed out, 'Il lettore non sa un tubo neanche dei patarini, dei catari e dei valdesi'),[9] and for playing a sadistic game with the reader of average education. In part, this criticism is just, but it is exactly the type of criticism that made the fortunes of the book: readers were fascinated by the illusion of easy and direct contact with the highbrow phantasms of the past. This is the power of postmodern literature, the ambition of which is to critique often inaccessible and obscure texts, to popularize the subtle mysteries of rigidly academic culture, and to defy the power of the unknown.

The same idea is at the basis of *Foucault's Pendulum,* which begins with a witty quotation from Agrippa's *De occulta philosophia* that teases the reader: 'Only for you, children of doctrine and knowledge, did we write this work. Examine the book, gather in that intention that we spread and arranged in various places; what we hid in one place, we manifested in another, so that it can be understood by your wisdom.' The invocation flatters the readers, 'children of doctrine and knowledge,' and ridicules their hubris, exposing the sadistic game of the author, who is planning to veil or make manifest the most unexpected references. But quoting Agrippa means much more than this. By citing him, Eco takes his place in the tradition of the *paradox*, a genre common in the Middle Ages and the Renaissance. The author of the paradox takes up the less likely argument of a debate, the one that goes against vulgar opinion, and supports it throughout; Agrippa, for example, writes *Of the Nobility and Excellence of the Feminine Sex* (1529). Sometimes the debate is not serious, and the writer limits his work to a play with language, but at other times it is crucial, so the author must be cautious. That is why Agrippa writes his warning to readers, urging them to read between the lines and choose for themselves what is serious and what is not, inviting them to a suspension of judgment that is typical of the sceptical tradition.[10] It is also why Eco chooses to refer to Agrippa in his first approach to the readers of his second novel.

The question of whether Eco's explanations satisfy his readers' quest for knowledge is idle, because the book suggests that perhaps there is no knowledge and that our efforts to link together our abductions often result in dangerous assumptions (as for Casaubon), especially when we overexert our imaginations. The scientific/positivistic description of the pendulum that opens the novel, with its aura of explicable inexplicability, works to break down the barrier of fake mystery that surrounds some of the obscure but common phenomena that take place before our eyes.

The dialogue of the couple visiting the Conservatoire and admiring the pendulum in fact summarizes the whole plot. The woman cannot understand why, if everything moves, the geometric central point does not. Furthermore, she does not care to understand. The man has lost the ability to marvel and tremble before infinity and the unknown. In the end, their commonsensical behaviour condemns them, but at the same time it saves them from falling into the trap Casaubon could not avoid: the belief in certainty, the idea that somehow, somewhere there is a plan that controls the mechanisms of the world and of society.

Both William and Casaubon have fallen for this powerful idea, and come to discover, in the end, that there is no plan, or, better, that the plan constructed by their imaginations has taken on a life of its own and revolted against them. It is a minor matter whether or not the plan was already in God's mind: that is something we will never know.

Either you are Rabelais, says Eco, or you are Descartes.[11] Either one accepts Order and laughs from within it with the intention of making it explode, or one pretends to reject it so as to restore it in different forms. We can have no doubt as to Eco's position. Even his 'serious' semiotics, painstakingly set forth in his theoretical works and examined in the first chapters of this study, seems aimed at disrupting the order from the inside. Using the vocabulary and methodology of structuralism, he erodes its foundations by establishing in its place what he calls 'the theory of the lie,' and continues the story with a book on serendipity, which I will examine in the last part of this chapter.

## The 'Bustine di Minerva'

Beginning in the 1960s, Eco contributed to monthly and weekly magazines a series of short essays meant as comments on contemporary events and issues. These were then collected in various volumes, including the three *Diari minimi* (1963, 1992, and 2000), *Il costume di casa* (1973), *Dalla periferia dell'impero* (1977), *Sette anni di desiderio* (1983), and *Sugli specchi e altri saggi* (1985).[12]

Notable in these essays is not only their sharp analysis of cultural phenomena, but also the characteristic wit accompanying their narration. The structure and rhythm of these *pastiches* seem spontaneous and natural, but a closer look reveals that they are astutely planned and based on conscious adoption of comic devices. Eco has written on categories of the comic on various occasions, in his essays on Pittigrilli,[13] Pirandello,[14] and Achille Campanile,[15] but his learned practice in no way spoils the freshness of approach and striking effect of these writings.

First of all, their genre. Eco includes them in the genre of the *pastiche*, but admits that the 'diario minimo' (minimal journal) is already becoming a genre in its own right, containing comment on societal customs, literary parody, fantasy of various kinds, and nonsense.

The influence of these superficially simple *divertissements* was greater than even Eco could have imagined. For example, a new organization was founded in Paris, *Transcultura*, which, responding to the parody in the essay 'Industry and Sexual Repression in a Society in Northern Italy,'[16] invited African and Asian anthropologists to study Western society in European cities.[17] Furthermore, some of these short writings came to be referred to as major studies, for example, the 'Fenomenologia di Mike Bongiorno'[18] (The Phenomenology of Mike Bongiorno) and 'Filosofi in libertà'[19] (Philosophers on the Loose). Others testify to Eco's political engagement and influence, with their ironic critique of Italian customs and, more globally, of the weaknesses of Western society.

These short essays seem to have no connection with medieval culture, but in fact many of them refer to the authors and themes of the Middle Ages. For example, Eco dedicates *Dalla periferia dell'impero* to

Beatus of Liebana, Virgil of Bigorre, and Honorius of Autun, three illustrious medieval scholars. He begins the book with a letter from a member of the confraternity of the wise (himself) to the emperor of Western civilization, the American president Gerald Ford. The letter displaces in time a contemporary issue, but does so in a language that mixes Latin ('Ad Geraldum Fordum Balbolum, Foederatorum Indiarium ad Occasum Vergentium Civitatum Principem')[20] with references to contemporary personalities such as Ford, Rumor, Andreotti (Andreozio), Saragat (Saragazio), and Kissinger (Chisingero).

The request being respectfully forwarded by the intellectual sounds like a desperate appeal, but it is also a biting criticism of how Italian politicians, thanks to the magnanimity of Geraldus Fordus, have been able to manipulate and corrupt the public sphere. Here Eco is resorting to a rhetorical device. First, he is comparing two different things, the situation of contemporary Italian politics and the condition of a small and insignificant Roman province at the time of the powerful Roman Empire. Second, he is using an old-fashioned rhetorical writing style to describe a contemporary issue. The effect of the analogy is clear and causes the reader to smile, because, as Aristotle had said, the essence of the enjoyment of wit is the recognition on the part of the hearer ('hence neither superficial enthymemes are popular ... nor ones that we do not understand when they are said, but either those of which recognition occurs as soon as they are spoken').[21]

In his discussion of irony and the comic in *Tra menzogna e ironia*, Eco makes clear who his predecessors are in the philosophical analysis of wit: Aristotle, Freud, and Bergson (to which list we could add Emanuele Tesauro and many others). The father of the rhetoric of wit, Aristotle, had already identified witticisms as artful constructions and as metaphors by analogy. Many of Eco's 'minimal' essays are constructed in this manner, but Eco himself identifies other important categories of wit, clearly distinguishing among wit, the comic, and humour, and between the comic in life and the comic in the text. While the comic in life has to do with physiology, the comic in the text is provided by rhetorical devices such as the rhythm of the narration. It is the comic in the text that better pertains to Eco's analysis.

The distinction among wit, the comic, and humour is clear, but all can be present in the same text at the same time. Wit is an apt association of thought and expression, the superimposition of two images, in other words what Aristotle calls a proportion. In Freudian terms, we could call it a 'condensation,' producing three different effects that

Freud categorizes as *Witze, Kalauer,* and *Klangwitze.* For the definition of the comic, Eco has recourse to Pirandello, who defines it as 'avvertimento del contrario' (recognition of the contrary). For Aristotle, Eco says, 'the comic was something wrong which appears when, in a chain of happenings, an event is introduced which alters the usual order of the facts.' For Kant, 'laughter is produced when an absurd situation causes our expectation to dissolve into nothing' (*Tra menzogna,* p. 63).

What is necessary, Eco adds, is that the person who laughs is not affected by the absurd situation, as Hegel has theorized, and can maintain a sense of superiority. As soon as this sense of superiority dissolves and one understands that he or she could be affected or fall into the same situation, the laughter becomes a smile, and what was *comical* becomes *humorous.*

On the basis of this distinction, we could conclude that what provokes a smile in the reader of Eco's essays is a mixture of wit and humour. In fact, there is never anything purely comical. Consider, for example, the essay entitled 'Verso un nuovo medioevo'[22] (Towards a New Middle Ages), based on a hypothesis of Roberto Vacca regarding the possibility of the collapse of our civilization due to the degradation of the systems of the technological era, to their having become too complex to be controlled even by an efficient managerial apparatus. Eco mentions a few things that can be seen as harbingers of this decay:

> First of all, a great peace that is breaking down, a great international power that has unified the world in language, customs, ideologies, religions, art, and technology, and then at a certain point, thanks to its own ungovernable complexity, collapses. It collapses because the 'barbarians' are pressing at its borders; these barbarians are not necessarily uncultivated, but they are bringing new customs, new views of the world. These barbarians may burst in with violence, because they want to seize a wealth that has been denied them, or they may steal into the social and cultural body of the reigning Pax, spreading new faiths and new perspectives of life. (*Dalla periferia dell'impero,* p. 74)

> Excess of population interacts with excess of communication and transportation, making the cities uninhabitable not through destruction and abandonment but through a paroxysm of activity. The ivy that slowly undermined the great, crumbling buildings is replaced by air pollution and the accumulation of garbage that disfigures and stifles the big restored buildings. (77)

The change within the big cities appears to be a medievalization of space, but whereas in the Middle Ages people abandoned the city because of decline in population and the difficulty of transportation, today the opposite is taking place because of an excess of population.

The paradoxical idea of a return to the Middle Ages, which should strike us as comical and which is presented be means of a sapient use of wit, instead causes a certain sadness in us. While we smile at the idea that air routes today are not very dissimilar to medieval pilgrimage routes, and that tourist guides back then listed churches in the same way that today they list motels and Hiltons, still we feel a certain *horror vacui*. We recognize that this type of change could very soon interfere with our own future, and our smile turns to a grimace. This is what Eco defines as humour: rather than feeling superior or detached, we identify with a situation, as with Don Quixote's refusal to acknowledge that the dreams he is after are possible only in the chivalric literature of a bygone era.

The comic rises from the violation of a rule, but does so among those who 'have so absorbed the rule that they also presume it is inviolable' (*Tra menzogna e ironia*, p. 275), so the rule is reaffirmed; humour, by contrast, represents criticism of the rule. According to this way of thinking, wit and the pun are kin to humour, as they arouse distrust of language 'in its fragility' (278). Alain Cohen has written: 'Laughter is part of the processes within the universe of language and discourse, as rich and as complex as they are themselves. Laughter cannot be apprehended as a separate phenomenon within discourse and action. Determinations of topic-switch, focus-switch, code-switch, tempo-switch or other effects pertinent to the pragmatic organization responsible for the laughter effect may point to perhaps necessary but not enough to sufficient conditions.'[23]

In fact, each episode of his own life that Eco recounts in his 'minimal diaries' is connected with the critique of a larger issue. For example, 'How to Travel with a Salmon' offers not basic advice about travelling, but a cultural commentary on the value of computers in today's society. The criticism comes about through the comic vicissitudes of the author, who in order to save a smoked salmon recently bought in Stockholm empties the hotel room refrigerator to make place for the fish and in the end is charged a lot of money because the computer, owing to a previous glitch, refuses to acknowledge that he had not drunk all the beverages contained in the refrigerator. The author is able subtly to criticize the unreliability of the machine, and does so by making the reader smile over our strange trust and distrust of modern technology.

In the essay on Campanile, Eco insists that the comic is produced by recognition and can therefore fail if the author of a joke rationally explains its significance. Campanile, according to Eco, does that once in a while, but that does not diminish his superiority, because what makes his sketches particularly comic is the way the comic is introduced by the text: language making fun of itself is what makes Campanile's word games natural reagents. His writings could never have been celebrations of the status quo, because they ridiculed the rhetoric of a certain kind of paraliterary culture and worked towards the parodying of stereotypes. Eco quotes various examples, but a single one can help clarify Campanile's intentions and achievement:

'I would never have expected this from you!' said Filippo.

'If I had imagined you would take it like this ...' Filippo signalled to him to keep silent. With his head in his hands he started crying like a lambkin. Guerrando's heart ached, and he would willingly have comforted his friend, if he had not been the least appropriate person to do so. Because he felt sincere affection for Filippo. He told him. His lover's husband looked at him in tears.

'It's all over, it's all over,' he cried.

Yes. This was the saddest thing: that it was all over, and also between the two men. How much worthier was Filippo's friendship than Susanna's unfaithful love! Now it was all over: the night card games, the nice conversations between the two men, who got along so well, the dinners, the jokes, the outings. Guerrando expressed to Filippo his sincere pain and his regret for the end of their friendship.

'You wanted it!' said Filippo, still crying. 'Now it can never be fixed.'

'Why not?' said Guerrando. 'It depends only on us.'

Filippo incinerated him with a glance.

'Don't you think,' he said, 'that everybody would laugh at me? It can't be done, it can't be done.'

And he started crying again.

'Let's meet secretly,' said Guerrando. 'Let's meet in hidden places, where nobody knows. I have a small apartment.'

'Shut up!' said the old man.

'No, Filippo,' said Guerrando mildly, 'you need to understand me and to understand my sincere desire to fix things.'

He said to comfort him: 'I suspect that woman cheated on me too.'

Filippo moaned: Out of pity for his betrayed friend? Out of pain for the news of his wife's betrayal?

Nobody ever knew.

He said simply: 'I will throw her out of the house.'

'Thank you,' said Guerrando.

'Actually,' he said, 'I will kill her.'

'No,' said Guerrando, 'why do you want to kill her?'

'Okay,' said the friend, 'I won't kill her.'

He felt a little better.

'Now,' he said, 'I have to confess one thing that will make you laugh. When I said "You're my wife's lover ..."'

'Well?'

'I was joking.'

'What a stupid joke!' cried the other. 'See? See what happens when you joke like this? Next time take it easy.'

He looked at his friend timidly.

'Then,' he said, 'if you throw your wife out of the house, I will still be able to come to your place? We could still play cards at night?'

Filippo was torn. But the temptation was strong. Suddenly he decided. He extended his right hand.

'All right,' he mumbled, 'but on one condition.'

'Tell me.'

'That nobody know.'

'Nobody will ever know anything,' whispered Guerrando. 'I swear. We will do everything possible so that nobody knows.'

'Be careful not to compromise me,' said the old man, 'it's a matter of honor. I expect maximum secrecy.'

'Filippo,' said the other seriously, 'I am a gentleman.'

'And most of all,' added Filippo, raising his finger, 'that my wife never hears.' ( *Tra menzogna e ironia*, pp. 75–7)

It is the play with language that provokes humour, and humour, like other human activities, can take different forms. For Eco, we are the only species capable of laughing owing to our consciousness, and it is only the consciousness that we are going to die that makes us capable of laughing about our condition. That is why irony, almost like 'wit' in Tesauro, can run the risk of becoming a metaphysical principle: the only way in which we can make the idea of death bearable is by laughing about it and so producing an estrangement-like effect. George Santayana expressed this idea: 'The most profound philosophers ... by the force of intense reflection, which discloses to them that what exists is unintelligible and has no reason for existing ... are driven to the alternative of saying that existence is illusion and that the only reality is something beneath or above existence. That real existence could be radically comic never occurs to these solemn sages; they are without one ray of humor and are persuaded that the universe must too be without one.'[24]

The idea of the comic and of irony as transcending the fundamental questions of existence is important in Eco's thought and in postmodern criticism. Irony as a mode of existence and a theory of self-detachment has been explicit since Kierkegaard's *The Concept of Irony*. Although presenting a highly traditional notion of language that goes back to Plato, in which words are equated with false currency, Kierkegaard discusses Socratic irony in contemporary terms. Socrates, he notes, was using irony not to conceal a superior truth, but simply to mystify, to negate. This is a very postmodern idea, that of language playing with itself, where the irony is directed not towards hidden meanings but towards signifiers themselves.

Critics such as Candace D. Lang have studied irony and humour as critical paradigms, defining the ironic critic as one who is subservient to conceptualization, ready to study linguistic functions as revelations of meaning and authorial intentions, whereas the humourist critic 'accords a priori to language a constitutive role in thought and therefore in the ego.'[25]

Although Lang admits that she hopes to arrive at a new sense of ironic discourse rather than a terminology, I find her definition of humour problematic, because it completely neglects the idea of laughter, of 'recognition,' and of affectability. She calls the texts of Robbe-Grillet, Sollers, and Barthes 'humorous,' in that they cast 'doubt upon the supposed priority of the signified and, consequently, the priority of the cogito itself.'[26] Following Eco, we could object that humour, as a sub-species of the comic, is associated with a variety of different states. The definition given by Lang is more a description of contemporary art and criticism than a qualification of irony and humour as disruptive of our systems of expectation and linguistic rules. Humour implies an actual smile, not only a metaphysical thought.

Interestingly, Eco remarks in his essay 'Pirandello ridens' that all those who wrote on humour were not humorous writers: Aristophanes, Molière, Groucho Marx, and Rabelais did not write on humour, whereas a serious thinker like Aristotle, a pietist like Kant, a rigorous philosopher like Hegel, a 'spleenetic' poet like Baudelaire, an existentialist like

Kierkegaard, a metaphysical writer like Bergson, and a psychoanalyst like Freud all wrote about it. Pirandello is not very dissimilar to these authors. In fact, Pirandello's definition of humour, according to Eco, is problematic and probably closer to the definition of 'irony,' because in the very moment of reflection which Pirandello defines as producing humour, we see that there is nothing funny about the situation in question. We might smile, because we recognize our human fragility, but we smile for the same reason that we cry. Who, then, is a humorous writer?

What makes Campanile a humorous writer, for Eco, is his working on the distortions of language, well summarized in aphorisms such as: 'There are rules made only of exceptions. They are very much confirmed.' Anticipating by decades the artifices of the *nouveau roman*, Campanile plays with the abnormality of what appears normal, presenting as normal the exact contrary of logical behaviour.

To return to Eco's use of humour and irony in the *diari minimi*, what we have is very different from a Campanile-style play with language or a Pirandellian reflection on the phoniness and unreality of the human condition; it is a direct lashing out at a social phenomenon, which is presented as a lie to the general public. Concerning American trains, for example, Eco refers to Protestant ethics and to political correctness. Taking the train in the U.S.A. is, for Eco, not a choice but a punishment, and the irony is that, unlike the glamorous images of them provided in Hollywood films, American trains are dirty and used only by the poor. White police saunter around and, dangling their batons, in the spirit of political correctness kindly ask vagabonds what they are doing inside the station and seraphically suggest that outside is a beautiful day.

Another example is his reflection on cultural expectations, when he comments on the typical conversation of Italian taxi-drivers, who take for granted that the customer wants to talk about soccer. The conversation, if directed to someone like Eco, would sound like this:

'Did you see Vialli?'
    'No, he must have come when I was not there.'
    'Are you going to watch the game tonight?'
    'No, I need to work on the second book of the *Metaphysics*, you know, the "Stagirita."'
    'Well, watch and then let me know. I think Van Basten could be the new Maradona, what do you think? But I would keep an eye on Hagi.'[27]

Eco critiques the possible closed-mindedness of fans who cannot conceive that a person might have different interests, but also comments on the largeness of their *encyclopaedia*. He comments that if he were to take the driver's place and insist on a conversation on the same level, it would sound something like this:

'Did you hear the last CD by Frans Brüggen?'
  'What?'
'The *Pavane Lachryme*. I think it's a little slow in the beginning.'
'Sorry, I don't understand.'
'I mean Van Eyck, the Blockflöte.'
'I am not ... Do you play it with an arch?'
'Oh, I understand, you don't ...'
'I don't.'
'Interesting. Did you know that to have a hand-made Coolsma you have to wait three years? Then it's better a Moeck made of ebony. It's the best, at least among those available. Gazzelloni told me. Listen, can you get to the fifth variation of *Derdre Doen Daphne D'Over*?'
'Actually I'm going to Parma ...'
'Oh, I understand, you play in F and not in C. It's more rewarding. I discovered a sonata by Loeillet which ...'
'Leié who?'
'But I'd like to see you with Telemann's "Fantaisie." Can you do those? You are not using the German handling, are you?'
'You see, the Germans, the BMW is a great car; I respect them, but ...'
'I understand. You use the baroque handling. Right. Listen, those of St Martin-in-the-Fields ...'[28]

Here Eco uses a type of humour more like Campanile's, playing with two levels of language and two minds that go in different directions: we perceive incongruity. But the criticism much more directly targets a social phenomenon (no matter whether the criticism is just or not), which shows how Eco goes beyond the textual humour of Campanile.

His position here is that of the hibernated medieval scholar who looks at and reflects on contemporary society with curiosity, keeping a distance from his actual objective, writing between the lines, and leaving it to the reader to interpret what has gone awry.

Eco's humour and irony move beyond post-structuralist thought, as the language game is not there for its own sake but involves a cultural critique. It is the inability of post-structuralist thinkers and semiotics to deal with matters outside the text that cultural studies thinkers have blamed on critics such as Eco. But as we saw in chapter 3, at least in the case of Eco it is a false charge, and semiotics can establish a liaison between texts and situations.

## The Power of the False

In a lecture entitled 'The Force of Falsity' delivered in 1994–5 at the University of Bologna and later published in *Serendipities: Language and Lunacy* (1998), Eco develops the idea that a great deal of human history has been based on false beliefs: 'Belief in gods, of whatever description, has motivated human history, thus if it were argued that all myths, all revelations of every religion, are nothing but lies, one could only conclude that for millennia we have lived under the dominion of the false' (2).

He starts out by quoting a witticism by Thomas Aquinas, who in *Quaestio Libetale XII*, 14, wonders 'utrum veritas sit fortior inter vinum et regem et mulierem' (whether truth were stronger than wine, kings, and women). Aquinas' subtle reply is that the four things cannot be compared because they belong to different categories, but somehow they are similar because they stir the human heart: wine produces drunkenness, women produce sensual delectation (*sic*), kings control the human intellect by the force of law, and truth moves the speculative intellect. The Doctor of the Church concludes that truth is stronger, because our animal forces depend on our intellectual ones.

If this is the power of truth, asks Eco, how is it possible that so much of our history has been controlled by false ideas? The Ptolemaic system confused historians and navigators for centuries (although everybody knew the earth was round); the Donation of Constantine founded for centuries the temporal power of the popes; the letter of Prester John served as an alibi for the expansion of the Church in the East; and the *Protocols of the Elders of Zion* inflamed not a few fanatics.

Some of these fabrications produced negative effects, others produced positive ones; nevertheless, they prove that humankind has accepted ideas that would chiefly serve their promulgators and conserve their power, in spite of surrounding disbelief. The fact that a big part of our history has been so biased 'should make us alert,' says Eco, 'ready to call into question the very tales we believe true, because the criterion of the wisdom of the community is based on constant awareness of the fallibility of our learning' (*Serendipities*, p. 20).

We should therefore respect searchers for truth like William of Baskerville or Casaubon, even if they arrive at wrong results. What matters is that their constructed plans bear good consequences. In the case of William, although he admits his failure in devising the apocalyptic plan (in chapter 7 we will examine whether he is actually wrong), he is able to stop the murders and expose the murderer. Casaubon shows us the risks we run when we go too far with our interpretations.

Irony and humour help us maintain a sceptical distance from the series of delusions constantly offered to humankind, and they are fundamental in Eco's vision of the world. His vision, though, is not one of disenchantment: he looks at the world and human history with the eyes of a curious child, never wearied by discovery of its shortcomings, its contradictions, and its marvels. It is this freshness of approach and the humour with which he imparts information that constitute the fascination of Eco's works.

He seems to smile at us from a miniature portrait painted by a medieval master, challenging the 'plans' that claim their truth as the one truth, having already mined the foundations of these plans with his critical system: the foundation of the ambiguity of signs. That is why he so reminds us of medieval scholars such as William of Ockham, who, having shrewdly ruled that theology is subordinate to logic, goes on to critique every single syllogism, or of Agrippa and Rabelais, who show that it is possible to support the most contradictory arguments using the supporters' own weapons.

'Rabelais knew that laughter can change the world much more than gunpowder, which had been invented a little earlier by another friar, who was properly called Berthold the Black.'[29] Even his fiction supports a medieval/Renaissance principle (although it has often been labelled as postmodernist): it is not a work of imagination, but a tool for theoretical reflections. I will analyse in the next chapter how a genre such as the detective story was manipulated by Eco for theoretical purposes, and why it has been such a favourite of so-called postmodern authors.

# 7 The *Whodunit* and Eco's Postmodern Fiction

The objective of this chapter is not to demonstrate whether or not Eco's novels are postmodern. The term, as I have mentioned, is problematic, owing to different critical definitions and different critical perspectives on it. Furthermore, Eco, as a philosopher, is a self-conscious author well aware of his postmodern position, as I suggested in chapter 4. The question of the postmodernism of Eco's fiction is therefore easily answered; the voluminous literature on the subject deals with the problems involved.

Of more interest for this study is how the relation between Eco's treatment of medieval and of postmodern theory is played out in his fiction, and whether his combination of the two allows for the formulation of a particular kind of postmodernism. I alluded to this matter in chapter 4, but I would like to return to it in a more specific way.

According to Lyotard, postmodern authors write without following pre-established rules, and their texts therefore cannot be judged by the application of familiar categories.[1] So, although we can say that *The Name of the Rose* and *Foucault's Pendulum* are detective novels, these works do not follow exactly the techniques of the traditional *whodunit*. Stefano Tani has attempted to study *The Name of the Rose* as a particular kind of detective novel,[2] which he defines as an 'innovative anti-detective novel,' but he finds himself at a loss and concludes that the novel eludes categorization. It clearly contains the typical ingredients of traditional detective fiction (a Sherlock Holmes–type detective, mirrors, a

The second section of this chapter is a modified reprint of the material as it appears in *Semiotics 1998*, ed. C.W. Spinks and John Deely (Bern: Peter Lang, 1999).

labyrinth, and a map), but the fact that they are treated ironically situates the book in a particular position within the genre.

The most evident sign of its distinctiveness is that the murder mystery is solved not thanks to the skills of a cerebral detective, but almost randomly. The sense of crisis William feels after he discovers that his plan was mistaken is utterly postmodern and moves beyond medieval sensibility ('I behaved stubbornly, pursuing a semblance of order, when I should have known well that there is no order in the universe,' p. 492). The medieval detective, therefore, goes beyond his time, assuming a postmodern identity, and declares to his disciple that the universe has no order. The primary role of faith would have made such an assertion impossible in the mouth of a Franciscan friar of the Middle Ages.

Medieval and postmodern philosophy are interwoven in the novel, combined and blurred by the author in a brilliant way, and the interweaving problematizes our vision of postmodern philosophy and challenges its uniqueness. It is not that William is a precursor of Wittgenstein or that Wittgenstein is an Ockhamist;[3] it is much more a matter of defining the order of the world by subsuming two perspectives that, at first consideration, appear extremely different.

Eco's decision to adopt the ingredients and plot of the detective story is partly at odds with the placing of his characters in a medieval milieu. We know well that the detective novel is a relatively modern creation traceable back to Edgar Allan Poe's 'The Murders in the Rue Morgue' in the 1840s and to Dickens' first detectives (such as Inspector Bucket in *Bleak House*). The earliest point of origin might be Voltaire's *Zadig* (1748), whose hero is a protodetective using 'inductive reasoning.'

In Italy, the detective novel did not exist before 1929, when Mondadori, a prestigious publishing company, introduced a series of British mystery novels, which became very popular. Soon, however, fascist censorship prohibited the circulation of detective novels.[4] It is therefore only after the Second World War that mystery stories such as Carlo Emilio Gadda's *Quer pasticciaccio brutto de via Merulana* (*That Awful Mess on Via Merulana*, 1946) and Leonardo Sciascia's *A ciascuno il suo* (1966) can be found.

Italian authors were never fascinated by 'Northern Gothicism,' and nightmare and bloody material have been excluded since the beginning. The Italian detective novel took on a different enterprise. As Tani argues, because of the 'snobbish and elitist concept of literature descended from the Italian classical tradition and exacerbated by the genre's connotation of escapist fiction,'[5] Italian writers often experimented with the genre in a parodic way, or else exploited its techniques for higher artistic purposes (as in the case of Sciascia and Oreste del Buono).

Eco belongs to the latter tradition. Not a detective writer by profession (like Borges, Nabokov, and Robbe-Grillet), Eco adopts the genre as an ideal mechanism for displaying contemporary chaos and postmodern sensibility. Subverting the rules of detective fiction, providing a non-solution instead of a clear explanation, allows him to attack the traditional novel, with its postulated rules and implied order. Tani identifies this attitude not only in Eco but in many postmodern authors, such as Borges, Pynchon, and Calvino, and characterizes the shift in the detective novel as a perfect watershed between modernism and postmodernism. These authors, he writes, exploit the conventions of the genre, making of them a mechanism without purpose: 'Serious novelists do not even try to "improve upon" detective fiction but rather use the form as a scrapyard from which to dig out "new" narrative techniques to be applied to the exhausted traditional novel; the detective novel clichés are like the spare pieces of an old car that cannot run anymore but, if sold as parts, can still be worth something.'[6]

The change in the detective novel is an increasing interest in the cognitive aspects of the detection process. For Raymond Chandler, the detective is a 'man' in search of a hidden truth. More and more this quest for truth becomes an analysis of human cognitive abilities and understanding of the world. In a Sherlock Holmes novel, 'reality' is easily and splendidly reconstructed by the cerebral work of a rational detective, whereas in postmodern detective fiction 'reality' is questioned: 'What [the detective] soon discovers is that the "reality" that anyone involved will swear to is in fact itself a construction, a fabrication, a fiction, a faked and alternate reality – and that it has been gotten together before he ever arrived on the scene. And the Op's work therefore is to deconstruct, decompose, deplot and defictionalize that "reality" and to construct or reconstruct out of it a true fiction, i.e. an account of what "really" happened.'[7]

William of Baskerville discovers at the end of The Name of the Rose that his account of the murders was nothing but a fiction, a beautiful construction he had created, a projection of his own desire. Although he had defictionalized Bernardo Gui's explanation of the murders as works of the devil and as reflecting God's anger at the disorder reigning in the abbey, he ends up reconstituting a false explanation.

David Richter has argued that, looking at the stream of murders as a whole, William's apocalyptic plan might not be entirely mistaken. In fact, the abbot (victim number six) suffocates, 'recalling the prophecy of the sixth angel and death by suffocation, the monstrous horsemen who kill by "smoke and sulphur" which "issue from their mouth."' The last death, that of Jorge, who kills himself devouring the poisoned pages of the mysterious book, 'recalls the last angel of Revelation, who gives John a scroll and tells him "Take it and eat ... And I ... ate it; it was sweet as honey in my mouth, but when I had eaten it my stomach was made bitter."'[8]

If Richter is right, Eco is playing with the reader's judgment: are we supposed to distrust signs, or are we supposed to believe in an enigmatic order imposed from above? In any case, William would still be wrong in his abduction, since he believed the murderer was purposely committing murders along the lines of the Apocalypse. In the case devised by Richter, the linearity of the apocalyptic murders was never in Jorge's mind: it would have been planned by a mysterious 'force' beyond human control.

This represents a fantastic clash of the postmodern radical deconstruction of traditional rationalism with a slight Ockhamistic touch: 'Est ubi nunc ordo mundi?' William of Ockham, despite his critique of universals and his undermining the possibility of science with his refusal of the 'adequatio,'[9] believed that there is order in the world, although it might be contingent and changing. If the order changes, it is because God wanted it to, and God is not a careless tyrant, but a loving God who arranges what is best for humankind.[10]

When William asserts that there is no order in this world, he goes beyond the area of uncertainty opened up by Ockham, and his position is closer to Wittgenstein's, who wrote: 'My phrases demonstrate that the person who understands me, in the end recognizes them as meaningless, when this person has gone through them – on them – above them (he must, so to say, throw away the ladder he used to climb up). He must surpass these phrases in order to see the world right ... The idea sits on our nose like a pair of glasses, and what we see, we see through them. We never come to the thought of taking them off.'[11]

For Wittgenstein, phrases are meaningless once they have been surpassed, but necessary in order to lead us to concepts. Ockham, however, believed that phrases and expressions, thanks to the conclusions of syllogisms, could be the basis for science. That is why he considers logic the superior science. For Wittgenstein, as for William of Baskerville, expressions and syllogisms can help us arrive at concepts and meanings, but by themselves they prove nothing and must therefore be rejected once one has come to an understanding – like the eyeglasses on our nose, which can be discarded once we have an idea of the object. This is the understanding to which William comes when he finally discovers the 'truth' and realizes that he can get rid of the suppositions that had blinded him.

William's crisis reflects the condition of knowledge of contemporary developed societies, which has been called by philosophers 'the postmodern condition.' The term represents what Lyotard has seen as an 'internal erosion of the legitimacy principle of knowledge.'[12] Because of the decline of narrative as a discourse of legitimization, we have arrived at a delegitimation of science. According to Lyotard, positive science is not a form of knowledge, but, like many other disciplines, what Wittgenstein called a 'language game,' a game that can be defined through its own rules. Because science does not look for 'consensus' through the use of a narrative, speculative philosophy is 'forced to relinquish its legitimation duties'[13] and is therefore facing a crisis.

After years of mourning for the loss of philosophy, however, the nostalgia for the lost narrative has vanished, and Wittgenstein's theory of language games triumphs. According to the German philosopher, legitimation of knowledge can derive only from linguistic practice and communicational interaction: 'Wittgenstein's strength is that he did not opt for the positivism that was being developed by the Vienna Circle, but outlined in his investigation of language games a kind of legitimation not based on performativity. This is what the postmodern world is all about.'[14]

Despite his fascination with Wittgenstein, Eco could not have stopped at the German philosopher's theory of language games. Linguistics does not satisfy cognitive inquiries and, as we know, is for Eco superseded by semiotics. As a philosopher, Eco is conscious of the erosion of the legitimacy principle of knowledge, but he does not surrender to a nonreferential game of 'signifiants.' Signs do refer to signs, and signs are 'something.'

If *The Name of the Rose* in the end emphasizes the defeat of William the semiotician, it does not declare the uselessness of semiotic research. For Peirce, semiosis is a temporal process that in moving from interpretant to interpretant does not arrive at truth, but does arrive at a final interpretant: 'The final interpretant is the interpretation, to which every interpreter "is destined to come," when the sign is sufficiently considered.'[15] Semiosis is not an empty process and, although at times it misleads us, it follows a teleological path, which moves towards the growth of cognition.

'But imagining mistaken orders you have nevertheless found something,' says Adso to William after he has testified to his pessimism. 'You said something very nice Adso, thank you,' replies William. The plummeting of the *aedificium* interrupts their conversation, but the idea that the seven-day adventure gave rise to 'something' concludes the novel. Adso as narrator meditates on the pain of not knowing the hidden meaning of the story he has recounted, but the fact that he struggles to put together fragments and to recollect makes us sympathetic towards the patient work of recomposition involved in unrewarded scholarship.

Later, Eco would regret that his emphasis on the weaknesses of semiotics and semiosis encouraged a movement towards exaggerated openness. Deconstruction interpreted Peircian semiosis as a meaningless drift, as a self-referential process that does not advance cognition. This was against what Peirce had declared: 'A sign is something by knowing which we know something more.'

Because of the academic expansion of the Derridean method, Eco decided after *The Name of the Rose* to write a book that would warn against the danger of deconstruction, since he wanted to give an example of how a dissemination process does not leave the world unchanged. This book would be *Foucault's Pendulum*. Like William of Ockham (*Quodl. Septem* 8), he maintained that even a simple act such as raising a finger creates change, because it shifts the relations between the finger and the rest of the universe (*Kant e l'ornitorinco*, p. 229).

Given Eco's struggle to talk about what is left of legitimate human knowledge, I cannot agree with John Deely when he writes that Eco's theory 'reaches the boundary between late modernity and postmodernity without completely crossing the line.'[16] One could even refer to Eco's thought as post-postmodern, at least in its intent.

In recent years, Eco has been occupied in rethinking the role of semiotics in connection with the transformation brought by the cognitive sciences. Finding their contribution useful but not satisfying, in *Kant e l'ornitorinco* (1997) he reaffirms the validity of Peircian semiotics and scours the paths of Western philosophy beginning with Kant, looking for an answer to a simple but historically tormenting question: 'How can we distinguish an elephant from an armadillo?' Aware of the end of 'grand narratives,' he resorts to parables, like that of the platypus, to illustrate the complexity of our cognitive functions, whose abilities cannot be dismissed by simply renouncing the Object. With typical humour, he declares from the beginning his perplexity and indecision ('Some time ago I was uncertain, but now I am not so sure' – a quotation by Boscoe Pertwee, eighteenth century, from Gregory the Great), and admits that his work does not lead to a systematic conclusion; but he provokes us into thinking about whether we should abandon a philosophical research that focuses on knowledge in favour of a linguistic game that legitimizes only itself.

A study of the theory of abduction as it is employed in *The Name of the Rose* and disregarded in the film version will help illustrate some aspects of this discussion.

### The Theory of Abduction and *The Name of the Rose*

Eco wanted no comparison to be drawn between the novel *The Name of the Rose* and the film version by the director Jean-Jacques Annaud, since they were two completely different works. But I would like to use both of them in order to make a theoretical point not so much about the semiotics of film, but about the metaphysics and epistemology behind *The Name of the Rose*, and Eco's use of medieval philosophy. In doing so, I will also link the discussion to the concept of 'truth.'

The film *The Name of the Rose* constitutes a peculiar object for semiotic analysis: one could analyse the film without considering its relation to the novel, but its relation to the novel in terms of semiotic theory is of great interest. One semiotic aspect emphasized in the novel but erased in the film is the theory of abduction.

Some scholars (for example, Ruggero Puletti in the introduction of his *Il nome della rosa*) have denied a direct link between the novel and Eco's semiotic theory and have struggled to connect the book to the tradition of the historical novel, tying it, on account of its intertextuality, to different literatures. But I believe that Eco's novel, notwithstanding its richness and multiple interests, is in fact a tribute to the theory of abduction that Eco elaborated from Peirce. The film, however, does not follow the novel in this respect, perhaps seeking to minimize the theory for the sake of the theatre audience; in consequence, it oversimplifies Eco's attempt.

The direct evidence for the first part of my argument is the quantitative preponderance of the use of abductions in Eco's text. For the second part of the argument, it will be sufficient to show how the film's alteration of some of the episodes of the novel, its profoundly different choices, demonstrate Annaud's disregarding this philosophical concern.

Eco's clearest explanation of abduction, which he also calls a vulgar-ization of Peirce's idea of abduction, is contained in the essay 'Abduc-tion in Uqbar,' published in English in the collection entitled *The Limits of Interpretation*. There Eco distinguishes among deduction, induction, and abduction. Deduction, he says, proceeds from a (true) Rule and, by means of a case, predicts a Result with absolute certainty. The ex-ample Eco uses, which has been much referred to, is as follows: There is a sack of white beans; if we take out some, we can assume without looking that they are white. In the case of an induction, from a number of results I can infer that they are cases of the same rule, and I arrive at the formulation of the rule. Using the same example: There is a sack of unknown content; we pull out a handful of beans, and we see that they are white. If we repeat the procedure, after a sufficient number of trials we can infer that all the beans in the sack are white. Abduction is different and more risky, because with it we are facing a strange or unexplainable result, and we must consider whether the result repre-sents a rule. In the example, there is a sack of beans on the table, and nearby there are some white beans; we can make the conjecture that the sack on the table contains white beans. The abduction is the conjec-ture we make in trying to consider the strange result as an instance of a rule. An abduction is the most economical explanation of a certain case. At this point, we must test our abduction against reality or against the historical consensus of the community, and see if it corresponds, without any guarantee that the hypothesis is correct. This is where the theory of abduction is connected with metaphysics, because, in order to test the conjecture against reality, we must first have a certain idea of reality.

When I first conceived this analysis, Eco's *Kant e l'ornitorinco* had not been published. I was pleased, therefore, to discover later that Eco had returned to the idea of reality, metaphysics, and epistemology in that book, and had developed material that had been systematized in *A Theory of Semiotics* twenty years before.

What Eco had discussed back then was how to resolve the dualism between reality and language. His was a slightly different dualism from the one previously studied by metaphysics, since his concern was not the connection between reality and the human intellect but the consti-tuting of an independent science of signs. In the later book, however, Eco discusses the connection between signs and reality, which presents itself as a philosophical problem; in answer to the question raised, Eco reinterprets Kant's metaphysics and follows Peirce's semiotic method, in believing that the intellect can know and study signs and that we can know reality only through a conjectural notion of truth.

In *The Name of the Rose*, with its interest in the idea of abduction – which is at the core of Eco's theory of knowledge and interpretation – we see the implicit epistemological background and its foundation in medieval scholasticism. There, against contemporary theories such as deconstruction, which have attempted to destroy the metaphysics of presence, Eco uses the Ockhamistic idea of *economy* in order to explain the link between human language and reality. Truth stands often, he says, in the most economical explanation, in the explanation that cuts out, thanks to Ockham's razor, all unnecessary categories and simplifies the human conjecture. In this sense, while other theorists have tried to find an anti-centre creating a logic of suspicion, Eco has returned to the humility of the human intellect and to the idea of unlimited semiosis.

I see Eco's method as a way of 're-structuring' philosophical and literary criticism, and I consider it extremely powerful, especially at this point in theoretical thinking, when some criticism continues to float in the shallow waters of de-centring and of denying any possible knowledge of the real, giving rise to a hermeneutical process that does not recognize boundaries.

To arrive at this result, Eco saw the possibility of recovering what is still valid in Thomas Aquinas' and Ockham's philosophy, their forbidding the idea of a Cartesian split, and he opposed early modern hermeneutic and hermetic principles, which looked at signs searching for clues revealing occult relations (see, for example, *Foucault's Pendulum* and *Interpretation and Overinterpretation*).

In *The Name of the Rose*, William of Baskerville proceeds using the method of abduction. Sometimes he is successful, as in the famous episode of the horse Brunellus, but at the end of the book he fails, his series of abductions being in fact wrong, and thus proves Peirce's theory that our choices can be subject to fallibility.

The episode concerning the horse Brunellus, at the beginning of the novel, is a precious example of how William's reasoning proceeds, and it sets out the method for the rest of the book. The scene can be summarized briefly. The Franciscan William of Baskerville, enacting a medieval (and more thorough) Zadig, approaches the Benedictine abbey to which he has been directed in the company of the Benedictine novice Adso, and just before reaching the door of the abbey he sees the footprints of a horse. When the monks who are chasing the horse meet William on the trail, he informs them that Brunellus, the abbot's favourite horse, black, five feet tall, with a sumptuous tail and small hooves, a small head, thin ears, and big eyes, has turned to the right. Amazed that William can so perfectly describe a horse he has never seen, the gatekeeper of the abbey follows William's directions and eventually finds the horse as instructed. William infers that the horse of his possible world corresponds to the horse of the world posed by his interlocutors, and ends up being right.

Explaining the episode to Adso, William comments that the world speaks to us through signs, through an infinite reserve of symbols. Observation of nature and inference are the method of reasoning William chooses in order to combine his world of signs and the world posed by the *cellarius* who is in charge of recovering the horse.

The Brunellus episode, as Teresa Coletti has stressed,[17] is emblematic not only of William's method of operation, but of Eco's theoretical method as well: in order to explore the truth, William studies signs and makes a series of conjectures or meta-abductions (Eco, 'From Aristotle to Sherlock Holmes'). Eco starts from the principle that reality exists and can be investigated, as long as 'the old method is upheld of observing, listening to, comparing, and thinking' (Eco, 'Semiosi naturale e parola nei *Promessi sposi*, pp. 1–2).

Eco wrote those words in his commentary on Alessandro Manzoni's *The Betrothed*, and they express the deep semiotic concern at the core of *The Name of the Rose*. William is perfectly right in his series of assumptions, and gives a demonstration of his semiotic abilities to his pupil and to the monks of the abbey, but his intellectual pride later will be called into question.

In 'Postille a Il nome della rosa,' Eco writes:

> Not by chance the book begins as if it were a detective story (and continues to beguile the naive reader, right up to the end, to the point that the naive reader may not even realize that it is a detective story in which little is discovered, and the detective is defeated). I believe people like detective stories not because of the murders, or because there is a celebration of a final order (intellectual, social, legal, or moral) over the chaos of guilt. It is because the detective novel represents a story of conjectures in a pure state. (524)

Here Eco admits that the appeal of his story, the trap he has set for the reader, consists in the pleasure of making conjectures, and in fact Eco's text as a detective novel aims to detect and interpret signs – from the little note left by Venanzio on the scriptorium, to the ink appearing on the corpses' fingers and tongues, to the behaviour of the various monks, and to the labyrinthine structure of the library.

Even Bernardo Gui, the powerful representative of the Inquisition, towards the end of the book makes abductions. For example, he interprets the objects found in Salvatore's possession (a black cat and other witch's paraphernalia) as signs of the presence of the AntiChrist; but he makes a wrong abduction because his accusation is based not on precise observation of reality, but on preconceptions. Nobody is incapable of making wrong abductions; even William's theory concerning the murders in the end turns out to be wrong. But the message is still that one should persist and try to get at the truth through careful research, and in fact this message is even reinforced by William's fallibility. Bernardo Gui, by contrast, links his chain of abduction to the supernatural, a method that William criticizes exactly as his namesake William of Ockham would have criticized it, saying that the mind is not capable of such a thing.

The film erases the epistemological and metaphysical principle of abduction almost completely, finding more comfort in the straight narration of the story. In fact, the viewer of the film is left with the idea that William is always right, a medieval Sherlock Holmes, and his weaknesses are never commented on. He solves the murders without ever believing the theory of the signs of the Apocalypse suggested by Jorge and constantly stressed by Adso. In the film, William remains unshakeable in his judgment, whereas in the novel he acknowledges his own weakness. In commenting on the Brunellus episode, for example, he admits that, in spite of the signs observed and notwithstanding his acumen, his abduction could have been wrong; but how else can knowledge advance?

We are all aware of the connection between *The Name of the Rose* and Conan Doyle's Sherlock Holmes stories, in particular *The Hound of the Baskervilles*, which is clearly echoed in William's name, but we are also aware of what is different in Eco's novel. Both Sherlock Holmes and William proceed in their investigations by abduction, but the Conan Doyle character's conjectures are always right. Sherlock Holmes is a vivid demonstration of the capacity of fiction to twist reality according to our will. William, by contrast, often makes wrong conjectures, and his fallibility corresponds more accurately to life.

Our knowledge is increased by our continuous attempts to explain reality. Throughout history, the advancers of knowledge have been those who, pursuing their research, have made the most courageous abductions.

In *The Name of the Rose*, the method most opposed to William's way of getting at the truth is that of Jorge, for whom knowledge needs no improvement: everything is already there, and our whole effort is to recapitulate it, and even to erase elements that seem to contradict it. This is why he is so adamant in preventing knowledge of Aristotle's second book on comedy, knowledge that would directly defy the scriptures in the matter of laughter.

Eco's book, then, is about the validity of semiotic inquiry in the pursuit of knowledge. Historical matters are undoubtedly important and also provide the origin of Eco's theory, but the interest of the story itself remains in the method of conjecture.

In his lectures on Manzoni's *The Betrothed*, Eco even speaks of a Galilean method of observation, which is about opposing accepted principles and trusting one's 'common sense.' Of course, William could not have known the Italian scientist, but Eco seems to suggest that the premises for his method were already present in Roger Bacon, William of Ockham, and Marsilius of Padua. In any case, the comment on the Galilean method presupposes a metaphysical comment, one that is at the core of Eco's philosophy: How do we proceed in our knowledge of reality? Can we achieve the truth? From which also follows, How do we interpret texts?

*The Name of the Rose* is a novel whose message lies in its method. Nature is known through careful observation, and knowledge is advanced through abduction. The book, therefore, brings together an epistemological and a metaphysical theory, which, in the story itself, is limited to the apparatus of the Middle Ages, but which can be developed to include the latest philosophical theories. Eco's message is a fictional example of the semiotic method: 'the study of signs in order to mention things or states of the world' (*A Theory of Semiotics*, p. 3). This is what William teaches his novice, and this is what Eco teaches his Model Reader.

In *The Name of the Rose*, the problem is posed only within a fictional account, and it lacks a definite metaphysical explanation, which the medieval philosophers could not have arrived at without the modern debate over Being and the Kantian discussion of transcendentals. Eco arrives at and perfects this explanation in *Kant and the Platypus*. Having written on texts, on intertextuality, on narrativity, and on interpretation, always posing the concept of the Dynamic Object as the terminus ad quem, Eco finally turns directly towards Being as something that poses limits to our freedom of speech, and discusses the Dynamic Object as terminus ab quo.

*Phenomena*, he says, do not say anything about *noumena*, because things live and grow according to an internal law that the intellect can only surmise. But, as Kant says, objects are organized in genus and species and we can try to identify those. When we do that, we schematize reality: from the observation of things, we infer a certain Rule, and in order to find this rule we need to hypothesize that a certain Result is a case of that Rule that needs to be constructed. This is nothing but an abduction (*Kant e l'ornitorinco*, p. 74). Kant would never have expressed himself in these terms; it was Peirce who elaborated the transcendental judgment in a semiotic way. But what is exciting and at the same time inevitable is that in order to explain the foundation of the epistemology of semiotics, Eco (and Peirce) needed to go back to the concept of abduction.

Abduction, therefore, as I have suggested, can be assimilated to what Kant called 'transcendental deduction,' because even though using the term 'deduction,' Kant was in fact indicating an inferential process of the mind that started from physical experience. Surprisingly enough, modern cognitive science has elaborated a method of mental knowledge that goes back to the Kantian deduction, proceeding in a way that corresponds to Peirce's and Eco's abductive method.

Ugo Volli, in an essay dedicated to object definition in the semiotics of Umberto Eco,[18] had raised the problem of the metaphysical basis of Eco's semiotic theory and concluded that semiotics was a surface science, because it studied the surface of phenomena without much concern for transcendental depth.

Lucrecia Escudero, in her essay on *Apocalittici e integrati*, defines semiotics as the science of the ephemeral or, as Eco himself has defined it, the science of 'next Thursday'; and the method of studying the ephemeral is the individuation of the categories that regulate codes and sign production.[19] But since, by definition, signs are substitutes for things, a theory of signs will always, according to Eco, be a science not of truth, but of lie.

As is often said, since our culture is based on communication, semiotic theory has developed a method of studying the *phenomena* of communication without paying great attention to the *noumena*. For Volli, this was the challenge semiotics had to face: it ought to take responsibility for the origin of its object. As Volli admits, Eco was concerned with the metaphysical problem, but it is emblematic that Eco decided to return to this topic in his most recent book, and it is interesting that his discussion of the problem is not dissimilar to that offered by cognitive science.

Abductions, as well as transcendental reasoning, are invariably radically undetermined: there is always an infinite number of hypotheses that are compatible with the evidence. Accordingly, we could say that a science of signs is not possible, because, even if we were able to eliminate the implausible hypotheses, an infinite number of possible abductions would remain.

Like what Owen Flanagan describes in his book *The Science of the Mind*, Eco's project is 'to postulate the simplest, most comprehensive, and predictive hypotheses about cognitive mechanisms compatible with the data and the rest of science.'[20] For Eco, this postulation was Ockham's theory, and it is the principle William follows in his attempts to understand the murders in the abbey.

In spite of recent attempts to attack semiotics on this ground, I believe it is enough to grant to semiotics the dignity of a science. In fact, it is the errors and the mechanisms of correction that make semiotics a science. Even though this science will never provide an exhaustive explanation of reality, like other forms of science it can lead towards an explanation, notwithstanding what Flanagan calls its 'epistemological afflictions.'

William with his fallibility represents far more than the medieval man of science; he represents the semiotician in general, who follows the semiosic chain that connects one sign to the other. His intellect, like a semiosic machine, is unstoppable and fallible. As Roberto Pellerey suggests, putting the mind in a particular disposition also raises up the ontological falseness.[21]

In the Brunellus episode, William answers Adso's question regarding 'essences,' defending the importance of individuality. Yes, the horse footprints could have expressed the idea of a horse as 'verbum mentis,' but in that particular time and place, those footprints said that one particular horse had passed there. William also explains that only the sight of the horse Brunellus, when caught up with by the monks, gave him full knowledge of what he had abducted. Only then was he able to test whether his reasoning had brought him close to truth.

It is interesting to notice how the film substitutes a different episode for the Brunellus one. Brunellus completely disappears, and William, when he reaches the abbey, makes two different abductions: first, he interprets the behaviour of a monk, which allows him to locate the restroom, and second, he interprets Adso's behaviour and then explains to him where the restroom is, identifying his need and providing him with the right suggestion. These, no doubt, can be considered abductions, but I would argue that they completely miss the intertextual link and the level of sophistication with which Eco had commented on the same topic in the Brunellus scene, and oversimplify his philosophical affirmations.

Immediately after the Brunellus episode, Eco in the book introduces a conversation between William and the abbot (Adso is pretending to sleep, but he overhears it). This dialogue is extremely important, since William, a good Ockhamist, refuses to connect the first death in the abbey, that of the young monk Adelmo, with the presence of the devil, and refuses by admitting human inability to deal with complicated chains of cause and effect: 'Because reasoning about causes and effects is a very difficult thing, and I believe the only judge of that can be God. We are already hard put to establish a relationship between such an obvious effect as a charred tree and the lightning bolt that set fire to it, so to trace sometimes endless chains of causes and effects seems to me as foolish as trying to build a tower that will touch the sky' (30).

Following the philosophy of William of Ockham, William of Baskerville asserts his theory of a clear separation between religion and science, faith and reason, Church and empire; but William's trust in the human intellect implies also the consciousness of its limits. That is why, even though both William's and Bernardo Gui's abductions are wrong, there is a difference: William admits to being wrong and is ready to start again in his search, and so reveals the importance of intellectual humility.

As I have remarked, Annaud's film, by stressing William's rightness, erases from Eco's theory the important idea of *fallibilism,* which Peirce defined as 'the doctrine that our knowledge is never absolute but always swims, as it were, in a continuum of uncertainty and of indeterminacy.'[22] In the novel, fallibilism is considered a condition for knowledge itself, whereas in the film fallibility is limited to William's recanting his defence of a translator on trial for heresy, a moral problem.

Jean-Jacques Annaud seems to have missed all this and has offered his audience a more 'straightforward' detective story. It is often historically accurate in its reconstruction and sometimes provides stunning and comical representations of the novel's characters (as in the case of Salvatore). But the film has deprived the story of the novel's philosophical implications.

## Medieval Aspects of a Postmodern *Whodunit*:[23] The Computer and the Kabbalah

Eco's second novel, *Foucault's Pendulum*, so far in this study has been discussed in connection with the theoretical works. There remain at least two aspects of the novel that deserve to be mentioned here: its embracing and postmodern subversion of the genre of the detective novel, and the links instituted in it with medieval philosophy.

The detective novel, as studied by Peter Bondanella,[24] has certain characteristics in common with textual interpretation, and it is clear that at the core of *Foucault's Pendulum*'s are a critique of deconstruction practices and an exploration of the dangers of hermetic semiosis. Eco was influenced in this direction by Harold Bloom's lectures[25] at the University of Bologna, delivered before *Foucault's Pendulum* was written. Eco afterwards taught a seminar on hermetic semiosis (1986–7), and his students continued his research, publishing their results in *L'idea deforme: Interpretazioni esoteriche di Dante* (The Distorted Idea: Esoteric Interpretations of Dante, 1989). Although some of their essays reached conclusions that Eco would probably not endorse, the collection as a whole developed a relatively complete outline of Eco's theories of interpretation. These theories would be set forth by Eco himself in *I limiti dell'interpretazione* (1989; *The Limits of Interpretation*, 1990) and in *Interpretation and Overinterpretation* (1990).[26]

We looked in chapter 4 at how these theories are debated in the novel and presented in the terms of a fictional account. Here we will examine further how Eco bridges the gaps between literary theorists and detectives, diabolical conspirators and occult philosophers.

*Foucault's Pendulum* is a 'cosmic' *whodunit*, involving a centuries-long cosmic plot organized by different groups of individuals in different countries, who embrace a similar belief. The idea of conspiracy must have been suggested to Eco by the dismantling in Italy of a secret organization called the 'Loggia P2,' which collected under its banner a number of well-known politicians and business representatives. This secret society aimed at controlling important spheres of Italian public life, and its uncovering preoccupied the national media. The idea of secret associations controlling the affairs of the world has by no means been left behind, and continues to make its presence felt in contemporary society.

Eco approaches the subject with his usual irony and places the origin of the problem in the Middle Ages, with the destruction in 1307 by Philip the Fair of the Templars, an order of knights formed in the period of the Crusades. After the order was dismantled, it is said, a group of its knights took refuge in Scotland, where they came to be involved with a lodge of Freemasons. From that came the unproved link between the Templars and Freemasonry.

The Templars are discussed in the novel in connection with the manuscript brought to Garamond Publishing by an old fascist officer, a Colonel Ardenti, who believes the Templars had a plan to conquer the world. He has discovered a document in Old French, and he believes that, once it is decoded, it will reveal an international conspiracy involving not only the Templars but the Rosicrucians, the Freemasons, the quest for the Grail, the Jews, and the Nazis.

When the three principal characters of the book, Casaubon, Belbo, and Diotallevi, set out to decipher the document, they participate in a game of interpretation, but this game becomes reality when the members of a secret society find out about it. In the beginning, the three colleagues enjoy the multiplicity of connections they can derive from a simple piece of paper, as they explain the whole of human history from the Crusades to the Holocaust, but in the end they suffer because their too perfect fantasy has been converted into reality: 'If you invent a plan and others carry it out, it's as if the Plan exists' (655).

The secret document in the end turns out to be a simple laundry list, and, with typical humour, Eco quotes an ironic sentence from Woody Allen's *Getting Even*,[27] along with Lia's interpretation of the document in chapter 106: 'List n.5, six shirts, six pairs of underwear and six handkerchiefs, has always intrigued scholars, fundamentally because of the complete lack of socks' (563).

The readers, as interpreters and semioticians, become detectives, motivated to search among different levels of conjecture. As Lois Zamora has noted, readers do not become allies of the 'sleuths' in their quest for understanding, since it is clear that they are going too far. Instead, readers are left with their scepticism and without a hero to cling to; and the main character, Casaubon, does not triumph over his enemy, but is the author of his own demise (although we are not told what will happen to him).[28]

Casaubon is driven by a wistful longing for some centre of meaning, but he betrays his own rules, as often happens with experienced readers (including scholars, professors, and students). Because Casaubon is lacking a direction, the reader is left in an ambiguous realm in which everything is decentralized. The only fixed point in the universe seems to be the pendulum, as Casaubon says at the beginning of the novel, but in fact there are many similar pendulums throughout the world (237).

Various murders take place. The first, which turns out not to be a murder, is that of Colonel Ardenti, who disappears the day after visiting Garamond and talking to Belbo and Casaubon about his project on the Templars and the world conspiracy. On the track of the supposed murderers is Chief of Police De Angelis, whose name not only reflects his angelic nature but is also the name of one of the first Italian detective novelists, Augusto de Angelis (1888–1944). The principal character in his stories, De Vincenzi, is 'a pensive commissioner gifted with a poetic sensitivity,'[29] like De Angelis. As a detective, De Angelis seems to head in the right direction, but he never really arrives at a solution of the mysteries.

The second person to disappear is a medium, a girl from Picatrix, a Milanese circle of 'mysterosophic' studies. In investigating this murder, De Angelis acts as Lia does: he gives a pragmatic answer, the most economical explanation. The girl's boyfriend, in his view, was implicated in a bad drug deal and therefore disappeared, taking the girl with him; the conclusion is very different from Casaubon's. But De Angelis disappears for long stretches of the novel and is far from being the main investigator. This is of course Casaubon, who upon his return from Brazil opens a cultural information agency and becomes an investigator of knowledge, 'the Sam Spade of culture,' as Belbo calls him.

The most interesting part of his job is his collection of information and the way in which he catalogues the different pieces. He uses reference cards that link subjects with subjects by way of association, like the process of unlimited semiosis, so that everything connects with everything else.

From this point on, the detective story becomes a search for information, with Casaubon, Belbo, and Diotallevi working on the Hermes Project, which involves the publication of texts on hermeticism and gnosis. Like a detective story, the project becomes a search for 'truth,' as Aglié points out, because the subject becomes knowledge itself, and the books the characters examine speak about books: 'The Isis Unveiled books must deal with the exact same subjects as all the others. They confirm one another; therefore they are true. Never trust originality' (276).

De Angelis reappears occasionally, and makes some of the same moves Casaubon is making. They end up in the same libraries looking for the same books. De Angelis is a sophisticated 'cop,' who looks for clues in books and finds references to universal conspiracies. Both he and Casaubon let themselves be drawn by their thirst for spectacular information and their fever of suspicion. As Aglié says, 'For the police, the more things you know or pretend to know, the more powerful you are. It doesn't matter if the things are true. What counts, remember, is to possess a secret' (339).

We do not know exactly which parts of the Plan De Angelis understood, but the last we hear of him is when Belbo calls him for help, and he says he is about to leave for Sardinia, where he has been transferred. We sense that he is somewhat frightened, so he must have surmised the dangers of the situation.

From this point on, Casaubon continues his search in isolation. He watches things happen without participating. Even when he witnesses the murder of his friend Belbo and of Belbo's girlfriend Lorenza, he does not intervene but runs away. He doubts his own vision, and since he is in an overexcited state, we never know if what he narrates has actually happened. Nevertheless, in the end he is, as a detective, successful, because he finally understands; but what he understands is that there is nothing to understand: there is no Plan; there is no Map; and Malkut is Malkut and nothing else. The problem is that, if he were to tell this secret, nobody would believe him, and what is the purpose of understanding, if others refuse and continue to interrogate? (641) And anyway, it is too late: 'The greatest wisdom ... is knowing that your wisdom is too late. You understand everything when there is no longer anything to understand' (640). The detective Casaubon draws a metaphysical conclusion. As Alain Cohen puts it: '*Whodunits* capture the spectator's imagination because to some extent they still partake of the Aristotelian tragic dimensions of pity (for the other), fear (for oneself) and catharsis (with all its complex history). They do so because they are also constructed with impeccable logic while at the same time the puzzles therein contained provide metaphysical comment upon the human condition.'[30]

In actuality, there was nothing to discover. Even the supposedly murdered Colonel Ardenti reappears in the end. Everything that Casaubon and his friends thought they ought to discover, they had created themselves. Casaubon, therefore, as Tani concludes, is an anti-detective: 'The anti-detective is like the Kierkegaardian ironist who knows that the only way to remain free (not imprisoned in the fiction and its serialization) and somehow superhuman is to choose not to choose (not to solve the mystery), since choice is a limitation of freedom and of the power of creativity as it turns the potential into actual.'[31]

Like William of Baskerville, Casaubon concludes that there is no order in the universe, and, even more important, that there is no map. As an anti-detective and as an unreliable narrator, Casaubon defies the rules of the traditional detective novel and, like Borges' Lönnrot, finds out that he himself is the victim of the conspiracy.

The book itself is an anti-detective novel, because its rules no longer define the genre but a human attitude towards life: the acceptance of the non-logical and the idea of life as a mystery.[32] This is what makes anti-detective novel writers postmodern.

The even more original aspect of Eco's work is a link with the historical past. The traditional detective novel always presents a reconstruction of the past, but in general the time span that concerns the solution of the crime is limited to a few weeks or months, occasionally a few years. Eco's story makes use of a much longer time span: the origins of the mystery go back to the creation and dissolution of the Order of the Templars in the Middle Ages.

The solution that Ardenti and Belbo think the diabolicals have found resides in a fourteenth-century document, which is a copy, not an original, and the original is missing: as Baudrillard would put it, it is a copy of nothing at all, a component of postmodern dissimulation.

In looking back to the medieval Templars, Eco suggests a connection between the contemporary and the so-called pre-modern world, and emphasizes that our sense of suspicion and our fear of conspiracy were not unknown in that era. He enables us to see a link between the dismantling of the 'P2 Loggia' and the persecution of the Templars by King Philip the Fair. Worried by the Templars' excessive power and riches, Philip ordered their arrest and forced them to confess to crimes they had not committed. The history of the Templars is immediately juxtaposed with the story of a student protest in Milan in the early 1970's and the subsequent police attack. Belbo and Casaubon evoke the Third Crusade and the conquest of Ascalonne: history is seen as a repetition of recurring events, and the Middle Ages is presented as the cradle of human precariousness. In a way, the contemporary world resembles more the pre-modern than the modern world, as it returns to that era's irrationality and obsession with reading the world. Even postmodern aesthetics relies more on the pleasure of repetition found in medieval aesthetics than on the anxiety for innovation typical of modern aesthetics.[33]

Contemporary popular culture, including the detective novel, respects the idea of a repetitive plot and of seriality. *Foucault's Pendulum* in part illustrates this aspect of postmodern aesthetics, especially in its game of intertextual quotations (see chapter 5) and its incorporation of some of the traditional elements of the detective story, but at the same time it transcends it. In its innovative structure and its particular role played by its unusual detective, this novel introduces many 'independent variables,' as Omar Calabrese has called them. This is not, therefore, pure repetition, since variations are potentially infinite, and the text becomes infinite as well.[34] That kind of enterprise, says Eco, needs a critical reader, an audience able to play with its own encyclopaedic competence: 'The ingenuous spectator, at first frustrated, overcomes his frustration and transforms himself into a critical spectator who appreciates the way in which he was tricked.'[35] The reader Eco hypothesizes for the 'era of repetition' is similar to the one he had in mind for his work.

That Eco is following a highly precise scheme is evident (see chapter 4). As I have pointed out, the plot is simple, but the course of events is complicated by continuous back and forth movement between the different time periods, by the reading of Belbo's memoirs, and by the recollections of the young protagonist. The time and space dislocation often gives the narrative a dreamlike effect. The reader at times feels enchanted and lost owing to the labyrinthine structure of the novel, which is supposed to resemble the structure of the Torah and therefore the structure of life.

The idea that everything is connected to everything else also seems mirrored in the structure of the novel, as we move with a spirallike movement towards the centre, constituted by the moment of realization. The structure is like that of the serpent Kundalini, referred to in the text, and represents the longest possible way of getting to the core; or, even better, like 'an infinite onion, which has its centre everywhere and its circumference nowhere. Initiation travels an endless Möbius strip' (*Foucault's Pendulum*, p. 621).

It also mirrors a human body the order of which has been disrupted by a mutated cell that has started to diffuse a tumour. The cell takes shape in the body of Diotallevi, the Torah scholar, who dies of cancer at the end: 'I'm dying because I convinced myself [literally, my cells] that there was no order, that you could do whatever you liked with any text' (567).

One cannot say, then, that there is no order, if by mistaking a letter or a number we can produce catastrophic results. But the system is highly complex, and the human yearning to map it out can bring us to excesses: 'Son, be cautious in your work, because it is divine work, and if you omit one letter or write one letter too many, you destroy the whole world' (565).

There is only one way to face 'the mystery of life,' and that is with a sense of irony. This is Belbo's typical response when someone is behaving as the bearer or the keeper of a secret: 'ma gavte la nata' (literally, take the cap off). He says it to Lorenza, his girlfriend, when she is acting as Sophia, the mother of the world, an attitude that will cost her her life; and he says it just before dying, facing the arrogance of his enemies. It is a gesture of resistance, of refusal to comply with nonsense. 'He somehow knew that, fragile as our existence may be, however ineffectual our interrogation of the world, there is nevertheless something that has more meaning than the rest' (623). In his life of missed opportunities, Belbo is thus able to say no to nonsense and to understand truth for the briefest moment. One can do that only before dying, because the human condition is such that one cannot avoid interpretation and the search for meaning.

## In the Swing of the Pendulum

Between the critique of certainty in *The Name of the Rose* and the critique of uncertainty in *Foucault's Pendulum*, Eco needed a balance, a third novel that would reflect the more recent state of his philosophical theory.

The Middle Ages has always attracted Eco for the way in which scholars were able to combine observation of the physical world with a sense of wonder at the mystery of nature. He had found in Aquinas this perfect combination, and a superior way of applying Aristotelian theory to the study of theology.

According to philosophers such as Foucault, at a certain point in human history there is a shift in paradigm, and our view of the world starts to coincide more and more with that of positive science. We are now still moving in the same direction, but we have not yet reached the other side of the arc described by the pendulum. In the seventeenth century, the era of the Baroque, the theory of knowledge seems perfectly torn between a scientific and a mystical view of nature. Although we may have moved forward since then, Eco contends, our era closely resembles that era. He goes so far as to call the postmodern the 'NeoBaroque.'

This is the topic of *The Island of the Day Before*, in which we meet the interesting character Father Caspar Wanderdrossel, a Jesuit who perfectly blends medieval man and baroque/neobaroque modernity. He is medieval in his careful observation of plants and animals, and very much baroque in his attempts to reconcile his scientific knowledge with the Bible and other sacred texts. In his exploration of the Great Flood, for example, he arrives at the conclusion, from observing nature, that forty days of rain, no matter how strong, could never have filled the whole earth and covered the mountains. This, for him, does not mean that the Bible is wrong; one cannot dispute the authority of sacred texts. Father Caspar comes to the witty conclusion that God must have taken water from the past, from the day before.

The method Father Caspar devises for calculating longitude is based on the scientific observation of Jupiter's satellites through a telescope mounted on a complex device called *Instrumentum Arcetricum*, which, according to the Jesuit, was described (but never built) by Galileo. The mounting of the strange machine creates the opportunity for a perfect comic sketch. When, after various attempts, Roberto has finally succeeded in hoisting the armoured Father Caspar on the chair onto the top of the 'metallic castle,' he drops the pendulum that was supposed to calculate the time. Turning around to look at the clock, he spills the ink, and trying to catch it, he causes the clock to fall. When Father Caspar, excited by what he is seeing through his telescope, looks down and sees what has happened, he explodes with a ludicrous, angry exclamation – 'Himmelpotzblitzsherrgottsakrament!' – and falls into the tank full of oil. The rudimentary character of early scientific machines is parodied here, but it contributes to make this awkward genius (a mixture of Leonardo and Galileo) a likeable character.

Another character who in many ways resembles Father Caspar, and who is also a Jesuit, is Father Emanuele, the confessor to whom Roberto goes to find reconciliation and peace after having been disturbed by the Pyrronian scepticism of Saint-Savin. Father Emanuele, based on the historical figure Father Emanuele Tesauro (1592–1675), is also an inventor. He has put together a machine he calls the Aristotelian Telescope, which is like the one described by Tesauro in his major work; but this telescope is peculiar because it is not constructed with lenses but composed of drawers and moving rollers that allow letter combinations. The purpose of this machine is to create witty metaphors, to accumulate and combine definitions, so as to allow us to see through words. Only through artificial eloquence can we understand how nature speaks.

Father Emanuele is similar to Father Caspar in his ingenuity, but at the same time he is his opposite. His invention completely excludes the observation of nature; it studies the world through language and is almost the prototype of a computer. It represents a completely artificial way of dealing with knowledge. Roberto often seems to have assimilated Father Emanuele's method and to have looked at nature through its frame: 'Both Art and Nature are fond of machination, and that is simply what the atoms themselves do when they aggregate in this way or in another' (*The Island of the Day Before*, p. 101).

Roberto, like Casaubon, is a particular kind of detective. The mysteries he wants to explore concern the secrets of the *Daphne* and its arcane mission, and the search for the Intruder who inhabits the ship with him. His method of detection is far from that of a Sherlock Holmes. He begins his search drunk and in fear, thinking his hunt could be infinite and taking pleasure in slowing it down. When he finally discovers a footprint of the Intruder, he knows that somebody is there. A duel of wit begins between the two: Roberto arranges all the clocks on the deck, like traps that cannot be avoided, and the Intruder moves them all around during the night and liberates a few animals; then the Intruder places a large stuffed animal in Roberto's bedroom, and Roberto finally decides to draw a map of the ship. Although the Intruder is able to outwit Roberto with his many tricks, in the end Roberto triumphs. He understands, thanks to his map, the existence of a hidden receptacle; he knocks down a thin partition wall and finds the old man pointing a gun at him.

Here Roberto has adopted an abductive investigative approach that allows him to move in his textual universe. On the second-last page of the novel, the twentieth-century narrator asks if this universe has an order, thereby transforming the detection process into a metaphysical question, the same question as in the other two novels. The essence of the mystery and the answer to Roberto's questions seem to be in the orange dove, which is not a dove but a tropical bird that cannot be named out of the vocabulary available to Roberto. According to Father Caspar, one must see it first. As we learn in chapter 26, the dove is an important sign because it has been allotted different meanings by the Egyptians, the Greeks, the Jews, the early Christians, and so on; it is understandable, therefore, that Roberto gives it particular importance. Since the dove is on the island, it too lives in the past, and it becomes for Roberto the past that he must recuperate. That is why Roberto's story involves a continuous back and forth movement between past and present, especially in the first half of the novel. In the second half, thanks to Father Caspar, Roberto seems to live more in the present, but his mind immediately reverts to rewriting the past as soon as the Jesuit disappears; the last chapters represent a merging of the written past (Roberto's romance) and the present (see figure 4).

Roberto sacrifices himself for the dove, for a multi-faceted emblem: 'But if a symbol or hieroglyph must be chosen as something to die for, its meanings should be multiple, otherwise you might as well call a spade a spade, an atom an atom, a void a void' (352). The dove represents for Roberto the unfathomability of witty messages. In other words, the dove means so much that one must admire it as a pure hieroglyph that neither says nor hides, but simply shows (353): it is a revelation in itself.

Like Casaubon, who understands only in the end, Roberto has a moment of revelation just before disappearing. After he has set fire to the *Daphne* and dived into the ocean, he sees the orange dove, whose flight represents the process of unlimited semiosis. The voyage stops only as we face death.

In her essay '"Dove" Is the Dove,' Claudia Miranda underlines the similarity of the dove's flight to a 'fugue' (fuga),[36] and in fact the book is full of musical references. 'Daphne,' 'Tweede Daphne,' 'Orainge,' and 'Doen Daphne d'over Schoone Maeght' are all compositions of the seventeenth-century Dutch composer Jonkheer Jacob Van Eyck (ca. 1590–1657), who was also blind – a little like Roberto, whose eyes ache and are covered with dark glasses.

When Roberto goes to Amsterdam in preparation for his voyage, he stops at a Dutch city and enters its cathedral. In a chapel next to the choir is a man dressed in black with his eyes wide open. This bell-master ('der Musycin en Directeur vande Klok-werken, le carillonneur, der Glockenspieler,' 232), who keeps replaying the same melody, 'Doen Daphne d'over Schoone Maeght,' is nobody other than Jacob Van Eyck. On the *Daphne*, then, Roberto listens to this melody repeatedly, since it is the only music coming from the mechanical organ at the bottom of the ship (Roberto does not know how to substitute the cylinder in order to play different songs). The *Daphne* itself is 'a Dutch fluyt, or flute, or flûte, or flyboat, or fliebote' (8), a musical instrument that produced a melody played by wind and water, a memory of the transformation of a divine creature into an arboreal substance (342).

The variations on the beautiful motif 'Doen Daphne d'over Schoone Maeght' reflect the mutable play of appearances that repeat themselves over and over in the disorder of our experience. Music, which presents multiple problems in terms of semiotic analysis, seems to be the perfect

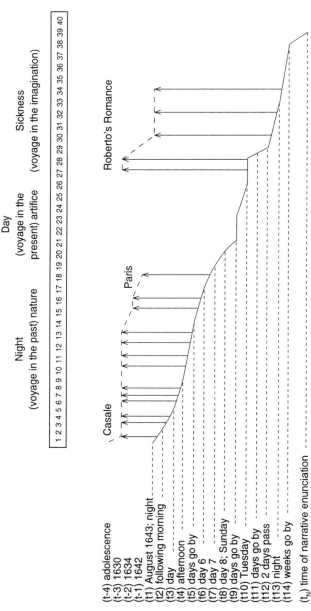

Figure 4. The time line of *The Island of the Day Before*

metaphor for the universe: 'Did an order that He had imposed on the Universe still exist? Perhaps He had imposed many, from the beginning; perhaps He was prepared to change them day by day; perhaps a secret order existed, presiding over the constant change of orders and perspectives, but we were still destined never to discover it, to follow instead the shifting play of those appearances of order that were recorded at every new experience' (512).

The metaphysical aspect of this idea is in fact a profound semiotic problem. Eco has criticized Saussure's semiology for its inadequacy in terms of a semiotics of music. If the concept of sign is understood as a 'totality' of signifier and signified, the 'sign nature' of music is easily called into question, since signification constitutes a major problem for the interpretation of sound. In other words, it is not so difficult to create new sound 'signifiers,' but it is extremely difficult to find new 'signifieds' for them.[37] The problem is not whether music means anything, but whether it is possible to explain 'how' it means.

Many theoreticians, including Eco and Nattiez, have found it profitable to return to Peirce's ideas of the Interpretant and the Dynamic Object in order to explain how music signifies. The Peircian Interpretant is useful because it goes beyond the definition of a term and implies a more complex interpretative process. Eco writes: 'That a cat is not only a domestic feline, but also the animal that zoological classifications define as *felix cattus*, the animal adored by the Egyptians, the animal that appears in Manet's *Olympia*, the animal that was a delicacy in the Paris besieged by the Prussians, the animal Baudelaire sang of ... the favourite animal of witches and so on, are all *interpretations* of the expression /cat/' (*Semiotica e filosofia del linguaggio*, pp. 108–9).

The sign refers to an object through an unlimited chain of interpretants. In the case of music, the 'object' it refers to is better understood as Peirce's Dynamic Object, 'a sort of *Ding an sich* determining the sign, but which, from the nature of things, the Sign cannot express, except in the "phantasmatic" form ... of the Immediate Object.'[38]

The chain of interpretants that Eco lists for 'cat' reflects the chain of interpretants of the 'Dove' highlighted in *The Island of the Day Before*. In reality, unlimited semiosis represents a circle that 'closes every second and never closes at all' (*Lector in fabula*, p. 46), an infinite aspiration to something one will never have: 'Is this not the highest point of the most generous desire?' (*The Island of the Day Before*, p. 331). Although the interpretant increases our understanding of the sign, the problem for the interpretation of music is its translation into another sign system. A musical sequence, according to Eco, rouses different expectations in the listener, 'so that music appears as a semiotic system in which every expressive situation is open to different interpretations and therefore has different *interpretants*.'[39]

The interpretants of the Dove, although they might never take Roberto to the possession of the Object, lead him to an increased understanding of it; in the same way, listening to the five variations on Van Eyck's melody do not take him to something precise, but bring him closer to nature's witty message.

As Otto Christensen argues, music in the Baroque period helps to connect level of expression with emotional content.[40] Music as a materialization of the composer's interior movements is a later idea, belonging to the eighteenth century. For the Baroque, then, there is a framework founded in 'a common understanding of the meaning deposited in music,'[41] and based on the concept of intersubjectivity. And like the music, the Dove is there to signify that the world speaks to us through signs, not for the purpose of concealing from us, but for the purpose of 'showing' us. We do not need to fumble in the recesses of secret conspiratory connections, but simply acknowledge the multiple levels of the book and reflect on the contemporary loss of the baroque framework.

Is the novel, then, simply a story about an unhappy lover, condemned to live under an exaggerated sky? (512) Of course it is much more. The novel has multiple meanings, like the dove; and it also refers to the most recent reflections in Eco's theory. As I have said, after *The Name of the Rose* and *Foucault's Pendulum*, *The Island of the Day Before* re-establishes the balance between the two poles of interpretation, between order and disorder, between the *Punto Fijo* and the Dove, between medieval and postmodern semiotics.

Nevertheless, if I had to choose one of the possible readings of the novel, I would say that *The Island of the Day Before* is Eco's most musical and melancholic meditation on time and on life and death.

Why have I never thought of death, and of the wrath of a laughing God? Because I was following the teachings of my philosophers, for whom death is a natural necessity, and God is He who into the disorder of the atoms introduced the Law that composes them in the harmony of the Cosmos. Could such a God, master of geometry, produce the disorder of Hell, even if out of justice, and could He laugh at the subverting of every subversion?

No, God does not laugh, Roberto said to himself. He bows to the Law that He Himself willed, the Law that wills the body to decay, as mine is surely decaying in this decadence. (463)

Roberto was 'thrown' onto the *Daphne* – and Eco writes the novel – in order to reflect on the question that haunts every philosopher: What is the mystery of the beginning? Which eternity preceded us? matter or God? Only by meditating on this question can one be liberated from anxiety about non-Being and be committed to the stupor of Being.

Eco's latest novel, *Baudolino,* cannot be called a detective novel. Although a *whodunit* kind of plot is present in the suspected murder of Frederick the Great, this line of the story is given relatively little presence. Furthermore, at the end of the book, the murder is accounted for as possibly an accident.

In the discussion between Baudolino and his friends concerning responsibility for the death, Baudolino does act as a semiotician/detective, but this episode has secondary importance in the novel. Much greater importance is given to the story of the fantastic voyage and to the matter of rewriting history from an individual perspective.

In fact, as suggested in this chapter, even in *The Island of the Day Before* the protagonist is a peculiar type of detective, less intent on solving a murder case than on discovering his own mind in relation to the natural world.

We can conclude, therefore, that in his last two novels Eco has shifted not only his narrative interest, but his semiotic interest as well. Baudolino makes abductions, but his most characteristic habits are playing with language and taking advantage of rhetorical possibilities. He enjoys employing the power of language to manipulate and interfere with reality. In this sense, then, maybe Baudolino is the ultimate postmodern detective, since he is able to construct not just his own story or the story of his friends, but history as well.

The following chapter will examine *Baudolino* in this light, keeping in mind Eco's concern about the question of fallibility. Once again, it is not just the fallibility of the main character, the detective, that is at stake but also the fallibility of our entire learning. Although finding the truth is ultimately impossible, the wisdom of a community rests on the ability to recognize failures and constantly call into question the tales we once believed true.

# 8  *Baudolino* and the Language of Monsters

Umberto Eco's most recent literary production, *Baudolino* (2000), like his previous novels combines fiction and historical detail. Once again, history blends with a plot that seems oriented towards the detective novel. But this time the theme of the fantastic journey in unexplored lands in the manner of Marco Polo's *Milione* prevails over the search for accountable murderers and the struggle for the semiotic solution of a puzzling enigma. One mysterious death does occur at the core of the novel, but its investigation is forgotten for approximately two hundred pages and is explained as a simple accident towards the end.

As in *The Name of the Rose* (1980), the story takes place in the Middle Ages, and Eco takes advantage of the cultural and intellectual traits of the time to discuss and represent important semiotic questions concerning the disestablishing concept of 'monster,' which represents a peculiar case for semiotics, and concerning the ideas of truth and falsity. In his book *Serendipities: Language and Lunacy*, he had discussed how certain historical fakes succeeded in diverting human history, and had asserted the power of the false. *Baudolino* appears as a collection of such fakes, a forceful example of how lies have been exploited throughout history for political motives and have served as a precious reminder of the fallibility of human knowledge. As Eco writes in *Serendipities*, 'Recognizing that our history was inspired by many tales we now recognize as false should make us alert, ready to call constantly into question the very tales we believe true, because the criterion of the wisdom of the community is based on constant awareness of the fallibility of our learning' (20).

This chapter is a modified reprint of the material as it appears in *Semiotica* 144 (2003).

The book narrates the life and adventures of Baudolino, the hero of the story, born in 1137 or 1138 into a family in humble circumstances in Alessandria, a town in Piedmont, which was in fact founded after Baudolino's supposed birth (Alessandria is also the city where Eco himself was born). As a result of his genius, his wit, his ability to assimilate foreign languages immediately (he speaks German, Greek, Turkish, Latin, and the language of the Frascheta, a Piedmontese dialect), and a serendipitous encounter, Baudolino is adopted as a son and counselor to Frederick the Great (nicknamed in Italy *Barbarossa,* Red-beard), the notorious emperor of the Holy Roman Empire, whose reign extended from 1152 to 1190.

Eco's book without doubt pays homage to his beloved home town and his ancestors, in whom he recognizes qualities and traits, vices and virtues that are common among the people of the area even today, and with which he identifies: a certain acumen, a curiosity, and a blasé attitude. Baudolino is brilliant and imaginative, ironic and resourceful; he looks at his interlocutors 'di sottecchi' – with a suspicious glance – (19), as if warning them not to take him seriously. This detail calls to mind the image of Eco the intellectual, once again uniting the major qualities of the adept semiotician.

*Baudolino* starts with an excerpt from the *Kronica Baudolini,* which Baudolino supposedly wrote in 1155 in the language of the Frascheta, his area of origin. This hilarious short piece, drafted on the stolen parchment of the *De duabus civitatibus historia* by Bishop Otto, would constitute, in the logic of the narrative, one of the first texts written in the *volgare,* the language of the people; different from the Latin used in official documents, in fact it is written in the style of the *Placito capuano* (written in 960), the first documented Italian written text.[1] Because Baudolino is using an idiom not usually put down on paper, the spelling of the words varies and the expressions come straight from the oral language, paragraphs are linked incorrectly, and little punctuation is used. Ideas pour out of Baudolino's pen as in a stream of consciousness. For example, he narrates of his encounter with Frederick:

> Raconto questa Chronica se no non si capise come è andata quella sera ke c'era un nebione ke si taliava col cultello et dire ke era già aprile ma da noi fa nebbia anca d'agosto et se uno non è di quelle parti si capise bene ke si perde tra la Burmia et la Frasketa specie se non cè un sancto ke lo tira per il morso ed ecco ke io andavo a casa ke mi vedo di nanzi un barone su un kavallo tuto di ferro

il barone non il kabvallo era tuto di ferro con la spada che somiliava il
re di Ragona

I am telling this story because if I don't you wouldnt understand what
happened that evening with the fog so thick you could cut it with a knife
and it was already april but in our Parts theres fog even in august and if
your not from those Parts you get lost between Burmia and Frescheta
especially if there isnt a saint to take you by the bridle and there I was
heading for home when I saw right in front of me a baron on a horse all
covered with iron

it was the baron covered with iron not the horse and with a sword he
looked like the king of Arragon (5)

This is young Baudolino (not yet educated in the *studium* of Paris)
narrating his famous encounter with Frederick the Great, who was lost
in the fog of the Frascheta. The language is a mixture of dialect and
Latin and aims at reflecting Baudolino's soul, which is simple but not
naive, coarse but witty. Between the lines of the *Chronicle*, we can read
excerpts in Latin from Otto's manuscript, which Baudolino was unable
to erase, a detail that signifies the rewriting of history by this shrewd
and amiable liar.

After this introductory note, a third person narrator takes over. In
the second chapter, more than fifty years have passed (it is Wednesday,
14 April 1204), and we find ourselves in Constantinople. Baudolino is
about sixty-seven. We discover that it is his friend Niketas Coniate,
orator, chancellor, and supreme judge of the Byzantine Empire, who is
reading what is left of Baudolino's *Kronica*. Baudolino is narrating to
Niketas his marvellous adventures, arrogantly hoping that one day
Niketas will transfer them to paper and that the story of his life will be
handed down to future generations, as had happened with Marco Polo
and Rustichello. We learn very soon that Baudolino is a renowned liar
and that his fantastic accounts are, to say the least, artful and question-
able. Meanwhile, the fires of the crusaders are burning the city of
Constantinople to the ground.

### History, Fiction, and the Realm of Monsters

Many historical and cultural issues are discussed in the novel, for example, the autonomy of the *studia* or the universities of Bologna and
Paris, interest in the Orient and the fabulous Kingdom of Prester John,

the search for the Holy Grail, the shape of the cosmos, and certain of the myths that constitute an important part of the medieval imagination. But in the midst of the novel's picaresque adventures, linguistic games, and allusion to historical events, there come to the surface many contemporary issues and concerns.

History is therefore connected to the present, but it is also seen as a collective illusion. Baudolino, despite his good intent, surrounds historical events with believable and unbelievable lies. In fact, as Eco himself reveals in an interview given to the Italian magazine *Panorama*, our hero falsifies half of the 'Biblioteca d'Occidente' (Western Library), beginning with Otto's *De duabus civitatibus historia*, which he scrapes off in order to write his own *Kronika*: 'And the world conforms,' says Eco. 'Furthermore, it conspires and collaborates with him in the universal fiction. Baudolino not only practises fiction, he also acts on the collective illusion that produces History.'[2]

Eco, then, is interested in a serendipitous idea of history and in history as a continuous production of myths. Baudolino as narrator is the writer as Great Liar, whose truth is what befits the web of his or her encyclopaedic explorations. In Eco's exploration, there is more than just a journey from the West to the East and from history to fairy-tales. He takes us back to the past in order to make us reflect on the present: 'In rereading the past there is always a kind of pessimism of the eternal return. We realize that there has been less progress than we thought. I don't think that certain conversations between Ronald Reagan and his collaborators were less naive than those between Frederick and his advisers. And if Frederick the Great did not understand the spirit of the Italian *Comuni*, it seems that George Bush, Jr, does not even know where the Balkans are located.'[3]

The similarities do not stop here. Although in this fantastic tale populated by 'sciapodes,' 'blemmyae,' and satyrs it is difficult to recognize the present, the correspondences are closer than we might think. Although we no longer believe the kind of fascinating tales of monsters reported by Baudolino, our society is not entirely bereft of monsters. Jeffrey Jerome Cohen, in his introduction to *Monster Theory*, sees in fin de siècle America

a society that has created and commodified 'ambient fear' – a kind of total fear that saturates day-to-day living, prodding and silently antagonizing but never speaking its own name. This anxiety manifests itself symptomatically as a cultural fascination with monsters – a fixation that is born of the twin desire to name that which is difficult to apprehend and to domesticate (and therefore disempower) that which threatens. And so the monster appears simultaneously as the demonic disemboweler of slasher films and as a wide-eyed, sickeningly cute plush toy for children: velociraptor and Barney.[4]

New York City's East Village is no stranger to monsters, for it is impossible to miss the astonishing quantity of cultural material on the monstrous: films, comic books, vampire clothes, horrifying tattoos, monster costumes and books. All this strongly contrasts with the designer clothes stores, diamonds, and Disney stores of uptown Manhattan. It does not represent a simple demographic division, since one can travel easily from the different parts of town; instead, it replicates our deepest desires. When our curiosity brings us to explore the transgressive embodiments of our fears, we move anxiously among exotic surroundings, dark recesses, and sensual fashions; but we feel relieved when we reappear in the trafficked streets and quaint bistros of uptown. If the island of Manhattan is a metaphor of our inner duality, Eco takes us through a similar journey, from the court of Fredrick the Great to the Far East of the monstrous imagination, although often the two categories are reversed and superimposed.

A born liar, Baudolino can hardly distinguish between what is true and what he has invented. Niketas, on the other hand, is his semiotic alter ego, who strives to find the truth or at least a better interpretation of what Baudolino is narrating. Baudolino and Niketas represent the two forces of language: on the one side, the creative, which is able to give birth to the most exotic monsters, and on the other side, the truth-seeking. This duality of language, on which the arts and sciences are founded, allows us not only to create and invent, but also to revise and criticize what we have produced. The duality is also within the writer/semiotician Eco, who has created fictional works but also dedicated his life to analysing texts in search for truth. Often, in the book, we realize that the boundaries between the two are far from well defined.

Eco is offering both a critique of language in its infinite potential to create ex nihilo and therefore potentially founding the impossibility of knowledge, and an exaltation of the scientific power of semiotics, capable of detecting a certain 'truth' among the lies. As Otto teaches the receptive youth, 'The world condemns liars who do nothing but lie, even about the most trivial things, and it rewards the poets, who lie only about the greatest things' (43). If Baudolino wants to be a perfect liar, therefore, he should listen to other people's thoughts, in order to understand how people persuade one another on this issue or that.

In a way, it does not matter whether the information or the events are true, as long as in the narrative 'tout se tient': the details must fit in the larger picture. For example, Baudolino and his friends speculate about the legend of the Three Kings who went to see Jesus in Bethlehem. They are conscious that the story is problematic, as only one of the Gospels mentions the king, their names are uncertain, and their number is doubtful. When Baudolino by chance encounters the relics of the Three Kings in the cathedral of St Eustorgio in Milan, he gives them specific names, he fabricates the trajectory of their journey, and he invents a specific story about their descent from Prester John, a king-priest governing an empire in the Far East. Passing the tale on to the court historian Rainaldo, he makes sure that the facts appearing in the tradition are to his own and Frederick's advantage. The pursuit of the kingdom of Prester John for Baudolino is a game. His journey to the Far East in search of this legendary ruler is a dangerous move, but only in a restricted sense: he can either find the kingdom or make it up, as long as it satisfies the political interests of Frederick the Great.

In this sense, the Middle Ages was an extraordinary period in history. In the absence of a scientific method of verification, the powerful were able to falsify true things or present as true false things – for example, the famous letter by Prester John, supposedly directed to Frederick, that Baudolino concocts and the idea for which is stolen from him by the disingenuous Zosimo and shrewdly used by the advisers of the Pope. Although we might convince ourselves that today we have greater control, thanks to technological innovations such as DNA and chemical analyses, in fact strong forces in alliance with the media can still manipulate public opinion and the interpretation of facts.

The letter of Prester John is one of the famous historical fakes Eco describes in his book on serendipity. Purposely, Baudolino and his friends fabricate an ambiguous document, conscious that future interpreters will examine its linguistic nuances and distort the meaning according to their interest.

The Priest Johannes, by the power and grace of God and of Our Lord Jesus Christ, master of all those who rule, to Frederick, holy and Roman emperor, wishing him good health and perpetual enjoyment of the divine benediction ...

... In the breadth of our munificence, if you desire something that can procure for you pleasure, inform us, either by a word to our messenger or by a sign of your affection. Accept in exchange ... (136)

They cannot suggest anything specific, so they concur on something vague:

'... *accipe istam veram arcam*, accept this true ark ...'
'Not bad,' Rabbi Solomon said. 'It conceals and reveals at the same time. And it opens the path to the vortex of interpretation.' (139)

In this fashion, the hint as to the Holy Grail is less than explicit, and the door is open to various explanations. The content and style of the letter are clearly too naive for such a powerful and mystic ruler, too directed towards explaining concerns that are at the core of Western beliefs, but the letter will play an important historical role in the hands of the Catholic Church and in the exploration and expansion of the Christian West towards the Orient. Moreover, we are never completely sure whether Baudolino and his friends wrote the letter, since they make no immediate use of it and since they are also, apparently, under the influence of Abdul's precious 'honey,' the powerful drug that the legendary and deceitful Alaodin administered to his helpless prisoners.

Although nowadays we have and trust our scientific instruments to verify the authenticity of things and tell us where the truth lies, in many instances we realize that we cannot trust our sources of information. As in the Middle Ages, the powerful often control the direction of public opinion and therefore guide our political future. Eco points to this permanent feature of the human condition; we are condemned to dealing with the ambiguity of language and its distinction from 'reality,' a feature that medieval scholars clearly understood and that contemporary semioticians have repeatedly analysed.

**In the Land of Monsters**

After the mysterious death of Frederick the Great, which provides the detection episode in a narrative of adventures, Baudolino, together with his eleven friends Abdul, Rabbi Solomon, Borone, Kyot, the Poet, Ardzrouni, and the Alexandrines Boidi, Cuttica, Porcelli, Ciula, and Colandrino, sets forth on a journey in search of the Kingdom of Prester John. It is the end of June 1190.

From this point on, the historical events become secondary, and we follow our heroes in a fantastic expedition through a land of mystery. They possess a map of those areas beyond the ocean where humans lived before the Flood, and which also includes Paradise. After many discussions and disquisitions about the shape of the cosmos, they accept the route offered by Ardzrouni's map and, having crossed mountains and deserts, come to assorted cities inhabited by monstrous creatures. At first, these are men who walk with four hands, women with venomous serpents in their vaginas, naked humans who mate on the streets, men with testicles running down to their knees, anthropophagi, furry beings, gymnosophists, and fleas as big as frogs. At various points, our characters are attacked by scorpions, snakes, and the basilisk itself. The basilisk has a rooster's head and claws, yellow and bulging eyes, and the body of a serpent. It corresponds perfectly to the traditional image, as given in Pliny for example – which demonstrates the degree to which these monsters are the fruit of a literary imagination.

Following the basilisk and the frightful experience of the Abcasia forest,[5] where the deepest darkness reigns, our heroes encounter almost all the monsters described by ancient mythology and medieval tradition, starting with the harpies, birds with girls' faces, which fly onto the travellers' heads screaming: 'On what soil are you treading? Go back! You cannot violate the land of the gods! Go back and tread the land that was given you!' (349) Following the harpies, three beasts bar the advance of our heroes: a cat with fiery eyes, 'notoriously the messenger of Satan' (350); a chimera, with a lion's head, a goat's body, and a dragon's back; and a manticore, with a lion's body, a scorpion's tail, and an almost human head. The three figures are like monstrous versions of Dante's allegorical beasts – the leopard, the lion, and the she-wolf, representing lust, pride, and avarice, the illnesses of a humanity that has abandoned virtue and embraced evil. Baudolino and his friends valorously defeat them: the cat is quickly killed with one arrow in the centre of his forehead; the chimera is defeated by a shower of darts, exactly as happens in the myth of Bellerophon, who, flying over her on Pegasus' back, assails her with copious arrows; and finally the manticore, the most difficult to eliminate thanks to its human head, which according to medieval tradition is the seat of rationality. Being a cannibal, the manticore bites Abdul with its triple teeth, and it takes too long for his friends to open the monster's jaws and liberate him. As a result, he loses his life, dreaming of his unfortunate love.

The crossing of the Sambatyon, the stone river, represents the arrival of the fake kings into unknown territories, which not even the most courageous explorers had reached. In this vast mysterious territory, they soon meet a faithful friend, a sciapode. As described by Pliny, the umbrella-foot sciapodes are one-legged creatures whose enlarged foot can be used to protect them from the sun, and who move in jumps with surprising speed. They appear in every medieval chronicle of monsters, and their domains are located by the geographers and map-makers of the time. The sciapode is usually represented seated and pulling its one leg up above its head, and this artistic rendering tends to make the figure of a quasi-circle, which, according to David Williams in *Deformed Discourse*, one of the most interesting recent studies on the medieval theory of monsters, is reminiscent of the figure of the self-swallowing serpent.

This awkward being, called Gavagai in the novel, guides Baudolino and his friends to the city of Pndapetzim, the capital of the kingdom of Deacon John (designated successor to Prester John). This peculiar city is inhabited by many diverse beings. We immediately meet a representative of the blemmyae, creatures with a human body but no head, and with eyes, nose, and mouth on their chests; later we encounter some panotii, beings of human appearance with very long ears. In addition to these, the kingdom is populated by pigmies, single-eyed giants, Nubians, tongueless beings, eunuchs, cameleopards, unicorns, and satyrs who-are-never-seen. The most interesting characteristic of these groups, aside from the physical aspect, the differences in which do not seem to influence their consideration of one another, is that they have different religious beliefs. As Gavagai innocently reveals to our heroes, they are unable to differentiate in terms of physical characteristics and consider themselves all good Christians, but they disagree on one thing, the nature of Christ:

'... All good Christians and faithful servants of the Deacon and Presbyter.'
'You are not friends because you are different?'
'What you say? Different?'
'Well, in the sense that you are different from us and –'
'Why I different you?'
'Oh, for God's sake,' the Poet said. 'To begin with, you only have one leg! We and the blemmyae have two!'
'Also you and the blemmyae if you raise one leg, you have only one.'

'But you don't have another one to lower!'

'Why should I lower a leg I don't has? Do you lower third leg you don't has?'

Boidi intervened, conciliatory: "Listen, Gavagai, you must agree that the blemmy has no head.'

'What? Has no head? Has eyes, nose, mouth, speaks, eats. How possible if has no head?'

'But haven't you noticed that he has no neck, and above the neck that round thing that you also have on your neck and he doesn't?'

'What means noticed?'

'Seen. Realized that. You know that.'

'Maybe you say he not entirely same as me; my mother couldn't mistake him for me. But you too not the same as this friend because he has mark on cheek and you no. And your friend different from that other one black like one Magi, and him different from that other with black beard like a rabbi.'

'How do you know I have a rabbi's beard?' Solomon asked hopefully, obviously thinking of the lost tribes, and deducing from those words a clear sign that they had passed through here or were living in this kingdom. (366–7)

Gavagai refuses to differentiate in terms of bodily characteristics; what distinguishes the different groups are beliefs. For example, the blemmyae are *phantasiastoi*: they believe Christ is not of the same nature as God; he is not word become flesh, but pure appearance, a *phantasma*. The sciapodes believe instead Arius' heresy,[6] and the tongueless people are Messalian, that is, they are convinced that one can get to heaven only by means of silent and continuous prayer.

Eco of course has in mind the medieval disputes about the nature of Christ that so agitated the Western world. These disputes are reflected in the confused domain of these monsters, whose physical characteristics seem a distorted manifestation of their will to sustain differences in thought. Furthermore, the monsters are unable to grasp their exterior distinctions, and rely on a different kind of semiotics. Longer ears are not markers: all individuals differ in terms of the measurement of specific body-parts, and these do not constitute their essence. The distinguishing element is a fundamental belief. To belong to a specific group, one must embrace its ideas, without possibility of dissent. This is why, when the Poet and Baudolino attend one of the reunions of the blemmyae, they are not permitted to bring up serious contradiction of their doctrine; empty debates, however, are acceptable.

The irony of the episode relies on the fact that Eco is not merely alluding to a problem of the historical past, but reflecting on the typically human tendency to distinguish, differentiate, and categorize. Even within the disorderly world of these unlikely beings, who parody human behaviour, a system tends to be constituted. Even when external markers are transcended, futile internal convictions draw boundaries. If we feel like deriding these ridiculous characters, blind and immersed in their inconclusive dilemmas, we need simply think of contemporary political situations, in which human beings can hardly see beyond their noses and for centuries have been entangled in fights. We might think of the Middle East, but Eco certainly also has in mind the Italian political situation.

A common concern about a possible invasion by the White Huns keeps these monster tribes united; in fact, the Poet, having gained control of the organization of the defence army, is able to exploit the abilities of each group to form a powerful and efficient militia. Before the attack, there is a solemn moment in which all the diverse cohorts chant the Pater Noster in their own languages, the effect being that of a choir of multiform sound. But in the moment of truth, when the Huns attack, the giants begin insulting the sciapodes, the pigmies start hitting the blemmyae, and so on, so that the Huns are able to take advantage of the internal squabbling and effortlessly slaughter their weakened adversaries. A few moments is sufficient to demonstrate the implacable discord existing among the various groups, and once again the inability of humankind to fight under a common banner, immediate danger notwithstanding, is caricatured. Baudolino and his friends are forced to escape and are afterwards captured by Alaodin's soldiers, the cynocephali or dog-headed beings, who keep them prisoner for years.

During his stay in the kingdom of the Deacon and before the invasion of the Huns, Baudolino meets a beautiful damsel, Hypatia, with whom he falls deeply in love. In appearance, she is completely human, and for days the two lovers meet by a lake and converse about philosophy. Hypatia belongs to a group of women, descendants of the Egyptian philosopher Hypatia (370–415), who are trying to keep alive the memory of Plato. Because Christianity had triumphed in her territory, the historical Hypatia was persecuted and finally killed. Her followers kept her beliefs alive by living a life completely without men. Baudolino's

Hypatia meets him in secret and explains to him the meaning of apathy, a condition of perfect estrangement from human emotions that implies a deeper knowledge of the causes of good and evil. Hypatia in the end breaks her apathy in her new-found love for Baudolino.

In the beginning, their affection is 'platonic,' but later Baudolino is overwhelmed by his passion and, in a moment of physical fervour, discovers that Hypatia's legs are goatlike. Baudolino understands that this is because the conceivers of the 'Hypatias' are the satyrs[7] who-are-never-seen. At first taken aback, Baudolino soon accepts his lover's peculiarity, since he recognizes that he is indifferent to her physical characteristics.

### *Baudolino* and Negative Theology

For much of the novel, Baudolino and his friends live surrounded by monsters. When our hero tells the story to Niketas, the latter sometimes expresses disbelief, but more often he is carried away by his friend's enchanting tales:

> As Niketas knew very well, that Baudolino wasn't sincere by nature; and if it's difficult to believe a liar when he tells you, for instance, that he has been to Iconium, how and when can you believe him when he tells you he has seen creatures that the most lively imagination would be hard pressed to conceive, and he himself is not sure of having seen?
>
> Niketas had determined to believe in a single thing, because the passion with which Baudolino spoke of it bore witness to its truth: that, on their journey our twelve Magi were drawn by the desire to reach a goal. (324)

Baudolino had certainly read about these unusual creatures of the unknown world in the Library in Paris, where he had conducted his studies. In fact, his accounts do not contradict the medieval treatises on monsters, such as the *Livre de merveilles*, the *Hortus sanitatis*, *Le monstre*, the *Cité de Dieu*, the *Monstrorum historia*, *Monstres*, the *Buch der Natur*, the *Historiae animalium*, the *De universo*, the *De natura bestiarum*, and other bestiaries.

Monsters are a particularly interesting subject for philosophy and semiotics. They are figures whose bodies are nothing but an image of them, an image that exists only in the human consciousness and unconscious. 'If one could see them one would discover the link between matter and thought, what Being consists of!' says the hermit in Flaubert's *Temptation of Saint Anthony*.[8]

Caught up in Baudolino's shrewd lies and fantastic narration, the naive reader might think that Eco has forgotten about more theoretical concerns, especially semiotic analysis; but the critical reader would be aware of the semiotic importance of the concept of the monster for both medieval and contemporary thought. In the Middle Ages, the monstrous is perceived as necessary for explaining the relation between matter and thought and therefore for understanding God. Because theologians of the period warned against an anthropomorphic representation of God, the only way to speak about God was through the negation of every possible affirmation concerning God.[9] The only way to talk about God was through paradox: the One and the Many, the Beginning and the End, the transcendent and the immanent, and so on. Hypatia explains these concepts to Baudolino:

God is unique, and he is so perfect that he does not resemble any of the things that exist or any of the things that do not; you cannot describe him using your human intelligence, as if he were someone who becomes angry if you are bad or who worries about you out of goodness, someone who has a mouth, ears, face, wings, or that is spirit, father or son, not even of himself. Of the Unique you cannot say he is or is not, he embraces all but is nothing; you can name him only through dissimilarity, because it is futile to call him Goodness, Beauty, Wisdom, Amiability, Power, Justice, it would be like calling him Bear, Panther, Serpent, Dragon, or Gryphon, because whatever you say of him will never express him. God is not body, is not figure, is not form; he does not have quantity, quality, weight, or lightness; he does not see, does not hear, does not know disorder or perturbation; he is not soul, intelligence, imagination, opinion, thought, word, number, order, size; he is not equality and is not inequality, is not time and is not eternity; he is a will without purpose. Try to understand, Baudolino: God is a lamp without flame, a flame without fire, a fire without heat, a dark light, a silent rumble, a blind flash, a luminous soot, a ray of his own darkness, a circle that expands concentrating on its own center, a solitary multiplicity; he is ... is ... He is a space that is not, in which you and I are the same thing, as we are today in this time that doesn't flow. (427)

Here the Pseudo-Dionysian corpus is of essential importance; according to this thinker the most suitable representation of being is achieved 'by resorting to the most inordinate, absurd, and monstrous images.'[10] By deforming the representation of a thing, artists called 'into question the adequacy of the intellectual concept of the thing in relation to its ontological reality.'[11] The monster thus raises concerns about the relation between the sign and its object or, as Pierce would say, between the sign and its *ground*.

All this has a larger point, that of underscoring the limitations of human discourse as a means of representing reality, and of erasing the boundary between the real world and a possible world. Hence, the importance of the idea of lying in Eco's novel. Baudolino, marked from the beginning as an arrant liar, continues to construct his own life, other people's lives, and, in the end, history itself through his fantastic narration, to the point that the reader is often left wondering which part of what he recounts is historically 'true.' Notwithstanding its impossibilities, Baudolino's story could have been possible. If we believe Baudolino when he tells us that Frederick the Great died in 1190, do we believe him when he says that he was born in 1137 or 1138, or when he describes himself as Frederick's adviser at many important moments during his reign? He is not a reliable narrator, but maybe his overall position is one of truthfulness, because at least we are warned against his tendency and suspect his accounts. What we know is that Baudolino tells lies 'a fin di bene' (for a greater good), and by denying his monsters it might be possible to arrive at a higher truth: is this not the role of fiction?

The discussion between Panufzio and Niketas in the last chapter of the novel sets forth this idea. Niketas decides not to include Baudolino's tale in his *Historia*, because, although a great story, it would reveal things better left unsaid. Panufzio urges Niketas, for example, not to mention the traffic in fake religious relics, fearing that Christians would lose their faith in sacred objects: 'In a great Historia small truths can be altered so that a greater truth can stand out' (522).

> 'It was a beautiful story [says Niketas]. Too bad no one will find out about it.'
> 'You surely don't believe you're the only writer of stories in this world. Sooner or later someone – a greater liar than Baudolino – will tell it.' (521)

In the end, we learn not only that Baudolino is a liar, but that the narrator is an even bigger liar. We are therefore left with a pile of information that is mined at its own foundation, having been informed that it is supposed to take us to a greater truth. But what is this greater truth, according to Eco's work?

In the Middle Ages, the idea was widespread that there is something in language beyond the sign's signification of a concept, a kind of natural relation between the human intellect and the real. The human mind can access the real only indirectly, through a metalanguage, 'through the poetic and rhetorical constructions of the paradoxes, ambiguities, grotesqueries, and monstrosity of mediaeval art and legend, which sufficiently deform the normal process of signification so as to urge the mind beyond the restriction of language and logic.'[12] If language is unable to access truth, truth must be approached through contradictions and anti-logical thought. This would explain the importance of the concept of monster in the medieval imagination and its frequent appearance in treatises. Sometimes the images are decorative or the descriptions pretexts for rhetorical exercises, but often they are a vehicle for philosophical and spiritual enquiry. Deformity became a tool to probe the secrets of form and substance.

The greatest paradox is the concept of God-made-man, which was a subject of great debate in the Middle Ages; Eco devotes an entire chapter to discussion of the different shades of interpretation of the question. Their different beliefs concerning the nature of Christ are what divide the various groups of monstrous creatures.

Augustine had described the paradox of knowing and speaking in this manner:

> Before you perceived God, you believed that thought could express God. Now you are beginning to perceive Him, and you think that you cannot express what you perceive. But, having found that you cannot express what you perceive, will you be silent, will you not praise God? ... 'How,' you ask, 'shall I praise Him?' I cannot now explain the small amount which I can perceive in part, through a glass darkly (*in aenigmate per speculum*) ... All other things may be expressed in some way; He alone is ineffable, Who spoke, and all things were made. He spoke, and we were made; but we are unable to speak of Him; His Word, by Whom we were spoken, is His Son![13]

Language has a double nature, like Christ. Through language, one can express material and immaterial meaning, and thereby make possible a confusion between the thing and the representation of it, a confusion medieval scholars well understood. In addition, language tends to 'impose' its own form upon the world.

John Scotus Eriugena made available the thought of Pseudo-Dionysius to the West, but he transformed Dionysius' system of representation – based on the dyad of the similar and the dissimilar – into a triadic one: the similar, the dissimilar, and the monstrous. He demonstrated the utility of the category of the monstrous by developing two kinds of allegory: allegory *dicti et facti* and allegory *dicti non (autem) facti*. The first derives its images from nature and history, whereas the second is a purely spiritual discourse.[14] There is a difference between constructing the object through logical discourse and pointing to the object in itself. We must therefore distinguish between the monster as a sign and the monster as a 'thing.'

Augustine's distinction between 'literal' and 'figurative' sign is therefore useful; for example, the sign 'ox' indicates both the existing animal (literal) and, figuratively, one of the apostles. A monster is both a 'literal' sign, since the medieval thinker believed in the physical existence of monstrous creatures, and a 'figurative' one. In this sense, the sign elevates the human mind beyond nature and towards the divine. 'There is,' writes Williams, 'paradoxically, no difference between the monstrous sign and what it stands for, since the sign, signifying "nothing," stands only for itself.'[15]

According to Isidore of Seville, the monster is a contradiction not of nature but of human epistemological categories. Nothing reveals the limitations of human understanding more than the monster. To give a clear example, the monster hermaphrodite contradicts our distinction between male and female. Notwithstanding this contradiction, the medieval thinker attempted the classification of monsters, in a quite paradoxical way imposing order on disorder and producing a taxonomy of chaos. The taxonomy Eco attempts when he groups the monsters according to their religious beliefs results in absurdity and is therefore ironic.

According to Williams, Dionysius' is a pessimistic semiology, because the author insists upon the inadequacy of the sign and upon 'the ultimate failure of the sign to present really the thing that it signifies.'[16] It would be surprising to learn that this is the concept Eco would like to endorse in his novel; but this seeming pessimism is in fact optimism, because it discourages an excessive reliance on the rational and warns against facile anthropomorphism.

In Western culture, two epistemological traditions prevailed, rooted in Greek philosophical thought, the Aristotelian and the Platonic: the first prefers the principle of mimesis and proceeds through analogy, the *via positiva*, whereas the second prefers dissimilitude, the *via negativa*; the first uses similarities as the basis for understanding, whereas the second negates the similitude of signs in order to uncover their profound dissimilitude: 'To name someone is to differentiate, to put aside during the description his or her unity with other beings/things, and so, to call him John is to say and to know what he is not; not an animal, but human; not female, but male; not Peter, James, or any other man, but this one defined, contained, isolated individual ... Negative or apophatic theology has the strength of liberation from the limitations of predication.'[17]

For Dionysius, affirmation and negation are not opposites, because contraries are resolved in a triadic process, according to the model of the Christian Trinity, in which the different nature of the persons is brought into union by a mysterious connection. Whereas St Thomas continued the development of the analogy of being through three different categories (analogy of attribution, analogy of inequality, and analogy of proportionality), Scotus Eriugena, rewriting the Pseudo-Dionysian corpus, emphasized even more the application of a triadic system, consisting of *resemblant, dissemblant,* and *teratological* signification. The monster – in Greek, τεραξ – because of the inappropriateness of the sign for the signified calls into question the mind's confidence in analogy and similitude and creates an intellectual disturbance of our categorical system of signification.

Despite the uneasiness with negation and gnosticism often demonstrated in the West, both the cataphatic and the apophatic traditions continued and developed. The problem was that they developed separately, so negation was relegated to religion, metaphysics, and poetry. Notwithstanding this development, the representation and description of monstrous figures continued steadily through the centuries and has persisted to this day, when, although we might not believe in such creatures, we still ornament our buildings with gargoyles and other devilish beings to represent the human hubris that caused the destruction of the Tower of Babel. We recognize that our thirst for analogical knowledge has taken us very far, perhaps too far, to the point where we need the monstrous to respond to our affirmative discourse and to our evaluation of human knowledge. As Williams explains, 'The monster bridges the gap between contraries in an aesthetic defiance of logical rule; it provides the third term, the copula, the mediation, between all those entities doomed, by logic and language, never to be joined. Such a union remains illogical, indeed absurd, but it is an absurdity that raises paradox out of its purely logical function and places it at the center of ontology.'[18]

According to Williams, the monster shows a combination of what is and what is not, transgresses natural categories, contradicts the limits of being, transgresses the law of the excluded middle, refuses the adequation of real with intellect, and 'challenges the epistemological authority of form, structure, and identity.'[19]

Thus, the monster became and remains a prominent concept. Deformity implies the loss of form, which is seen as repulsive, and therefore death. Remembering St Bernard's stern reaction to the monstrosities he observed on cathedral walls, we understand the fear of some medieval thinkers who believed that disorder and lack of form could bring chaos in the structures of the mind. Baudolino has a similar reaction when he contemplates the aborted foetus that he had conceived and that came out of the emaciated body of his deceased wife Colandrina:

'It was a little monster,' he said, after a moment, 'like the ones we imagined in the land of Prester John. The face had tiny eyes, like two slits, a very thin chest, with little arms that looked like a polyp's tentacles. And from its belly to its feet it was covered with fine hair, as if it were a sheep ... I had generated not a portent but a horrible thing. My son was a lie of nature. Otto was right, but more than he had thought; I was a liar and I had lived the life of a liar to such a degree that even my seed had produced a lie. A dead lie. And then I understood ...' (231–2)

In Baudolino's era, the conviction was widespread that the foetus generated inside the mother's body was influenced by immaterial events, including things that the mother would observe or read about. If the child did not resemble the father, it was automatically regarded as a monster. Baudolino realizes by looking at the little monster he has conceived that the lies he has 'simply' told have been reflected in his own physical progeny. But even more than that, Baudolino's son reflects the other son that he conceives later with Hypatia. Hypatia, the virgin creature and daughter of the satyrs who-are-never-seen, who was pregnant when she abandoned Baudolino, has the lower body of a goat. It is therefore ironic that the son of the fully human Colandrina resembles Baudolino's future companion; but, in effect, the foetus mirrors Baudolino's own monstrosity, which is mainly a discursive one.

**The Power of Falsity: Baudolino's Own Monstrosity**

Baudolino is not only a liar, but a polyglot as well, and polyglots were considered monsters in the Middle Ages because they negate the distinction achieved after the fall of the Tower of Babel. It was believed that polyglots lured human beings by speaking their language and then ate them. Although Baudolino is not a cannibal, the seductive power of his mendacious language causes the downfall of some of his enemies and friends, including the death of his beloved Frederick.

Frederick dies in the intriguing castle of the ingenious Ardzrouni, who practises various scientific experiments. He owns, for example, Archimedes' mirrors, which he uses to protect the castle from possible enemy assaults; he possesses a device in the form of a funnel that allows him to communicate from room to room, and mechanisms that automatically open doors; furthermore, he experiments in producing a vacuum with complicated machinery, a subject immensely interesting to Baudolino's friend Borone. On the morning when Baudolino finds Frederick lying unconscious on the floor, he and his friends formulate numerous hypotheses as to the cause of death, but a plausible explanation is not given until chapter 38, when our heroes are in Constantinople and accuse one another of being responsible for the murder. Each of them could have caused, either voluntarily or involuntarily, the death of the sovereign, including Baudolino.

The mysterious death belongs to the detective story, often central in the general plot of Eco's novels. But what Ardzrouni is manipulating in his castle are the four elements that constitute the world: fire, air, water, and earth. Because these four elements mirror the four seasons and the four humours that comprise our bodies (blood, yellow bile, black bile, and phlegm), their imbalance causes diseases, insanity, and even cataclysms. The death of Frederick could have been caused by a lack of air in the room, by the fire in the fireplace, or by the water of the river; in any case, it represents a disturbance of the established order, and it is directly responsible for the journey of our heroes. Perhaps their adventures in the domains of the monsters are proof of their insanity or of the world's malady.

As I have tried to show, *Baudolino* is much more than just an adventure story in the manner of *Treasure Island*; it is more similar, for example, to *Gulliver's Travels* (to which there are explicit references). Although we can certainly consider the book a *Bildungsroman* or, as

Rocco Capozzi has suggested, an anti-*Bildungsroman*,[20] we learn very soon that the interest of the novel does not stop at its surface plot. Eco's novel is about paradox and about the ability of human language to represent and to express. Having been warned against Baudolino's lies, we read the novel suspecting his story and wondering about our capacity to detect truthfulness, as we move between fiction and history. Niketas, as the primary reader of Baudolino's story, doubts him as well; he compares him to a chameleon ('similar to a tiny goat,' 356), because he changes the tone of the narration according to the event.

According to Rosalie Colie, paradox is a thing crafted to deny and destroy 'systems.' She distinguishes three basic types: the rhetorical, the logical, and the epistemological. The liar is an example of the episte-mological type: 'The problem it presents is a special case of all "specula-tive," or self-referential operations – a special case, then, of what I call the epistemological paradox, in which the mind, by its own operation, attempts to say something about its operation.'[21]

In other words, we call into question both language's expressive power and our own interpretative capacity. We wonder which kind of narra-tion is more truthful, that which asserts itself or that which negates itself. 'Paradoxes are the monsters of truth,' said Balthasar Gracian (1601–55), a Spanish theologian who discussed at length the power and ambiguities of language.

God is the ultimate paradox. Because our understanding cannot grasp the Supreme Cause, we struggle to deepen our knowledge by saying what God is not, as does Pseudo-Dionysius: 'It is neither knowledge nor truth. It is not kingship. It is not wisdom. It is neither one nor oneness, neither divinity nor goodness. Nor is it a spirit, in the sense in which we understand that term. It is not sonship or fatherhood and it is nothing known to us or to any other being. It falls neither within the predicate of nonbeing nor of being' (*MT* 1048A).[22]

The monster as paradox is a projection, an embodiment of a certain cultural moment; etymologically it is that which 'reveals.' It escapes categorization and threatens a revolution in the logic of meaning. It is difference made flesh. As Jeffrey Jerome Cohen has written in his intro-duction to *Monster Theory*, 'Monsters are never created *ex nihilo*, but through a process of fragmentation and recombination in which ele-ments are extracted "from various forms" (including – indeed, espe-cially – marginalized social groups) and then assembled as a monster.'[23]

This strange mixture produces a certain fear, which, however we try to repress it, always seems to return. Medieval monsters are placed at the limits of the world, usually in the Antipodes, in Ultima Thule, or in the Indian Ocean, in realms of liberation where everything is possible and miscegenation is accepted. Baudolino embraces his fright and mates with a being half woman and half goat. His apprehension mixes with desire; his abjection attracts him even more to this extraordinary creature. As Julia Kristeva has written:

> There looms, within abjection, one of those violent, dark revolts of being, directed against a threat that seems to emanate from an exorbitant outside or inside, ejected beyond the scope of the possible, the tolerable, the thinkable. It lies there, quite close, but it cannot be assimilated. It beseeches, worries, fascinates desire, which, nonetheless, does not let itself be seduced. Apprehensive, desire turns aside; sickened, it rejects ... But simultaneously, just the same, that impetus, that spasm, that leap is drawn toward an elsewhere as tempting as it is condemned. Unflaggingly, like an inescapable boomerang, a vortex of summons and repulsion places the one haunted by it literally beside himself.[24]

When Baudolino talks to the eunuchs in charge of the kingdom of the Deacon (who is afflicted with leprosy), he learns of their scorn for the monsters, who are forced to live on the margins of the kingdom and made to believe what the eunuchs need them to believe in order to control them. Praxeas, the chief eunuch, says of them: 'They have lived here together for centuries, they have grown accustomed to one another, and refusing to see the monstrosity of their neighbors, they ignore their own' (382).

Baudolino is the only one who, in the end, recognizes his own monstrosity. When Panufzio, the blind expert, reveals to Baudolino that probably Frederick was still alive when Baudolino found him and that very likely he had died when Baudolino threw him into the river, Baudolino has a fit of despair. Overwhelmed by his responsibility for the death not only of Frederick but of the Poet as well, he disappears and later is found on a hermit's column outside the city. At first, he simply wants to meditate in solitude, but little by little he starts producing aphorisms in reply to all those seeking counsel from him. Once, a man arrives in desperation because his son has been hit by a hunter's arrows, and Baudolino tells him that unfortunately his son is already dead. When the response is proved to be true, a jealous priest begins throwing stones in his direction, accusing him of being responsible for the boy's death; the priest had been unable to perform any miracle.

Baudolino descends from the column and prepares to return to the East to search for Hypatia and his child: 'You saw for yourself,' he tells Niketas. 'The one time in my life I told the truth and only the truth, they stoned me' (518). Conscious that a life of lies produces monsters, and at the same time disappointed by a world that lives under illusions, Baudolino rides away towards the Kingdom of Prester John.

This is the end of Baudolino's story, and, despite this ending, the mystery of his identity deepens. We know by now that he is a linguistic monster, since his discourse is tainted by falsehood, but he also physically produces aberrations. While living on the column, he is compared to a small goat, which reminds us of Hypatia and of both Baudolino's sons. Maybe he has been able to hide his monstrous appearance from us and now, as a satyr (who-is-never-seen) and a follower of Bacchus, he smiles at us for our naivety.

Baudolino is a story-teller in both senses of the word, but although his stories are fictitious, their relevance lies in their deeper signification. If some of his friends pursue the things that are ('The things that count are the things that do exist,' says Boidi, 502), Baudolino, animated by a constant thirst for adventure, even in adversity carries on his search for something that is not, represented by the Kingdom of Prester John. He remains faithful to his dream, although Panufzio's words raise doubts in him for a short while. In the end, he chooses to turn his eyes from the truth, because if you find it you stop searching – 'that no one will kill his own dream by putting his hands on it' (502). Perhaps the ultimate (but not the only) message of the novel is this, that what is important is not the truth, but the search for it; not the result, but its pursuit. Despite God's punishment of Baudolino's hubris and all the involuntary mistakes, our hero's creations are well-meant – 'a fin di bene' – wrought in complete faith and out of respect for his fellows.

## Monsters between Chaos and Cosmos

During the course of their search for an identity, humans have forged a portrait of the 'perfect man' as a hybrid, incorporating characteristics from many different creatures[25] so that he can develop multiple implicit possibilities. By creating monsters, humans demonstrate their transgressive creativity. According to Giambattista Vico, the extreme shapelessness that is Chaos, which is represented in mythology by the god Orcus, ultimately coincides with the imagination and creation of the cosmos. But, says Vico, the poets gave Chaos the monstrous form of

Pan, the god of satyrs, who wander the Earth and have the appearance of men but the behaviour of uncivilized beasts. Both Vico and Eco interpret these myths as reflections of the ambivalent duality of human nature in all its aspects: body and soul, order and chaos, assertion and negation, animal and divine, natural and civil, rational and irrational. Monsters reflect all these conceptions, which are the projections of humans' own self-perception.

That is why monsters are such a rich subject, worthy of being revisited, and Eco does revisit the subject with his usual subtlety and erudition. Although his narration feels distant and characteristically is arbitrated by at least two intermediaries, we sometimes recognize more personal and direct concerns, which explain the dedication of the book to Emanuele, his first grandchild, who had been born recently. References to the mysteries of birth and the portents of nature are explicit throughout the novel, but beyond the autobiographical what fascinates our author is the deeply human process of conquering and mastering nature, even if that means deciphering monsters as signs. As Vico maintained, the logic of monstrosity shows 'how the founders of gentile humanity in a certain sense generated and produced in themselves the proper human form in its two aspects: that is, how by means of frightful religions and terrible paternal powers and sacred ablutions they brought forth from their giant bodies the form of our just corporature, and how by discipline of their household economy they brought forth from their bestial minds the form of our human mind.[26]

The transition from monstrous chaos to patriarchal order is secured by the transmission of the law of the father to the offspring and by the other pillars of civilization. In order to preserve these, our society needs heroes like Baudolino, willing to confront the monsters that guard our boundaries. Although today our monsters assume a different shape (it is not Proteus but a cyborg, not a Panotius but the aliens of *Star Wars*, not a satyr's child but embryonic stem-cell manipulation), they still make us face the 'Other,' which is ultimately our own self, and force us to meditate on difference and the grotesque products of human language.

# 9 Conclusion

Umberto Eco is a proud product of Italian intellectual life. He was a child gifted in everything (maybe, as he has written, with the exception of soccer!), and those who knew him were aware he would be success-ful. But very few would have predicted his great international 'exploit' as a novelist and as a theorist. I have tried to account for his personal success in terms of a felicitous theoretical choice, a blending of the medieval and the postmodern.

Medieval philosophy is somehow closer to contemporary thought than is so-called modern philosophy. We find, for example, that, like the thinkers of the post-Wittgenstein tradition, medieval authors distin-guished clearly between epistemology and a theory of the mind. For modern philosophy, the principal question regarded the possibility of knowledge and was an essentially epistemological debate concerning origin; for contemporary or postmodern thought, the principal ques-tion regards language and meaning. Medieval scholars, probably be-cause the epistemological debate was resolved in their faith, concen-trated many of their efforts on the study of logic, a discipline that assumed greater centrality in the twentieth century.

The similarities between postmodern and medieval consciousness form one of the many paradoxes of the contemporary age. As Linda Hutcheon says, 'Medieval hermeticism and contemporary postmodernism share the ability to juggle "complexity and contradiction" in what postmod-ernist architect Robert Venturi calls "the difficult unity of inclusion."'[1]

Because the present-day world is, as Terry Eagleton has bluntly said, 'an appalling mess'[2] and is therefore difficult to map, the critics who have attempted an explanation of its mechanisms have sometimes come to different conclusions, in a few cases to contradictory ones. Nevertheless, it is still possible to identify characteristics of the culture on which the majority of these critics would agree.

Like the Middle Ages, our historical period appears to be an epoch of transition, and it has called into question the values and the aesthetics of modernism; although some of the principles of modernism are still very much alive, its ideology is no longer definitive. 'Postmodernism,' then, is an appropriate denomination, because it contains the word 'modern' and at the same time reflects the surpassing of modernity.

Although Eagleton's view of this epochal change is generally negative, the adjectives he uses to define it both seem appropriate and are agreed upon by major scholars of postmodernism. Postmodernism presents 'a depthless, decentred, ungrounded, self-reflexive, playful, derivative, eclectic, pluralistic art which blurs the boundaries between "high" and "low" culture, as well as between art and everyday experience.'[3] This definition appears little different from the one architecture, the founding art of postmodernism, has given. Charles Jencks, one of the major scholars of postmodern architecture, has used many of the same adjectives to highlight the break with the past brought about by architects of the 1960s and 1970s.[4] For him, the chief characteristics of the new attitude are its eclecticism, its aggressive attitude to conventions, its use of traditions to make a comment, a historicism that pillages from disregarded historical works, its complexity, its ambiguity, its mannerism, its boredom with modernist aesthetics, its double-coding, its reflexivity, its surface wit, its participation in the public realm, its pluralism, and its interest in popular and local codes of communication.

The disagreements might arise with respect to the notion of historical depth (Jameson sustains that postmodernism theory is historically deaf) and Lyotard's definition of postmodernism as 'incredulity towards metanarratives,' which Jameson has critiqued and which I discussed in the conclusion of chapter 4. Nevertheless, the leap of postmodernism has to do with a certain suspicion of classical notions of truth, with scepticism about an ultimate ground of explanation, and with disbelief in the Real.

Jean Baudrillard, even if he shivers at the very mention of the word 'postmodernism,'[5] is the philosopher of this 'disappearance' of the Real: 'The very definition of the real has become: that of which it is possible to give an equivalent reproduction ... The real is not only what can be reproduced, but that which is always already reproduced: that is, the hyperreal ... which is entirely in simulation.'[6] Simulation represents the maximum expression of today's consciousness. Because the guarantor of the exchange of meaning – God – has disappeared, or better, is reduced to something that can be simulated, the whole system becomes 'a gigantic simulacrum.'[7] The key transition is when signs dissimulate nothing, when they simply refer to each other in 'an uninterrupted circuit without reference.'[8]

*Foucault's Pendulum* tried to respond to this idea of a real without origin and warned against the danger of such a concept. It is in response to this kind of provocation that, in recent years, Eco has returned to a discussion of the ontogenetic problem; in fact, he explores the question of Being in one of his most recent theoretical books, *Kant and the Platypus*. If we look at Eco's considerations in the light of Baudrillard's theory, Eco's insistence on the resistance posed by Being does not appear to be 'postmodern.' Eco would agree with the French theoretician on the idea of the cumulative character of our culture and on the importance of a layered revisitation of the past, but he would protest the idea of a semiotic without an ultimate Object, for how indistinct and faint this can be. Although in *The Island of the Day Before* the 'Dove' is a sign constituted by the accumulation of the interpretants built by the culture and represents the apex of unfulfilled desire, the appearance of its 'Orainge'[9] makes us sing. This difficult equilibrium demonstrates how the Peircian circle of unlimited semiosis is closed by the *final interpretant.*

Semiotics cannot avoid discussing Being, because it is that Something that causes sign production. There are, then, questions one should ask: To what do we refer when we speak? – as a terminus ad quem – and, What makes us speak? – as a terminus a quo. Peirce's Dynamic Object is what makes us speak: it is Something that urges us to speak, or at least makes us turn our attention to it.[10] Therefore, if we ask why there is Being instead of nothing, the answer is 'Perchè sì' (*Kant e l'ornitorinco,* p. 8), or, in more philosophical terms, being is *id quod primum intellectus concipit quasi notissimum.*

But being acts also as a limitation, and it is necessary to identify its *lines of resistance,* which pose certain boundaries, because we live 'in the horizon of the limit of being-for-death' (essere-per-la-morte) (37). This leads us to believe that there are even more limits. The limitlessness, Eco says, is only in our own desire for absolute freedom. In *Foucault's Pendulum,* A simple No as the answer to the computer's insistent question 'Do you have the password?' poses a limit to our stream of possible interpretations. 'Being comes towards us with "Noes," which are simply the affirmation that there are things we cannot say' (*Foucault's Pendu-*

*lum,* p. 391). We run into this kind of barrier every time we investigate reality. For Thomas Aquinas, even God is subject to physical limits, as he cannot undo what has been (*Kant e l'ornitorinco,* p. 41).

Once semiotics has recognized this balance between the multiple manifestations of Being and its resistances, it can proceed to explore the world; and explored the world Eco has, in a variety of possible ways.

The key to his success is that he has maintained throughout these years of searching a sense of wonder before life's masterpieces and oddities. Even dismantling the deepest mechanisms, which he has done rigorously on many occasions, he has always firmly believed that a theoretical explanation does not disrupt the magic but enhances our admiration.

If we look at one of his latest publications, the translation and analysis of Gérard de Nerval's *Sylvie,* we see that Eco continues to maintain this belief. The text creates a blue and purple atmosphere and obviously produces a dreamlike effect on the reader, which makes its interpretation difficult. Eco wants to discover why and how the text can create such dreamy and foggy effects, without fear of eliminating its magic: 'The more one knows about it, the more one can re-read it with renewed stupor' ('*Sylvie,*' p. 100).

### Experiences in Translation and Sulla letteratura

In October 1998, while working on the translation of *Sylvie,* Eco was invited by the Department of Italian Studies of the University of Toronto to deliver a series of specialized lectures on the text and translation. From those emerged a theoretical work entitled *Experiences in Translation,* published by the University of Toronto Press, in which Eco identifies the semiotic characteristics of translating.

In his customary story-telling fashion, Eco categorizes the various kinds of translation and reveals the hidden principles of text interpretation. He establishes very early that 'equivalence in meaning cannot be taken as a satisfactory criterion for a correct translation' (*Experiences,* p. 9), and that translating 'is not only connected with linguistic competence, but with intertextual, psychological, and narrative competence' (13). Translation is, for him, a special case of interpretation, 'in Peirce's sense': 'Interpreting means making a bet on the sense of a text, among other things. This sense that a translator must find – and preserve, or recreate – is not hidden in any pure language, neither a divine *reine Sprache* nor any Mentalese. It is just the outcome of an interpretive inference that can or cannot be shared by other readers. In this sense, a translator makes a *textual abduction*' (16).

Often the best translation is the one that is able to obtain the same effect as the source text, and the best translator is the one who can interpret and reword the text so that its 'guiding spirit' is preserved, with compensation for losses if necessary. Following Jakobson's and Hjelmslev's models, Eco identifies three types of translation: interpretation by transcription (the case of the Morse alphabet), intrasystemic interpretation (which takes place within the same language or the same semiotic system), and intersystemic interpretation (which is translation in the common use of the word, as it implies translation between languages and between semiotic systems).[11]

Once again, while pursuing poetic and aesthetic results, Eco nonchalantly provides the theoretical/semiotic ground for his project. What he defines as his 'common sense' approach is in fact a depiction of translation as a semiotic task resulting in an intriguing new typology.

Another of Eco's recent achievements is a collection of essays entitled *Sulla letteratura* (On Literature). This book, in which Eco takes into consideration major literary works and stylistic/rhetorical devices, reveals a continuity of interests, as Eco returns to some of his principal sources of inspiration. It is clearly written with the same acumen and in the same style as *Six Walks in the Fictional Woods* (1994). With his usual versatility, wit, and taste for interdisciplinarity, Eco discusses medieval masterpieces such as Dante's *Paradiso* and more recent authors such as Wilde, Nerval, Marx, and Camporesi. He goes back to *Don Quixote* and to the texts of Borges, but his chief interest is in discussing general literary principles, such as questions of style, poetics, symbolism, myth, form, the verbal representation of space, and intertextual irony.

Although the essays are focused on the principal aspects and function of literature, we often find Eco reflecting on his own writing. This is more pronounced in essays such as 'Come scrivo' (The Way I Write), 'Ironia intertestuale e livelli di lettura' (Intertextual Irony and Reading Levels), and 'Borges e la mia angoscia dell'influenza' (Borges and My Anxiety of Influence), but it is present even where Eco is not talking directly about himself, as in 'Il mito americano di tre generazioni antiamericane' (The American Myth of Three Anti-American Generations) and 'La forza del falso' (The Power of the False).

With this book, Eco reveals the mechanisms below and behind the stage. In a way, he plays the same game in his fiction, conveying certain emotions with a sapient manipulation of the narrative structure. Because he has analysed the narrative structures of other works so well, some critics have blamed him for mechanically constructing his own novels, but the ability to entrap the reader in a particular atmosphere is the mark of a great author.

Eco gave us a taste of the Middle Ages in *The Name of the Rose* and *Baudolino*, the flavour of the Italy of the 1970s in *Foucault's Pendulum*, and a magical sense of the artificial exotic in *The Island of the Day Before*. Especially in this novel, Eco has in part imitated the technique of *Sylvie*, sustaining the plot over the time span of a few days, using continual references to the past, and complicating the *fabula*. As he says of *Sylvie*, 'This text is constructed in an admirable way, in a play of symmetries, oppositions and internal references' ('*Sylvie*,' p. 101). Like *Sylvie*, *The Island of the Day Before* is a narration of a narration, which makes use of the same indefinite tense, the imperfect.

I stress this last aspect because it represents another example of Eco's virtuosic balancing of opposites. Like Father Caspar, he is a mixture of the mechanical engineer and the fanciful philosopher, which explains why he is one of the rare examples of a theorist-writer. It is a quality Eco has admired in medieval scholars, a lesson learned from Aquinas, who despite his rigorous system was a poet of the human condition.

Because our searching and conjecturing must always come to terms with our limitations, one of the more convincing aspects of Eco's method has been his conviction that 'we must face Being with gaiety (and even Leopardi's can be "gay science"), interrogate it, test its resistances, detect its openings, the never too explicit hints' (*Kant e l'ornitorinco*, p. 42). Maybe Eco has accomplished the alliance between laughter and wisdom that Nietzsche wished for in his *Gay Science*, as his platypus, smiling, places in a critical position the most sophisticated theories of knowledge.

In order to critique modern philosophy, Eco finds support in the medieval theory of signs and in the particular attitude of medieval scholars, who were patiently 'looking for a positive justification of earthly things, at the very least as an instrument of salvation' (Eco, *Art and Beauty in the Middle Ages*, p. 54).

It is understandable that, in elaborating his semiotic theory, Eco finds more support and assistance in medieval writings than in post-Renaissance philosophical treatises. That does not imply that medieval authors had found a solution to all the problems posed by the study of signs; in fact, for Eco, their conclusions need to be linked with more recent philosophical reflections. But this unification, rendered easier by an implicit similarity of points of departure, has given Eco the edge in his reflection on contemporary thought and culture. The theoretical choices were made possible by the vibrant resonating of history in Eco's brain, where it constitutes an empowering model for dealing with postmodern reality.

# Appendix A

ALPHONSE ALLAIS

**Un drame bien parisien (1890)**

**Chapitre 1**

*Où l'on fait connaissance avec un Monsieur et une Dame qui auraient pu être heureux, sans leurs éternels malentendus*

> *O qu'il ha bien sceu*
> *Choisir, le challan!*
>
> (Rabelais)

A l'époque où commence cette histoire, Raoul et Marguerite (un joli nom pour les amours) étaient mariés depuis cinq mois environ.

Mariage d'inclination, bien entendu.

Raoul, un beau soir, en entendant Marguerite chanter la jolie romance du colonel Henry d'Erville:

> L'averse, chère à la grenouille,
> Parfume le bois rajeuni.
> ... Le bois, il est comme Nini.
> Y sent bon quand s'débarbouille.

Raoul, dis-je, s'était juré que la divine Marguerite (*diva Margarita*) n'appartiendrait jamais à un autre homme qu'à lui-même.

Le ménage eût été le plus hereux de tous les ménages, sans le fichu caractère des deux conjoints.

Pour un oui, pour un non, crac! Une assiette cassée, une gifle, un coup de pied dans le cul.

À ces bruits, Amour fuyait éploré, attendant, au coin d'un grand parc, l'heure toujours proche de la réconciliation.

Alors, des baisers sans nombre, des caresses sans fin, tendres et bien informées, des ardeurs d'enfer.

C'était à croire que ces deux cochons-là se disputaient pour s'offrir l'occasion de se raccomoder.

## Chapitre 2

*Simple épisode qui, sans se rattacher directement à l'action, donnera à la clientèle une idée sur la façon de vivre de nos héros*

> *Amour en latin faict amor.*
> *Or donc provient d'amour la mort*
> *Et, par avant, soulcy qui mord,*
> *Deuils, plours, pièges, forfaitz, remord ...*

(Blason d'amour)

Un jour, pourtant, ce fut plus grave que d'habitude.

Un soir plutôt.

Ils étaient allés au Théâtre d'Application, où l'on jouait, entre autres pièces, *L'infidèle*, de M. de Porto-Riche.

Quand tu auras assez vu Grosclaude, grincha Raoul, tu me le diras.

Et toi, vitupéra Marguerite, quand tu connaîtras Mademoiselle Moreno par cœur, tu me passeras la lorgnette.

Inaugurée sur ce ton, la conversation ne pouvait se terminer que par les plus regrettables violences réciproques.

Dans le coupé qui les ramenait, Marguerite prit plaisir à gratter sur l'amour-propre de Raoul comme sur une vieille mandoline hors d'usage.

Aussi, pas plutôt rentrés chez eux, les belligérents prirent leurs positions respectives.

La main levée, l'œil dur, la moustache telle celle des chats furibonds, Raoul marcha sur Marguerite, qui commença dès lors, à n'en pas mener large.

La pauvrette s'enfuit, furtive et rapide, comme fait la biche en les grands bois.

Raoul allait la rattraper.

Alors, l'éclair génial de la suprême angoisse fulgura le petit cerveau de Marguerite.

Se retournant brusquement, elle se jeta dans les bras de Raoul en s'écriant:

Je t'en prie, mon petit Raoul, défends-moi!

## Chapitre 3

*Où nos amis se réconcilient comme je vous souhaite de vous réconcilier souvent, vous qui faites malins*

*'Hold your tongue,*
*Please!'*
. . . . . . . . . . . . .
. . . . . . . . . . . . .
. . . . . . . . . . . . .
. . . . . . . . . . . . .

## Chapitre 4

*Comment l'on pourra constater que les gens se mêlent de ce qui ne les regarde pas feraient beaucoup mieux de rester tranquilles*

*C'est épatant ce que le monde deviennent rosse depuis quelque temps!*
(Paroles de ma concierge dans la matinée de lundi dernier)

Un matin, Raoul reçut le mot suivant:

'Si vous voulez, une fois par hasard, voir votre femme en belle humeur, allez donc, jeudi, au bal des Incohérents, au Moulin-Rouge. Elle y sera masquée et deguisée en Pirogue congolaise. À bon entendeur, salut! Un ami'

Le même matin, Marguerite reçut le mot suivant:

'Si vous voulez, une fois par hasard, voir votre mari en belle humeur, allez donc, jeudi, au bal des Incohérents, au Moulin-Rouge. Il y sera, masqué et deguisé en Templier fin de siècle. À bonne entendeuse, salut! Une amie'

Ces billets ne tombèrent pas dans l'oreille de deux sourds.

Dissimulant admirablement leurs desseins, quand arriva le fatal jour:

Ma chère amie, fit Raoul de son air le plus innocent, je vais être forcé de vous quitter jusqu'à demain. Des intérêts de la plus haute importance m'appèlent à Dunkerque.

Ça tombe bien, répondit Marguerite, délicieusement candide, je viens de recevoir un télégramme de ma tante Aspasie, laquelle, fort souffrante, me mande à son chevet.

## Chapitre 5

*Où l'on voit la folle jeunesse d'aujourd'hui tournoyer dans les plus chimériques et passagers plaisirs, au lieu de songer à l'éternité*

> *Mai vouéli vièure pamens:*
> *La vido es tant bello!*

> (Auguste Marin)

Les échos du *Diable boiteux* ont été unanimes à proclamer que le bal des Incohérents revêtit cette année un éclat inaccoutumé.

Beaucoup d'épaules et pas mal de jambes, sans compter les accessoires.

Deux assistants semblaient ne pas prendre part à la folie générale: un Templier fin de siècle et une Pirogue congolaise, tous deux hermétiquement masqués.

Sur le coup de trois heures du matin, le Templier s'approcha de la Pirogue et l'invita à venir souper avec lui.

Pour toute réponse, la Pirogue appuya sa petite main sur le robuste bras du Templier, et le couple s'éloigna.

## Chapitre 6

*Où la situation s'embrouille*

> *I say, don't you think the rajah laughs at us?*
> *Perhaps, sir.*

> (Henry O'Mercier)

Laissez-nous un instant, fit le Templier au garçon de restaurant, nous allons faire notre menu et nous vous sonnerons.

Le garçon se retira et le Templier verrouilla soigneusement la porte du cabinet.

Puis, d'un mouvement brusque, après s'être débarrassé de son casque, il arracha le loup de la Pirogue.

Tous les deux poussèrent, en même temps, un cri de stupeur, en ne se reconnaissant ni l'un ni l'autre.

Lui, ce n'était pas Raoul.

Elle, ce n'était pas Marguerite.

Ils se présentèrent mutuellement leurs excuses, et ne tardèrent pas à lier connaissance à la faveur d'un petit souper, je ne vous dis que ça.

## Chapitre 7

*Dénouement heureux pour tout le monde, sauf pour les autres*

> *Buvons le vermouth grenadine,*
> *Espoir de nos vieux bataillons.*

(George Auriol)

Cette petite mésaventure servit de leçon à Raoul et à Marguerite.

À partir de ce moment, ils ne se disputèrent plus jamais et furent parfaitement heureux.

Ils n'ont pas encore beaucoup d'enfants, mais ça viendra.

# Appendix B

ALPHONSE ALLAIS

## Les Templiers (1887)

En voilà un qui était un type, et un rude type, et d'attaque! Vingt fois je l'ai vu, rien qu'en serrant son cheval entre ses cuisses, arrêter tout l'escandron, net.

Il était brigadier à ce moment-là. Un peu rosse dans le service, mais charmant, en ville.

Comment diable s'appellait-il? Un sacré nom alsacien qui ne peut pas me revenir, comme Wurtz ou Schwartz ... Oui, ça doit être ça, Schwartz. Du reste, le nom ne fait rien à la chose. Natif de Neufbrisach, pas de Neufbrisach même, mais des environs.

Quel type, ce Schwartz!

Un dimanche (nous étions en garnison à Oran), le matin, Schwartz me dit: 'Qu'est-ce que nous allons faire aujourd'hui?' Moi, je lui réponds: 'Ce que tu voudras, mon vieux Schwartz.'

Alors nous tombons d'accord sur une partie en mer.

Nous prenons un bateau, *souque dur, garçon!* Et nous voilà au large.

Il faisait beau temps, un peu de vent, mais beau temps tout de même.

Nous filions comme des dards, heureux de voir disparaître à l'horizon la côte d'Afrique.

Ça creuse, l'aviron! Nom d'un chien, quel déjeuner!

Je me rappelle notamment un certain jambonneau qui fut ratissé jusqu'à l'indécence.

Pendant ce temps-là, nous ne nous apercevions pas que la brise fraîchissait et que la mer se mettait à clapoter d'une façon inquiétante.

Diable! dit Schwartz, il faudrait ...

Au fait, non, ce n'est pas Schwartz qu'il s'appelait.

Il avait un nom plus long que ça, comme qui dirait Schwartzbach. Va pour Schwartzbach!

Alors Schwartzbach me dit: 'Mon petit, il faut songer à rallier.'

Mais je t'en fiche, de rallier. Le vent soufflait en tempête.

La voile est enlevée par une bourrasque, un aviron fiche le camp, emporté par une lame. Nous voilà à la merci des flots.

Nous gagnions le large avec une vitesse déplorable et un cahotement terrible.

Prêts à tout événement, nous avions enlevé nos bottes et notre veste.

La nuit tombait, l'ouragan faisait rage.

Ah! Une jolie idée que nous avions eue là, d'aller contempler ton azur, ô Méditerranée!

Et puis, l'obscurité arrive complètement. Il n'était pas loin de minuit. Où étions-nous?

Schwartzbach, ou plutôt Schwartzbacher, car je me rappelle maintenant, c'est Schwartzbacher: Schwartzbacher, dis-je, qui connaissait sa géographie sur le bi du bout du doigt (les Alsaciens sont très instruits), me dit:

– Nous sommes dans l'île de Rhodes, mon vieux.

Est-ce que l'administration, entre nous, ne devrait pas mettre des plaques indicatrices sur toutes les îles de la Méditerranée, car c'est le diable pour s'y reconnaître, quand on n'a pas l'habitude?

Il faisait noir comme dans un four. Trempés comme des soupes, nous grimpâmes le rochers de la falaise.

Pas une lumière à l'horizon. C'etait gai.

– Nous allons manquer l'appel de demain matin, dis-je, pour dire quelque chose.

– Et même celle du soir, répondit, sombrement Schwartzbacher.

Et nous marchions dans les petits ajoncs maigres et dans les genêts piquants. Nous marchions sans savoir où, uniquement pour nous réchauffer.

– Ah! s'écria Schwartzbacher, j'aperçois une lueur, vois-tu, là-bas?

Je suivis la direction du doigt de Schwartzbacher, et effectivement une lueur brillait, mais très loin, une drôle de lueur.

Ce n'était pas des feux de village, non, c'était une drôle de lueur.

Et nous reprîmes notre marche en l'accélérant.

Nous arrivâmes, enfin.

Sur ces rochers se dressait un château d'aspect imposant, un haut château de pierre, où l'on n'avait pas l'air de rigoler tout le temps.

Une de tours de ce château servait de chapelle, et la lueur que nous avions aperçue n'était autre que l'éclairage sacré tamisé par les hauts vitraux gothiques.

Des chants nous arrivaient, des chants graves et mâles, des chants qui vous mettaient des frissons dans le dos.

– Entrons, fit Schwartzbacher, résolu.

– Par où?

– Ah! Voilà ... cherchons une issue.

Schwartzbacher disait: 'Cherchons une issue,' mais il voulait dire: 'Cherchons une entrée.' D'ailleurs, comme c'est la même chose, je ne crus pas devoir lui faire observer son erreur relative, qui peut-être n'était qu'un lapsus causé par le froid.

Il y avait bien des entrées, mais elles étaient toutes closes, et pas de sonnettes. Alors c'est comme s'il n'y avait pas eu d'entrée.

À la fin, à force de tourner autour du château, nou découvrîmes un petit mur que nous pûmes escalder.

– Maintenant, fit Schwarzbacher, cherchons la cuisine.

Probablement qu'il n'y avait pas de cuisine dans l'immeuble, car aucune odeur de fricot ne vint chatouiller nos narines.

Nous nous promenions par des couloirs interminables et enchevêtrés.

Parfois, une chauve-souris voletait et frôlait nos visages de sa sale peluche.

Au détour d'un corridor, les chants que nous avions entendus vinrent frapper nos oreilles, arrivant de tout près.

Nous étions dans une grande pièce qui devait communiquer avec la chapelle.

– Je vois ce que c'est, fit Schwartzbacher (ou plutôt Shwartzbacher-mann, je me souviens maintenant), nous nous trouvons dans le château des Templiers.

Il n'avait pas terminé ces mots, qu'une immense porte de fer s'ouvrit toute grande.

Nous fûmes inondés de lumière.

Des hommes étaient là, à genoux, quelques centaines, bardés de fer, casque en tête, et de haute stature.

Ils se relevèrent avec un long tumulte de ferraille, se retournèrent et nous virent.

Alors, du même geste, ils firent *Sabre-main!* Et marchèrent sur nous, la latte haute.

J'aurais bien voulu être ailleurs.

Sans se déconcerter, Schwartzbachermann retroussa ses manches, se mit en posture de défense et s'écria d'une voix forte:

– Ah! Nom de Dieu! messieurs les Templiers, quand vous seriez cent mille ... aussi vrai que je m'appelle Durand ...!

Ah! Je me rappelle maintenant, c'est Durand qu'il s'appelait. Son père était tailleur à Aubervilliers. Durand, oui, c'est bien ça ...

Sacré Durand, va! Quel type!

# Notes

Where Eco's works are identified in the text by their English titles, page references are to the published English versions listed in the Bibliography. Where the works are identified by their Italian titles, the translation is my own.

## Chapter 1

1 Michael Caesar, *Umberto Eco* (Cambridge, 1999), p. 170.

## Chapter 2

1 In the preface to *Il problema estetico in Tommaso d'Aquino* (Milan, 1954), p. 7, Eco wrote: 'Le metodologie strutturali che si stanno imponendo nelle scienze umane hanno non poche parentele con certi aspetti delle metodologie scolastiche: e la rimeditazione della *forma mentis* scolastica puó servire come cartina di tornasole sia per controllare e perfezionare certe costruzioni contemporanee, sia per indicarne, se il caso, le loro ingenuità medievaleggianti.' 'The Structuralist methodologies which are increasingly used in the social sciences have some affinities with certain aspects of Scholasticism. Thus, reflection upon the scholastic *forma mentis* can serve as a kind of litmus test, both for analyzing and refining certain contemporary theories, and also for disclosing in some cases their medievalist subtleties,' *The Aesthetics of Thomas Aquinas*, trans. Hugh Bredin (Cambridge, Mass., 1994), p. viii.
2 Eco borrows the term from Deleuze; see *Semiotica e Filosofia del Linguaggio.*
3 In Italian by Bompiani in 1954 and 1970; in English by Harvard University Press in 1988.

4 In 1951, Eco became part of Azione Cattolica, a youth group of the Catholic Church whose objective is to understand and apply the values that characterize Christian living in the world. In the early 1950s, the organization was engaged in opposing the conservative policies of the then reigning pontiff, Pius XII. Eco wrote for the magazine of the group, *Gioventù cattolica*, for a few years, but left the organization in 1954.

5 See, for example, *Interpretation and Overinterpretation*.

6 See Roberto Pellerey, 'Thomas Aquinas: Natural Semiotics and the Epistemological Process,' in Umberto Eco and Costantino Marmo, eds, *On the Medieval Theory of Signs*, (Amsterdam, 1989), p. 83.

7 For an exhaustive account, see Jean Seznec, *The Survival of the Pagan Gods* (New York: Pantheon, 1953).

8 Nicolas Cusanus, *Of Learned Ignorance*, trans. Fr Germain Heron (London: Routledge & Kegan Paul, 1954), p. 8.

9 Ibid.

10 'All our greatest philosophers and theologians unanimously assert that the visible universe is a faithful reflection of the invisible, and that from creatures we can rise to a knowledge of the Creator, "in a mirror and in a dark manner," as it were. The fundamental reason for the use of symbolism in the study of spiritual things, which in themselves are beyond our reach, has already been given. Though we neither perceive it nor understand it, we know for a fact that all things stand in some sort of relation to one another; that, in virtue of this inter-relation, all the individuals constitute one universe and that in the one Absolute the multiplicity of beings is unity itself. Every image is an approximate reproduction of the exemplar, yet, apart from the Absolute image or the Exemplar itself in unity of nature, no image will so faithfully or precisely reproduce the exemplar, as to rule out the possibility of an infinity of more faithful and precise images, as we have already made clear,' ibid., p. 25.

11 Ibid.

12 Ibid., p. 47.

13 Eco, *Interpretation and Overinterpretation*, p. 34.

14 'Die Grenzen seines Lebensgefühl, die Schranken, die der unmittelbaren Nachempfindung der Natur gezogen sind, sind daher zugleich die Grenzen seines Wissens von ihr. Die entgegengesetze Form der Deutung zeigt jene Richtung der Naturbetrachtung, die, von Cusanus anhebend, über Leonardo da Vinci, zu Galilei und Kepler weiterführt,' Ernst Cassirer, *Individuum und Kosmos in der Philosophie der Renaissance* (Darmstadt, 1963), p. 58.

15 Analogical thinking is very much in use in this century's quantum mechanics, as most effects realized in those small proportions cannot be experimentally verified. Einstein was often bothered by what he called the *spukhafte Fernwirkungen* (spooky actions at a distance) that he could not see with his own eyes.

16 Nicholas, *Of Learned Ignorance*, p. 97.

17 Ibid., p. 102.

18 Michel Foucault, *Les mots et les choses* (Paris: Gallimard, 1966), p. 32.

19 See Eco, *Interpretation and Overinterpretation*.

20 John Deely, 'Looking Back to *A Theory of Semiotics*: One Small Step for Philosophy, One Giant Leap for the Doctrine of Signs,' in Rocco Capozzi, ed., *Reading Eco* (Bloomington and Indianapolis, 1997), p. 107.

21 A sign-function, according to Eco, is 'the correlation between an expression and a content based on a conventionally established code,' *A Theory of Semiotics*, p. 191.

22 Ludovico Geymonat, *Storia del pensiero filosofico e scientifico*, vol. 2 (Milan: Garzanti, 1970), p. 39.

23 Giordano Bruno, *On the Composition of Images, Signs, and Ideas* (New York: Willis, Locker & Owens, 1991), p. 4.

24 Ibid., p. 4.

25 Ibid., p. 5.

26 Eco gives an example of this on p. 280 of *A Theory of Semiotics*: in the twelfth century, the Dominican friars were called the 'dogs of God' ('domini canes'), because both the sememe 'dog' and the sememe 'friar' possess the same connotative marker: fidelity.

27 'Tutta la forza di ciascun Vocabulo significante ... consiste nel rappresentare alla mente umana la cosa significata. Ma questa Rappresentazione si può fare, ò col Vocabulo nudo e proprio, il quale non richieda niun'opera dell'ingegno: ò con alcuna significatione ingegnosa, che insieme rappresenti & diletti. Onde nascono due generali differenze della Oratione: l'una Propria e Grammaticale: l'altra Rettorica e Arguta,' Emanuele Tesauro, *Il cannocchiale aristotelico*, 1670, facs. repr. ed. August Buck (Bad Homburg, Berlin, Zürich, Gehlen, 1968), p. 235.

28 Tesauro defines as *proper* those words that are commonly used in the best age by the best composers to signify objects. The *proper* language is the one that has been used in the best age by the best people. In his discussion, Tesauro reveals his idea of language as an organism, which is born, lives, and then dies, as it is testified by the Latin language. It is now (in Tesauro's time) the turn of the Italian language, which was born from Latin, had its

youth in thirteenth-century Florence with Dante, Petrarch, and Boccaccio, and is now in the fullness of its 'virility,' being used by writers like Bembo and Marino, and being subject to the Crusca Academy, which 'improved the language, reducing the licenses to stable rules,' ibid., p. 244.

29 Unusual words, or *parole peregrine*, are for Tesauro those that really signify objects without the veil of metaphor, but that have 'the grace of novelty.' He divides them into PRISCHE, FORESTIERE, DERIVATE, MUTATE, COMPOSITE, and FINTE.

30 'PAROLA PELLEGRINA, VELOCEMENTE SIGNIFICANTE UN'OBIETTO PER MEZZO DI UN'ALTRO,' ibid., p. 82.

31 '... tutti gli obietti con le sue proprie parole successivamente si ci presentano,' ibid., p. 301.

32 '... la Metafora, tutti à stretta li rinzeppa in un Vocabulo: & quasi in miraculoso modo gli ti fà travedere l'un dentro all'altro. Onde maggiore è il tuo diletto: nella maniera, che più curiosa e piacevol cosa è mirar molti obietti per un'istraforo di perspettiva, che se gli originali medesimi successivamente ti venisser passando dinanzi agli occhi. Opera (come dice il nostro Autore) non di stupido, ma di acutissimo ingegno ...,' ibid., p. 82.

33 'La Metafora, quindi, prima ancora che modalità (figura) o disposizione della parola e del discorso a "dire" una cosa e a "significarne" un'altra, è riconoscimento della mobilità e della potenziale disposizione di un qualsiasi essere a divenire un "altro," fosse anche soltanto nel libero gioco di un'intelligenza associativa e permutante,' Mario Zanardi, 'La metafora e la sua dinamica di significazione ne *Il cannocchiale aristotelico* di Emanuele Tesauro,' *Giornale storico della letteratura italiana* 157 (1980): 321.

34 Ibid., p. 325.

35 Ezio Raimondi, *Letteratura barocca* (Florence, 1982), p. 22.

36 'Disordinatamente strutturalista, Tesauro sa comunque che non sono più i rapporti ontologici ma la struttura stessa del linguaggio che garantisce i trasferimenti metaforici.'

37 *The Aesthetics of Chaosmos* was originally the final chapter of *Opera aperta* (1962), but it was later removed from that work and published separately.

## Chapter 3

1 This essay was partially translated into English as 'Form and Interpretation in Luigi Pareyson's *Aesthetics*' and was included in the English edition of *The Open Work* (1989).

2 Pareyson, quoted by Eco in *La definizione dell'arte* (Milan, 1978), p. 22.

3 '... intendendo con questo che l'opera d'arte costituisce un fatto comunicativo che chiede di essere interpretato, e quindi integrato, completato da un apporto del fruitore. Apporto che varia con gli individui e le situazioni storiche e che viene continuamente misurato riferendosi a quel parametro immutabile che é l'opera in quanto oggetto fisico.'

4 'C'è infatti chi afferma che l'opera d'arte é sostanzialmente incompiuta, e quindi non s'offre al lettore se non reclamando ch'egli partecipi all'atto creativo dell'autore e lo prolunghi per conto suo con i più diversi e originali complementi. E chi così afferma si appella alla stessa intenzione dell'artista, il quale spesso preferisce il non finito al finito, talvolta proprio per evocare con l'indeterminatezza dello sfumato una misteriosa insondabilità di significati ...,' Luigi Pareyson, *I problemi dell'estetica* (Milan, 1966), p. 187.

5 'La massima scientificità dell'estetica non viene raggiunta stabilendo scientificamente ... le regole del gusto, ma definendo la a-scientificità della esperienza di gusto ed il margine che in essa va lasciato al fattore personale e prospettico.'

6 Andrea Tabarroni, 'Mental Signs and the Theory of Representation in Ockham,' in Eco and Marmo, *On the Medieval Theory of Signs*, p. 196.

7 'The interpretant can assume different forms:
   a) It can be the equivalent (or apparently equivalent) sign-vehicle in another semiotic system. For example I can make the drawing of a dog correspond to the word /dog/.
   b) It can be the index which is directed to a single object, perhaps implying an element of universal quantification ("all objects like this").
   c) It can be a scientific (or naïve) definition in terms of the same semiotic system, e.g. /salt/ signifies "sodium chloride."
   d) It can be an emotive association which acquires the value of an established connotation: /dog/ signifying "fidelity" (and vice versa).
   e) It can simply be the translation of the term into another language, or its substitution by a synonym' (Eco, *A Theory of Semiotics*, p. 70).

8 See Armin Burkhardt, 'Die Semiotik des Umberto "von Baskerville,"' in Armin Burkhardt and Eberhard Rohse, eds, *Umberto Eco. Zwischen Literatur und Semiotik* (Braunschweig, 1991).

9 Deleuze and Guattari have also represented a similar type of network as a rhyzome, with branches that go in every direction and open up the possibility of infinite connections.

10 The essay is collected in Norma Bouchard and Veronica Pravadelli, eds, *Umberto Eco's Alternative* (New York, 1998), pp. 25–38.

11 Ibid., p. 25.

12 Ibid., p. 35.

13 Tabarroni, 'Mental Signs,' p. 196.

14 Quoted in *Effetto Eco*, by Francesca Pansa and Anna Vinci (Rome, 1990), p. 43.

15 Quoted in 'Dove andremo a finire?' in Eco, *Diario minimo*, p. 97.

16 'Quanto più i mezzi di massa offrono spettacoli lontani dall'umano, dal dialogo, tanto più essi fingono l'intimità del conversare, della gioviale cordialità, come si può vedere (se l'animo basti) assistendo ai loro spettacoli, che obbediscono a un precetto segreto: interessa l'uomo a ciò che non ha per lui alcun interesse, né economico, né estetico, né morale,' ibid., p. 105.

17 'La poetica dell'opera "aperta" tende, come dice Pousseur, a promuovere nell'interprete "atti di libertà cosciente," a porlo come centro attivo di una rete di relazioni inesauribili, tra le quali egli instaura la propria forma, senza essere determinato da una *necessità* che gli prescrive i modi definitivi dell'organizzazione dell'opera fruita; ma si potrebbe obiettare (rifacendosi a quel più vasto significato del termine 'apertura' cui si accennava) che qualsiasi opera d'arte, amche se non si consegna matrialmente incompiuta, esige una risposta libera ed inventiva, se non altro perchè non può venire realmente compresa se l'interprete non la reinventa in un atto di congenialità con l'autore stesso.'

18 Caesar, *Umberto Eco*, p. 52.

19 This essay originally appeared in Vittorini's journal *Menabò* and later was included in subsequent editions of *Opera aperta*.

20 See Fortunato Pasqualino in *L'Osservatore romano* of 13 June 1962, quoted also in the introduction to *Opera aperta*, p. xiii.

21 'Caeterum in claustris coram legentibus fratribus, quid facit ridicula monstruositas, mira quaedam deformis formositas ac formosa deformitas? Quid ibi immundae simiae? Quid feri leones? Quid monstruosi centauri? Quid semihomines? Quid maculosae tigrides? Quid milites pugnantes? Quid venatores tubicinantes? Videas sub uno capite multa corpora, et rursus in uno corpore capita multa. Cernitur hinc in quadrupede cauda serpentis, illinc in pisce caput quadrupedis. Ibi bestia praefert equum, capra trahens retro dimidiam; hic cornutum animal equum gestat posterius. Tam multa denique tamque mira diversarum formarum ubique varietas apparet, ut magis legere libeat in marmoribus quam in codicibus, totumque diem occupare singula ista mirando quam in lege Dei

meditando. Proh Deo! Si non pudet ineptiarum, cur vel non piget expensarum?' quoted in Eco, *Apocalittici e integrati*, p. 17.

22  'Dai modelli divistici del cinema, ai protagonisti dei romanzi d'amore sino alle trasmissioni televisive per la donna, la cultura di massa per lo più rappresenta e propone situazioni umane che non hanno alcuna connessione con le situazioni dei consumatori e che tuttavia per essi diventano situazioni modello.'

23  Antonio Gramsci, *Letteratura e vita nazionale*, vol. 3 (Turin, 1954).

24  '... ogni sforzo di definire una forma significante senza investirla già di un senso è vano e illusorio, così che ogni formalismo assoluto altro non è che un contenutismo mascherato. Isolare delle strutture formali significa riconoscerle come *pertinenti* rispetto a una ipotesi globale che si anticipa sul verso dell'opera; non c'è analisi di aspetti significanti pertinenti che non implichi già una interpretazione e quindi un riempimento di senso.

In tal caso ogni analisi strutturale di un testo è sempre la verifica di ipotesi psico-sociologiche e ideologiche sia pure latenti. Tanto vale avere allora coscienza di questo fenomeno, per ridurre al massimo (senza pretendere di eliminarlo) questo margine di soggettività (o storicità) inevitabile.'

25  'Il Superuomo del feuilleton si rende conto che il ricco prevarica sul povero, che il potere è fondato sulla frode; ma non è un profeta della lotta sociale, come Marx, e quindi non ripara a queste ingiustizie sovvertendo l'ordine della società. Semplicemente sovrappone la propria giustizia a quella comune, distrugge i malvagi, ricompensa i buoni, ristabilisce l'armonia perduta. In tal senso il romanzo popolare democratico non è rivoluzionario, è caritativo, consola i propri lettori con l'immagine di una giustizia fiabesca; ma tuttavia pone a nudo dei problemi e, se non offre delle soluzioni accettabili, delinea delle analisi realistiche.'

26  Another type of criticism – for example, a review of *Apocalittici e integrati* by Piero Citati – concerned the use of instruments of 'high culture,' such as the theories of Kant and Husserl, to analyse 'low culture,' and expressed a fear that the future role of intellectuals would be to write films, comics, and popular songs (which to a certain extent has come to pass).

27  Eco's department library, although small, has all the characteristics he wishes for in a library. Unfortunately, the university library still seems far behind.

28  During mentions as an example the analysis of cigarette-smoking: semiotics, he says, would turn its attention to an image such as the 'Marlboro Man' and its connoting of freedom and masculinity, but would

leave untouched the question of uses, practices, and feelings, Simon
During, ed., *The Cultural Studies Reader*, 2nd ed. (London and New York:
Routledge, 1999), p. 5.

## Chapter 4

1 Elizabeth Freund, *The Return of the Reader* (London and New York, 1987),
p. 18.
2 Ibid., p. 156.
3 Louis Marin, *Le récit est un piège* (Paris, 1978), p. 8.
4 Henry James, 'The Figure in the Carpet,' in *The Figure in the Carpet and
Other Stories* (New York: Viking, 1986).
5 Eco, introduction to *Lector in fabula*, p. 5.
6 'The Lacanian acknowledgment of the autonomy of the symbolic as the
chain of the signifiers, by inspiring the new deconstructionist practices, has
now allowed the new and atheistic mystics of a godless drift, to rewrite indefinitely, at every new reading, the new Torah,' *Semiotica e filosofia*, p. 156.
7 The English translation appeared in the same year, with the title *The Role of
the Reader*; it also contains other essays, including some from *The Open Work*.
8 The chapter is entitled '*Intentio lectoris*: The State of the Art.'
9 Eco, *Six Walks in the Fictional Woods*, p. 126.
10 In Bouchard and Pravadelli, *Eco's Alternative*, pp. 63–79.
11 'So I might as well stay here, wait, and look at the hill. It's so beautiful!'
*Foucault's Pendulum*, p. 700.
12 Peter Carravetta, 'Hermenentic Aspects of Eco's Later Works,' in Bouchard
and Pravadelli, *Eco's Alternative*, p. 63.
13 '*Intentio lectoris*: The State of the Art,' pp. 44–63.
14 Algirdas J. Greimas, *Sul senso* (Milan, 1974), p. 188.
15 Richard Rorty, quoted in *Interpretation and Overinterpretation*, p. 12.
16 Jonathan Culler, quoted ibid., p. 14.
17 Eco, *Kant e l'ornitorinco*, p. 79.
18 'Pare che il gruppo dell'Oulipo abbia recentemente costruito una matrice
di tutte le possibili situazioni poliziesche e abbia trovato che rimane da
scrivere un libro in cui l'assassino sia il lettore. Morale: esistono idee
ossessive, non sono mai personali, i libri si parlano tra loro, e una vera
indagine poliziesca deve provare che i colpevoli siamo noi.' The OuLiPo
group was founded by poets and prose writers, including Queneau,
Calvino, Georges Perec, and Harry Mathews, who practiced 'procedural'
writing, a type of writing that involves a partial surrender of authors'
control over the production of the text. It was not the surrealist 'automatic'

writing, but it was a 'mechanical' writing that exploited the potential of the literary and the linguistic system.

19 See, for example, Roger Rollin in '*The Name of the Rose* as Popular Culture,' in M. Thomas Inge, ed., *Naming the Rose* (Jackson and London, 1988).

20 Susan R. Suleiman and Inge Crosman, *The Reader in the Text* (Princeton, 1980), p. 9.

21 See Inge, *Naming the Rose*, pp. 162–3.

22 'I have never doubted the truth of signs, Adso; they are the only things man has with which to orient himself in this world,' Eco, *The Name of the Rose*, p. 495.

23 See chapter 7 for a discussion of this point.

24 The Abbé Vallet wrote a book on Thomas Aquinas, in which Eco found the stimulus he needed for completing his doctoral dissertation. Eco recalls reading the book and having a moment of revelation, a moment of understanding; but many years later, when he went back to the book, he could not find the idea that had so inspired him, which was never there in the first place.

25 The story of Milo Temesvar (an author who never existed) is recounted by Eco in 'Prelude to a Palimpsest,' an introduction to the collection of essays *Naming the Rose*, and it is worth recounting it here. Milo was invented by a group of editors during the Frankfurt Book Fair in order to bring to light and satirize the widespread practice of paying enormous sums of money for all the rights to a book. One of the editors said, 'I bet that if we invent an author – let us say, Milo Temesvar – who has written a new novel, let's say "Let Me Say It Now," and that the New American Library has just paid $50,000 advance for an option on the manuscript, before the night is over, everybody will rush to obtain the foreign rights.' 'By 6:00 p.m. practically everyone was ready to sell his own soul in order to have Temesvar, and at 8:00 p.m., a well-known Italian publisher boasted at dinner: – Stop. I have just bought the foreign rights for the whole world,' p. xii.

26 Eco's assertion is even more important nowadays, seventeen years later, when the persuasion that one should write engaging only with the present has re-emerged, although in a different context. It is very clear that Eco does not disengage: 1968 is the time of his Model Author, and while he is fascinated by Adso's terrible story, the Soviet troops are invading Prague, so that he must flee to Linz. A reflection on the relation between Adso's story and the invasion of Prague would certainly not be idle.

27 'The criterion is simple: suspect, always suspect. One can read in transparency even a do-not-enter street sign,' *Foucault's Pendulum*, p. 399.

28 Isaac Casaubon (1559–1614) was a Swiss philologist who, in the early

seventeenth century, established that the *Corpus Hermeticum* had been written after the Christian era, and not, as was believed, in ancient Egypt by Hermes Trismegistos before the time of Moses.

29   The story starts at the beginning of the fourteenth century, when Philip the Fair destroyed the Order of the Templars. Since then, people have fantasized about a clandestine survival. Later, two other secret sects were created, the Rosicrucians and the Freemasons, which also cultivated an aura of mystery. In 1797, Abbé Barruel wrote his *Mémoires pour servir à l'histoire du jacobinism*, a novel that begins with the Templars, who through the Freemasons give rise to the Jacobins; the underlying thesis is that the Templars were responsible for the French Revolution. At the beginning of the nineteenth century, a notion circulated that the Jews had infiltrated the secret societies.

In 1864, Maurice Joly wrote a booklet against Napoleon III, in which Machiavelli talks with Montesquieu. Joly was arrested and finally killed himself. A few years later, Elie de Cyon in Russia rewrote the booklet substituting the figure of a political opponent for that of Machiavelli. When the anti-Semitic Russian chief of police, Pĕtr Ivanovic Rachowskij, found the booklet, eager to eliminate Cyon he changed the figure into a group of Jews. He elaborated the idea of a Jewish conspiracy against the czar. His plan was facilitated by the fact that the name Cyon recalls Zion.

Rachowskij's text constitutes the primary source for the *Protocols of the Elders of Zion*, which discusses a plan elaborated by the Jews to bring the whole world under their dominion. Even though this document could easily have been identified as a product of nineteenth-century France, when it reached the hands of Hitler nobody thought of a philological analysis, even though the *Times* in 1921 had discovered Joly's book and was identifying it as the source for the *Protocols*. The rest of the story is well known.

30   Eco's choice was certainly a response to Harold Bloom's lectures at the University of Bologna, which were delivered before *Foucault's Pendulum* was written. The lectures discussed Peirce's theory, but Bloom also presented his own theory of strong readings, according to which any strong reading of a work is necessarily a 'misreading.' These ideas were also developed in his *Kabbalah and Criticism* (New York, 1975).

31   Samuel Ben Samuel Abraham Abulafia (1240–92) was a thirteenth-century Jewish mystic who studied the infinite combinations of the Torah and developed a method for interpreting it that was highly influential in cabbalism.

32   'Chiunque di noi si stupirebbe, dopo aver sentito una lezione di Piaget sul come si percepiscono gli oggetti, incontrare un pittore che si proponesse

di dipingere "alla Piaget." Gli risponderemmo che, se le teorie di Piaget sono vere, esse definiscono ogni esperienza percettiva possibile e che dunque anche Raffaello dipingeva "alla Piaget." Cioè, non bisogna mai fare di una spiegazione teorica, un modello di operazioni pratiche. Non si deve fare di una estetica una poetica, non si deve fare di una metafisica dell'Essere un sistema di guida per autoveicoli (anche se gli autoveicoli e il nostro guidarli altro non sono che epifanie dell'Essere).'

33  Eco, 'Prelude to a Palimpsest,' p. xii.

34  We could include Eco's *Opera aperta* here.

35  Brian McHale, *Constructing Postmodernism* (London and New York, 1992), p. 171.

36  Ibid., p. 187.

37  Eco, while writing this novel, was also working on *The Search for the Perfect Language* (1993).

38  'The Fixation of Belief,' in Charles S. Peirce, *Philosophical Writings* (New York, 1995), p. 5.

39  Ibid., p. 6.

40  Ibid., p. 18.

41  Ibid.

42  Ibid., p. 4.

43  Ibid., p. 8.

44  Michel Foucault, *The Order of Things* (New York, 1994), pp. 48–9.

45  '[Nella forma barocca] viene negata proprio la definitezza statica ed inequivocabile della forma classica rinascimentale, dello spazio sviluppato intorno a un asse centrale, delimitato da linee simmetriche e angoli chiusi, cospiranti al centro, in modo da suggerire piuttosto una idea di eternità "essenziale" che non di movimento. La forma barocca è invece dinamica, tende ad una indeterminatezza di effetto ... e suggerisce una dilatazione progressiva dello spazio; la ricerca del mosso e dell'illusionistico fa sì che le masse plastiche barocche non permettano mai una visione privilegiata, frontale, definita, ma inducano l'osservatore a spostarsi continuamente per vedere l'opera sotto aspetti sempre nuovi, come se essa fosse in continua mutazione. Se la spiritualità barocca viene vista come la prima chiara manifestazione della cultura e della sensibilità moderna, è perchè qui, per la prima volta, l'uomo si sottrae alla consuetudine del canonico ... e si trova di fronte, nell'arte come nella scienza, ad un mondo in movimento che gli richiede atti di invenzione.'

46  Omar Calabrese, *Neo-Baroque*, trans. Charles Lambert (Princeton, 1992), p. 45.

47  Ibid., pp. 15, 29.

48  See Eco, 'Tra La Mancha e Babele,' in *Sulla letteratura* (Milan, 2002), pp. 114–27.

49  'Il vero eroe della Biblioteca di Babele non è la Biblioteca stessa, ma il Lettore, nuovo Don Quijote, mobile, avventuroso, instancabilmente inventivo, alchemicamente combinatorio, capace di dominare i mulini a vento che fa ruotare all'infinito.'

50  Mettale, *Constructing Postmodernism*, p. 4.

51  Donald Barthelme, *The Dead Father* (New York, 1976), p. 119.

**Chapter 5**

1  Lino Pertile, *La puttana e il gigante* (Ravenna, 1998), p. 8.

2  Quoted in Peter Bondanella, *Umberto Eco and the Open Text* (Cambridge, 1997), pp. 99–100.

3  Giuseppe Zecchini, 'Il Medioevo di Umberto Eco,' in Renato Giovannoli, ed., *Saggi su 'Il nome della rosa'* (Milan, 1999), p. 329.

4  Ibid., p. 331.

5  Rocco Capozzi, 'Intertextuality, Metaphors and Metafiction,' in Capozzi, *Reading Eco*, p. 399.

6  '... con un testo sacro non ci si possono permettere molte licenze, perchè c'è di solito una autorità ed una tradizione religiosa che rivendica le chiavi della sua interpretazione. Per esempio la cultura medievale non ha fatto altro che incoraggiare lo sforzo di una interpretazione infinita nel tempo, e tuttavia limitata nelle sue opzioni. Se qualcosa caratterizzava la teoria medievale dei quattro sensi era che i sensi delle Scritture (e per Dante anche della poesia profana) erano quattro, ma (i) questi sensi dovevano essere individuati seguendo delle regole ben precise e (ii) questi sensi, ancorchè nascosti sotto la superficie letterale, non erano affatto segreti, anzi-per coloro che sapevano leggere rettamente il testo-dovevano essere palesi,' in Maria Pia Pozzato, ed., *L'idea deforme* (Milan 1989), pp. 27–8.

7  Linda Hutcheon, 'Irony-clad Foucault,' in Capozzi, *Reading Eco*, p. 323.

8  Capozzi, 'Intertextuality, Metaphors, and Metafiction,' p. 389.

9  Rocco Capozzi, 'The Return of Umberto Eco: Baudolino *Homo Ludens*,' in *Rivista di studi italiani* 18 (Dec. 2000): 211–35.

10  Jorge Luis Borges, *Labyrinths*, ed. Donald A. Yates and James E. Irby (New York, 1964), p. 44.

11  Norris J. Lacey, ed., *Text and Intertext in Medieval Arthurian Literature* (New York and London, 1996), p. vii.

12  'I punti forza del racconto non sono affatto quelli in cui sta accadendo qualcosa di inaspettato; quelli sono i punti-pretesto. I punti forza sono

quelli in cui Wolfe ripete i gesti consueti ... L'attrattiva del libro, il senso di riposo, di distensione psicologica che è capace di conferire, è data dal fatto che, sprofondato nella propria poltrona o nel divano dello scompartimento ferroviario, il lettore ritrova di continuo e punto per punto quello che già sa, quello che vuole sapere ancora una volta e per cui ha speso il prezzo del fascicolo ... Un piacere in cui la distrazione consiste nel rifiuto dello sviluppo degli eventi, in un sottrarci alla tensione passato-presente-futuro per ritirarci in un *istante*, amato perché ricorrente.'

13 Rocco Capozzi, 'Intertestualità e Semiosi: L'*Education semiotique* di Eco,' in Giovannoli, *Saggi su 'Il nome della rosa*,' pp. 156–73.

14 Burkhardt Kroeber, 'Il misterioso dialogo di due libri: Eco e Calvino,' in Giovannoli, *Saggi su 'Il nome della rosa*,' pp. 68–75.

15 'La conoscenza come molteplicità è il filo che lega le opere maggiori, tanto di quello che viene chiamato modernismo quanto di quello che viene chiamato il *postmodern*, un filo che-al di là di tutte le etichette-vorrei continuasse a svolgersi nel prossimo millennio,' Italo Calvino, *Lezioni americane* (Milan: Arnoldo Mondadori, 1993), p. 126.

16 'Quella che prende forma nei grandi romanzi del XX secolo è l'idea d'una enciclopedia *aperta*, aggettivo che certamente contraddice il sostantivo *enciclopedia*, nato etimologicamente dalla pretesa di esaurire la conoscenza del mondo rinchiudendola in un circolo. Oggi non è più pensabile una totalità che non sia potenziale, congetturale, plurima.

A differenza della letteratura medievale che tendeva a opere che esprimessero l'integrazione dello scibile umano in un ordine e una forma di stabile compattezza, come la *Divina Commedia*, dove convergono una multiforme ricchezza linguistica e l'applicazione d'un pensiero sistematico e unitario, i libri moderni che più amiamo nascono dal confluire e scontrarsi d'una molteplicità di metodi interpretativi, modi di pensare, stili d'espressione. Anche se il disegno generale è stato minuziosamente progettato, ciò che conta non è il suo chiudersi in una figura armoniosa, ma è la forza centrifuga che da esso si sprigiona, la pluralità dei linguaggi come garanzia d'una verità non parziale. Com'è provato proprio dai due grandi autori del nostro secolo che più si richiamano al Medioevo, T.S. Eliot e James Joyce, entrambi cultori di Dante, entrambi con una forte consapevolezza teologica (sia pur con diverse intenzioni). T.S. Eliot dissolve il disegno teologico nella leggerezza dell'ironia e nel vertiginoso incantesimo verbale. Joyce che ha tutte le intenzioni di costruire un'opera sistematica e enciclopedica e interpretabile su vari livelli secondo l'ermeneutica medievale (e redige tavole di corrispondenze dei capitoli di *Ulysses* con le parti del corpo umano, le arti, i simboli) è soprattutto l'enciclopedia degli stili che realizza, capitolo per capitolo in *Ulysses* o convogliando la molteplicità polifonica nel tessuto verbale del *Finnegans Wake*,' ibid., pp. 127–8.

17  Georges Perec, *La vie mode d'emploi* (Paris, 1978), p. 16.

18  '... il disegno sterminato e insieme compiuto, la novità della resa letteraria, il compendio d'una tradizione narrativa e la summa enciclopedica di saperi che danno forma a un'immagine del mondo, il senso dell'oggi che è anche fatto di accumulazione del passato e di vertigine del vuoto, la compresenza continua d'ironia e angoscia, insomma il modo in cui il perseguimento di un progetto strutturale e l'imponderabile della poesia diventano una cosa sola,' Calvino, *Lezione americane*, p. 132.

19  Ibid., pp. 53–4.

10  Ibid., p. 54.

21  A notebook entry quoted by David Cowart in *Literary Symbiosis* (Athens and London, 1993).

## Chapter 6

1  'Yo sabía que tendría que inventar un libro misterioso para el fondo de mi novela, pero el que sea de Aristóteles ha sido casual. También fue casual que leyera el texto de Bajtin sobre Rabelais, que cayera en mis manos la "Coena Cipriani," *El país* (Madrid), 31 Jan. 1983.

2  Thomas Stauder, *Umberto Ecos 'Der Name der Rose'* (Erlangen, 1988), p. 63.

3  'Di Bakhtin si può dire che è un gigante perché supera di un balzo i formalisti russi a cui è stato sempre accompagnato, né rimane etichettabile soltanto come un semiologo. Ovvero lo è, ma nel senso più glorioso del termine, lega lo studio dei sistemi linguistici a quello della cultura, va al di là delle ricerche formali sulle parole, e offre nuove chiavi per interpretare altri linguaggi, quelli del corpo, del cibo, della festa. Soprattutto, ... dà un contributo capitale a una filosofia, a una estetica, a una semiotica del comico,' Eco, 'Corpo Dio,' *L'Espresso*, 3 Feb. 1980.

4  '*Gargantua e Pantagruel* si presenta da solo, basta prenderlo in mano per trovarlo gloriosamente moderno, post-avanguardie storiche, post-sessantotto, post-settantasette, gli autonomi col passamontagna e le brigate rosse coi loro pistolini fanno ridere di fronte al modo in cui questo fratacchione, con la penna d'oca, colpisce al cuore alcuni secoli di cultura, di morale, di politica, detronizza la Sorbona, volta il mondo a testa in giù e mette in scena proprio l'emarginazione, gli esiliati, la cultura reietta, la cultura della pancia, dell'uccello, del carnevale popolare, fa più rinascimento lui coi suoi frati e scolari che pisciano, scorreggiano,

s'ingozzano e recitano litanie falliche, che Michelangelo con le sue cupole
... e con tanta irriverenza ci restituisce una grande dignità, almeno per il
corpo, ma anche per l'anima. Perché un'anima capace di ridere è più
umana di quelle che piangono, teste Aristotele, "De Anima," libro terzo: tra
tutti i viventi l'uomo è l'unico essere capace di ridere,' ibid.

5  Henry D. Spalding, *Joys of Italian Humor and Folklore* (New York, 1980), p. 1.

6  Jeannine Horowitz and Sophia Menache, *L'humour en chaire* (Geneva,
   1994), pp. 35–6.

7  The 'Coena Cipriani,' attributed to a Carthaginian bishop but in fact
   anonymous, includes an episode in which all the characters of the Christian tradition – Jesus, Mary, King Herod, Solomon, etc. – eat together,
   drink, shout, steal, and slap each other, repeating their famous gestures in
   form of a parody. For Eco, it represents the triumph of material and
   corporal life and a moment of glorious freedom.

8  Quoted in Margherita Ganeri, *Il 'caso' Eco* (Palermo, 1991), p. 122.

9  Quoted ibid., p. 127.

10  Oubelmanine Zhiri, 'Paradoxes and the Renaissance,' University of
    California at San Diego graduate seminar, winter 1999.

11  Eco, *Diario minimo*, pp. 85–96.

12  The essays contained in these volumes have been translated into many
    languages under various titles. The English translations were partially
    collected under the following titles: *Misreadings* (1993), *Travels in
    Hyperreality* (1986), and *How to Travel with a Salmon* (1994).

13  This essay is contained in *Il superuomo di massa*, pp. 115–43.

14  In *Sugli specchi*, pp. 261–79.

15  One in *Sugli specchi*, pp. 271–9, and a longer, more recent version in *Tra
    menzogna e ironia*, pp. 53–97.

16  This essay is contained in *Diario minimo* (1963), pp. 66–84.

17  The essay presents a study of the *primitive* inhabitants of the city of Milan
    conducted by Melanesian anthropologists. This excerpt will serve to
    illustrate the tone and message of the parody: 'The day of the native
    Milanese follows the elementary solar rhythms. They wake up early in order
    to take care of the typical tasks of this population: collection of steel in the
    plantations, cultivation of metal profiles, treatment of plastic materials,
    trade of chemical fertilizers with the interior, sowing of transistors, pasture
    of scooters, breeding of Alfa Romeos, and so forth. But the natives do not
    love their job and do everything possible to avoid the moment in which
    they will begin it; what is curious is that the village chiefs seem to encour-
    age this, for example eliminating the usual means of transportation,
    uprooting the railway tracks of the primitive trains, confusing the circula-

tion with large yellow stripes painted along the paths (with the clear significance of a taboo), and, finally, digging big holes in the less expected places, in which many natives fall head first and are sacrificed to the local gods,' ibid., p. 71.

18 In *Diario minimo* and in English in *Misreadings*.

19 In *Il secondo diario minimo*, pp. 203–43.

20 *Dalla periferia dell'impero*, p. 7.

21 Aristotle, *The Art of Rhetoric*, trans. and ed. H.C. Lawson (London, 1991), p. 185.

22 In *Dalla periferia dell'impero*, pp. 187–211.

23 Alain J.-J. Cohen, '*Some Like It Hot*: Billy Wilder's Virtuoso Strategies of Laughter and Play,' in Gerald F. Carr, Wayne Harbert, and Lihua Zhang, eds, *Interdigitations* (Bern, 1999), p. 670.

24 Quoted in Candace D. Lang, *Irony/Humor* (Baltimore and London, 1988), p. 5.

25 Ibid., p. 6.

26 Ibid., p. 8.

27 Eco, *Il secondo diario minimo*, p. 138.

28 Ibid., p. 137.

29 'Rabelais sapeva che il riso può cambiare il mondo assai più della polvere da sparo, inventata poco prima da un altro frate, che giustamente si chiamava Bertoldo il Nero,' Eco, 'Corpo Dio.'

## Chapter 7

1 Jean-François Lyotard, 'What Is Postmodernism?' (1983), in *The Postmodern Condition*, trans. Geoff Bennington and Brian Massumi (Minneapolis, 1993), p. 81.

2 Stefano Tani, *The Doomed Detective* (Carbondale and Edwardsville, 1984), p. 72.

3 Karl Roland Schreiber, 'Est ubi nunc ordo mundi? Zum philosophiege-schichtlichen Hintergrund von Umberto Ecos Roman *Der Name der Rose*,' in Burkhardt and Rohse, *Umberto Eco*, p. 123.

4 Tani, *The Doomed Detective*, p. 28.

5 Ibid.

6 Ibid., p. 34.

7 Steven Marcus, quoted ibid., p. 23.

8 David H. Richter, 'The Mirrored World,' in Capozzi, *Reading Eco*, p. 274.

9 Medieval knowledge before Ockham was based on the concept of 'adequatio mentis ad rem,' meaning that there was a mysterious correspondence between the mind and things, between words and objects.

10 Schreiber, 'Est ubi nunc ordo mundi?' p. 151.
11 'Meine Sätze erläutern dadurch, daß sie der, welcher mich versteht, am Ende als unsinnig erkennt, wenn er durch sie – auf ihnen – über sie hinausgestiegen ist. (Er muß sozusagen die Leiter wegwerfen, nachdem er auf ihr hinaufgestiegen ist)'; 'Er muß diese Sätze überwinden, dann sieht er die Welt richtig ... Die Idee sitzt gleichsam als Brille auf unsrer Nase, und was wir ansehen, sehen wir durch sie. Wir kommen gar nicht auf den Gedanken, sie abzunehmen,' Ludwig Wittgenstein, *Tractatus logico-philosophicus* (Frankfurt: B.F. McGuinness/J. Schulte, 1989), pp. 4 and 101–3.
12 Lyotard, *The Postmodern Condition*, p. 39.
13 Ibid., p. 4.
14 Ibid., p. 41.
15 Hanna Buczynska-Garewicz, 'Semiotics and Deconstruction,' in Capozzi, *Reading Eco*, p. 167.
16 Deely, 'Looking Back,' p. 83.
17 Teresa Coletti, *Naming the Rose* (Ithaca, 1988).
18 Ugo Volli, 'Il Campo e la Soglia,' in Patrizia Magli, Giovanni Manetti, and Patrizia Violi, eds, *Semiotica: Storia, teoria, interpretazione* (Milan, 1992), pp. 78–88.
19 Lucrecia Escudero, 'Apocalittico e integrato,' in Magli, Manetti, and Violi, *Semiotica: Storia, teoria, interpretazione*, pp. 343–55.
20 Owen Flanagan, *The Science of the Mind* (Cambridge, Mass., 1991), p. 192.
21 Roberto Pellerey, 'George Berkeley. Un modello pansemiotico,' in Magli, Manetti, and Violi,' *Semiotica: Storia, teoria, interpretazione*, pp. 59–72.
22 In Charles Hartshorne and Paul Weiss, eds, *Collected Papers of Charles Sanders Peirce* (Cambridge, Mass., 1931–5), vol. 1, pp. 170, 171–5.
23 We are indebted for this expression to Alain Cohen, who first used it in his 'Lynch's *Lost Highway*: A Postmodern *Whodunit*,' *La Licorne/Whodunits* 8 (1999): 205–24.
24 Peter Bondanella, 'Interpretation, Overinterpretation, Paranoid Interpretation,' in Capozzi, *Reading Eco*, pp. 285–99.
25 Bloom, *Kabbalah and Criticism.*
26 The Italian translation, *Interpretazione e overinterpretazione*, was published in 1995.
27 Woody Allen, *Getting Even* (New York: Random House, 1971), p. 8.
28 Lois Zamora, 'The Swing of the "Pendulum": Eco's Novels,' in Capozzi, *Reading Eco*, pp. 328–47.
29 Tani, *The Doomed Detective*, p. 29.
30 Cohen, 'Lynch's *Lost Highway*,' p. 207.
31 Tani, *The Doomed Detective*, p. 146.

32  Ibid., p. 151.
33  See Eco, 'Innovation and Repetition: Between Modern and Postmodern Aesthetics,' in Capozzi, *Reading Eco*, pp. 14–15.
34  Ibid., p. 29.
35  Ibid., p. 22.
36  Claudia Miranda, '"Dove" Is the Dove,' in Capozzi, *Reading Eco*, pp. 362–86.
37  Eero Tarasti, ed., *Musical Signification* (Berlin and New York, 1995), p. ix.
38  Rosario Mirigliano, 'The Sign and Music: A Reflection on the Theoretical Bases of Musical Semiotics,' in Tarasti, *Musical Signification*, p. 49.
39  Eco, quoted ibid., p. 57.
40  Otto M. Christensen, 'Interpretation and Meaning in Music,' in Tarasti, *Musical Signification*, p. 87.
41  Ibid.

## Chapter 8

1  See Capozzi, 'The Return of Umberto Eco,' p. 233.
2  'E il mondo si adegua. Anzi, cospira e collabora con lui alla finzione universale. Baudolino non pratica solo la fiction romanzesca, agisce anche su quell'illusione collettiva che produce la Storia,' Eco, quoted in *Panorama*, November 2000.
3  'Nel rileggere il passato c'è sempre una specie di pessimismo dell'eterno ritorno. Ci accorgiamo che c'è stato meno progresso di quanto credevamo. Non penso che certe conversazioni di Ronald Reagan con i suoi collaboratori fossero meno ingenue di quelle tra Federico e i suoi consiglieri. E se Barbarossa non capiva lo spirito dei Comuni italiani, pare che George Bush jr. non sappia neanche dove stanno di casa i Balcani,' ibid.
4  Jeffrey J. Cohen, ed., *Monster Theory* (Minneapolis, 1996), p. viii.
5  Abchasia, in fact, is an autonomous republic of the former U.S.S.R., under the protectorate of the Republic of Georgia.
6  According to Arius' heretical interpretation, Christ is not the Son of God, but a human creature on whom God's word descended; he was not God incarnated, but a divinized man.
7  According to Greek mythology, the satyrs were creatures with both human and animal characteristics. They had a beard, horns, and goatlike legs. Hesiod wrote of them as good-for-nothing beings. They were famous for their luxurious instincts.
8  Quoted in David Williams, *Deformed Discourse* (Montreal and Kingston, 1996), p. 3.

9   Ibid., p. 4.
10   Ibid.
11   Ibid., p. 5.
12   Ibid., p. 9.
13   Quoted ibid.
14   Ibid., p. 10.
15   Ibid., p. 12.
16   Ibid., p. 26.
17   Ibid., p. 33.
18   Ibid., p. 59.
19   Ibid.
20   Capozzi, 'The Return of Umberto Eco.'
21   Quoted in Williams, *Deformed Discourse*, p. 46.
22   Quoted ibid., p. 48.
23   Cohen, *Monster Theory*, p. 11.
24   Julia Kristeva, *The Powers of Horror*, trans. Leon S. Roudiez (New York, 1982), p. 1.
25   See, for example, La Fontaine in his *Fables* and Pico della Mirandola in his *Oratio de dignitate hominis*.
26   Giambattista Vico, *The New Science*, 1774, trans. Thomas Goddard Bergin and Max Harold Fisch, 3rd ed. (Ithaca, 1968), p. 262.

**Chapter 9**

1   In Capozzi, *Reading Eco*, p. 317.
2   Terry Eagleton, *The Illusions of Postmodernism* (Oxford, 1996), p. vii.
3   Ibid.
4   Charles Jencks, *The Language of Post-Modern Architecture* (New York, 1977).
5   This piece of information comes from Alain Cohen's personal conversations with Baudrillard.
6   Jean Baudrillard, *Simulations*, trans. Paul Foss, Paul Patton, and Philip Beitchman (New York, 1983), p. 38.
7   Ibid., p. 10.
8   Ibid., p. 11.
9   'Orainge' is another of Jacob Van Eyck's melodies.
10   Primary attention, for Peirce, is the ability to direct the mind towards something.
11   In *Experiences in Translation*, p. 100, Eco provides the following diagram:
    1.  Interpretation by transcription
    2.  Intrasystemic interpretation

2.1.   Intralinguistic, within the same natural language
2.2.   Intrasemiotic, within other semiotic systems
2.3.   Performance
3. Intersystemic interpretation
3.1.   With marked variation in the substance
3.1.1. Interlinguistic, or translation between natural languages
3.1.2. Rewriting
3.1.3. Translation between other semiotic systems
3.2.   With mutation of continuum
3.2.1. Parasynonymy
3.2.2. Adaptation or Transmutation

# Bibliography

**Major Works by Umberto Eco**

*Il problema estetico in Tommaso d'Aquino.* 1954. Milan: Bompiani, 1970.

*Opera aperta.* 1962. Milan: Bompiani, 1997.

*Le poetiche di Joyce.* Milan: Bompiani, 1962.

*Diario minimo.* Milan: Mondadori, 1963.

*Apocalittici e integrati: Comunicazioni di massa e teorie della cultura di massa.* 1964.
  Milan: Bompiani, 1977.

*La definizione dell'arte. Dall'estetica medievale alle avanguardie; dall'opera aperta alla
  morte dell'arte.* 1968. Milan: Garzanti, 1978.

*La struttura assente.* 1968. Milan: Bompiani, 1996.

*Le forme del contenuto.* Milan: Bompiani, 1971.

*Il costume di casa.* Milan: Bompiani, 1973.

*Il segno.* 1973. Milan: ISEDI, 1974.

*Trattato di semiotica generale.* Milan: Bompiani, 1975.

*Il superuomo di massa. Retorica e ideologia nel romanzo popolare.* 1976. Milan:
  Bompiani, 1998.

*A Theory of Semiotics.* 1976. Bloomington: Indiana University Press, 1979.

*Come si fa una tesi di laurea.* Milan: Bompiani, 1977.

*Dalla periferia dell'impero.* Milan: Bompiani, 1977.

*Lector in fabula: La cooperazione interpretativa nei testi narrativi.* 1979. Milan:
  Bompiani, 1997.

*The Role of the Reader: Exploration in the Semiotics of Texts.* Bloomington: Indiana
  University Press, 1979.

*Il nome della rosa.* 1980. Milan: Bompiani, 1996.

*The Aesthetics of Chaosmos: The Middle Ages of James Joyce.* 1982. Trans. Ellen
  Esrock. Cambridge: Harvard University Press, 1989.

*Esercizi di stile* by Raymond Queneau. 1947. Trans. and ed. Turin: Giulio Einaudi, 1983.

*The Name of the Rose.* Trans. William Weaver. New York: Hartcourt Brace, 1983.

*Sette anni di desiderio.* Milan: Bompiani, 1983.

*Semiotica e filosofia del linguaggio.* 1984. Turin: Einaudi, 1996.

*Semiotics and the Philosophy of Language.* Bloomington: Indiana University Press, 1984.

*Sugli specchi e altri saggi.* Milan: Bompiani, 1985.

*Art and Beauty in the Middle Ages.* New Haven and London: Yale University Press, 1986.

*Travels in Hyperreality.* Trans. William Weaver. San Diego: Harcourt Brace, 1986.

*The Aesthetics of Thomas Aquinas.* 1988. Trans. Hugh Bredin. Cambridge: Harvard University Press, 1994.

'On Truth: A Fiction.' In *Meaning and Mental Representations.* Ed. Umberto Eco, Marco Santambrogio, and Patrizia Violi. Bloomington: Indiana University Press, 1988.

*Il pendolo di Foucault.* 1988. Milan: Bompiani, 1997.

*On the Medieval Theory of Signs.* Ed. Umberto Eco and Costantino Marmo. Amsterdam: John Benjamins, 1989.

*Foucault's Pendulum.* Trans. William Weaver. London: Secker & Warburg, 1990.

*The Limits of Interpretation.* 1990. Bloomington and Indianapolis: Indiana University Press, 1994.

*Interpretation and Overinterpretation.* 1992. Ed. Stefan Collini. Cambridge University Press, 1994.

*Il secondo diario minimo.* 1992. Milan: Bompiani, 1994.

*La ricerca della lingua perfetta nella cultura europea.* 1993. Roma: Editori Laterza, 1996.

*L'isola del giorno prima.* 1994. Milan: Bompiani, 1996.

*Sei passeggiate nei boschi narrativi: Harvard University, Norton Lectures 1992–1993.* 1994. Milan: Bompiani, 1995.

*Six Walks in the Fictional Woods.* Cambridge: Harvard University Press, 1994.

*The Island of the Day Before.* Trans. William Weaver. Orlando: Harcourt Brace, 1995.

*The Search for the Perfect Language.* Trans. James Fentress. Oxford: Blackwell, 1995.

*Kant e l'ornitorinco.* 1997. Milan: Bompiani, 1999.

*Serendipities: Language and Lunacy.* Trans. William Weaver. New York: Columbia University Press, 1998.

*Tra menzogna e ironia.* Milan: Bompiani, 1998.

*La bustina di Minerva.* Milan: Bompiani, 1999.

'*Sylvie*' by Gérard de Nerval. 1984. Trans. and ed. Turin: Giulio Einaudi, 1999.

*Baudolino.* Milan: Bompiani, 2000.

*Kant and the Platypus: Essays on Language and Cognition.* Trans. Alastair McEwen. New York: Harcourt Brace, 2000.

*Experiences in Translation.* Trans. Alastair McEwen. Toronto: University of Toronto Press, 2001.

*Baudolino.* Trans. William Weaver. Orlando: Harcourt Brace, 2002.

*Sulla letteratura.* Milan: Bompiani, 2002.

**Shorter Works by Umberto Eco**

'The Analysis of Structure.' *Times Literary Supplement* 27 (Sept. 1963), pp. 755–6.

'La critica semiologica.' In C. Segre and M. Corti, eds, *I metodi attuali della critica in Italia.* Turin: ERI, 1970, pp. 371–88.

'Codice.' *Versus* 14 (1976): 1–38.

'Peirce and Contemporary Semantics.' *VS* 15 (1976): 49–72.

'Tre donne sulle donne per le donne.' In Marina Federzoni, Isabella Pezzini, and Maria Pia Pozzato, eds, *Carolina Invernizio, Matilde Serao e Liala.* Florence: La Nuova Italia, 1979, pp. 5–27.

'Il cane e il cavallo: Un testo visivo e alcuni equivoci verbali.' *Versus* 25 (1980): 28–43.

'From Aristotle to Sherlock Holmes.' *Versus* 30 (1981): 3–19.

'Stele per Celli.' In Giorgio Celli, ed., *La scienza del comico.* Bologna: Calderini, 1982, pp. v–vii.

'Horns, Hooves, Insteps: Some Hypotheses on Three Types of Abduction.' In Umberto Eco and T.A. Sebeok, eds, *The Sign of Three: Dupin, Holmes, Peirce.* Bloomington: Indiana University Press, 1983, pp. 198–220.

'On Fish and Buttons: Semiotics and Philosophy of Language,' *Semiotica* 48 (1984): 97–117.

'Semiosi naturale e parola nei *Promessi sposi*.' In Giovanni Manetti, ed., *Leggere i promessi sposi.* Milan: Bompiani, 1989.

'Small Worlds.' *VS* 52–3 (1989): 53–70.

Foreword. In Omar Calabrese, *Neo-Baroque: A Sign of the Times.* Princeton: Princeton University Press, 1992, pp. vi–x.

'La maledizione del faraone.' *Sette: Corriere della Sera* (supplement to the Milanese daily), 1995, pp. 32–6.

'Ideologie e pratiche del reimpiego nell'alto medioevo.' In *Settimane di studio del Centro Italiano di Studi sull'Alto Medioevo*. Spoleto: Centro Italiano di Studi sull'Alto Medievo, 1999, pp. 461–84.

## Works by Other Authors

Aquinas, Thomas. *Summa theologica*. 1272. New York: Benziger, 1947.

Aristotle. *The Art of Rhetoric*. 3rd century BCE. Trans. and ed. H.C. Lawson-Tancred. London: Penguin, 1991.

Armstrong, Paul B. *Conflicting Readings: Variety and Validity in Interpretation*. Chapel Hill and London: University of North Carolina Press, 1990.

Artigiani, Robert. 'Image–Music–Pinball.' *Modern Language Notes* 107 (1992): 855–76.

Bakhtin, M.M. *Rabelais and His World*. Trans. Helene Iswolsky. Cambridge: MIT Press, 1968.

Barthelme, Donald. *The Dead Father*. New York: Pocket Books, 1976.

Barthes, Roland. *The Pleasure of the Text*. Trans. Richard Miller. New York: Noonday, 1994.

Baudrillard, Jean. *Simulations*. Trans. Paul Foss, Paul Patton, and Philip Beitchman. New York: Semiotext[e], 1983.

Bloom, Harold, et al. *The Anxiety of Influence: A Theory of Poetry*. New York: Oxford University Press, 1973.

– *Deconstruction & Criticism*. New York: Seabury, 1979.

– *Kabbalah and Criticism*. New York: Seabury, 1975.

Bondanella, Peter. *Umberto Eco and the Open Text: Semiotics, Fiction, Popular Culture*. Cambridge: Cambridge University Press, 1997.

Booth, Wayne C. *Critical Understanding: The Powers and Limits of Pluralism*. Chicago and London: University of Chicago Press, 1979.

Borges, Jorge Luis. *Labyrinths: Selected Stories & Other Writings*. Ed. Donald A. Yates and James E. Irby. New York: New Directions, 1964.

Bouchard, Norma, and Veronica Pravadelli, eds. *Umberto Eco's Alternative: The Politics of Culture and the Ambiguities of Interpretation*. New York: Peter Lang, 1998.

Boutet, Dominique, and Laurence Harf-Lancuer, eds. *Ecriture et modes de pensée au Moyen Age (VIIIe–XVe siècles)*. Paris: Presses de l'Ecole Normale Supérieure, 1993.

Buchler, Justus, ed. *Philosophical Writings of Peirce*. New York: Dover, 1995.

Burkhardt, Armin, and Eberhard Rohse, eds. *Umberto Eco. Zwischen Literatur und Semiotik*. Braunschweig: Ars & Scientia, 1991.

Caesar, Michael. *Umberto Eco: Philosophy, Semiotics, and the Work of Fiction.* Cambridge: Polity, 1999.

Calabrese, Omar. *Neo-Baroque: A Sign of the Times.* Trans. Charles Lambert. Princeton: Princeton University Press, 1992.

Calvino, Italo. *Lezioni americane. Sei proposte per il prossimo millennio.* 1986. Milan: Arnoldo Mondadori, 1993.

– *Se una notte d'inverno un viaggiatore.* Turin: Einaudi, 1981.

Cannon, JoAnn. *Postmodern Italian Fiction: The Crisis of Reason in Calvino, Eco, Sciascia, Malerba.* London and Toronto: Associated University Presses, 1989.

Capozzi, Rocco. 'Intertextuality and Semiosis: Eco's Education Sémiotique.' *Recherches Sémiotiques/Semiotic Inquiry* 3 (1983): 284–96.

– 'Palimpsests and Laughter: The Dialogical Pleasure of Unlimited Intertextuality in The Name of the Rose.' *Italica* 4 (1989): 412–28.

– 'Il pendolo di Foucault: Kitsch o neo/postmoderno.' *Quaderni d'Italianistica* 2 (1990): 225–37.

– ed. *Reading Eco: An Anthology.* Bloomington and Indianapolis: Indiana University Press, 1997.

– 'The Return of Umberto Eco: Baudolino *Homo Ludens*: Describing the Unknown.' *Rivista di studi italiani* 18 (Dec. 2000): 211–35.

– *Scrittori, tendenze letterarie e conflitto delle poetiche in Italia (1960–1990).* Ravenna: Longo, 1993.

Cappello, Giovanni. *La dimensione macrotestuale. Dante, Boccaccio, Petrarca.* Ravenna: Longo, 1998.

Cassirer, Ernst. *Individuum und Kosmos in der Philosophie der Renaissance.* Darmstadt: Wissenschaftliche Buchgesellschaft, 1963.

Celli, Giorgio. *La scienza del comico.* Bologna: Calderini, 1982.

Clayton, Tony, and Eric Rothstein. *Influence and Intertextuality in Literary History.* Madison: University of Wisconsin Press, 1991.

Cobley, Evelyn. 'Closure and Infinite Semiosis in Mann's *Doctor Faustus* and Eco's *The Name of the Rose.*' *Comparative Literature Studies* 26 (1989): 341–61.

Cohen, Alain J.-J. 'Lynch's *Lost Highway*: A Postmodern Whodunit.' *La Licorne/ Whodunits* 8 (1999): 205–24.

– '*Some Like It Hot*: Billy Wilder's Virtuoso Strategies of Laughter and Play.' In Gerald F. Carr, Wayne Harbert, and Lihua Zhang, eds, *Interdigitations: Essays for Irmegard Rauch.* Bern: Peter Lang, 1999, pp. 667–80.

Cohen, Jeffrey J., ed. *Monster Theory.* Minneapolis: University of Minnesota Press, 1996.

Coletti, Teresa. *Naming the Rose: Eco, Medieval Signs, and Modern Theory.* Ithaca: Cornell University Press, 1988.

– 'Pinball, Voodoo, and "Good Primal Matter": Incarnations of Silence in *Foucault's Pendulum.*' *Modern Language Notes* 107 (1992): 877–91.

Consoli, Joseph P. 'Navigating the Labyrinth: A Bibliographic Essay of Selected Criticism of the Works of Umberto Eco.' *Style* 4 (1993): 478–514.

Contini, Gianfranco. *Un'idea di Dante.* Torino: Giulio Einaudi, 1970.

Cotroneo, Roberto. *La diffidenza come sistema.* Milan: Anabasi, 1995.

Cowart, David. *Literary Symbiosis: The Reconfigured Text in Twentieth-Century Writing.* Athens and London: University of Georgia Press, 1993.

Cunningham, Valentine. *In the Reading Gaol: Postmodernity, Texts, and History.* Oxford and Cambridge, Mass.: Blackwell, 1994.

Deely, John. *New Beginnings: Early Modern Philosophy and Postmodern Thought.* Toronto: University of Toronto Press, 1994.

De Lauretis, Teresa. *Umberto Eco.* Florence: La Nuova Italia, 1981.

De Man, Paul. *The Resistance to Theory.* Minneapolis: University of Minnesota Press, 1986.

Derrida, Jacques. *De la grammatologie.* Paris: Editions de Minuit, 1967.

Eagleton, Terry. *The Illusions of Postmodernism.* Oxford: Blackwell, 1996.

Eberstadt, Fernanda. 'Eco Consciousness.' *Vogue,* Nov. 1995, pp. 196–8.

Espen, Hal. 'Man Overboard: 1600 and All That.' *New Yorker,* Aug. 1995, pp. 122–4.

Fiedler, Leslie. *The Dynamics of Literary Response.* New York: Oxford University Press, 1968.

Finke, Laurie A., and Martin B. Schichtman, eds. *Medieval Texts and Contemporary Readers.* Ithaca and London: Cornell University Press, 1987.

Flanagan, Owen. *The Science of the Mind.* Cambridge, Mass.: MIT Press, 1991.

Foucault, Michel. *The Order of Things: An Archeology of the Human Sciences.* New York: Vintage, 1994.

Frese, Dolores W., and Katherine O'Brien O'Keeffe, eds. *The Book and the Body.* Notre Dame and London: University of Notre Dame Press, 1997.

Freud, Sigmund. *Jokes and Their Relation to the Unconscious.* 1905. Trans. and ed. James Strachey. New York and London: Norton, 1989.

Freund, Elizabeth. *The Return of the Reader: Reader-Response Criticism.* London and New York: Methuen, 1987.

Ganeri, Margherita. *Il 'caso' Eco.* Palermo: Palumbo, 1991.

Gellrich, Jesse M. *The Idea of the Book in the Middle Ages.* Ithaca and London: Cornell University Press, 1985.

Giovannoli, Renato, ed. *Saggi su 'Il nome della rosa.'* Milan: Bompiani, 1999.

Goodheart, Eugene. *The Failure of Criticism.* Cambridge, Mass.: Harvard University Press, 1978.

Gramsci, Antonio. *Letteratura e vita nazionale.* Vol. 3. Turin: Einaudi, 1954.

Green, Arthur, ed. *Jewish Spirituality: From the Bible through the Middle Ages.* New York: Crossroad, 1986.

Greimas, Algirdas J. *Sul senso.* Milan: Bompiani, 1974.

Gritti, Jules. *Umberto Eco.* Paris: Editions Universitaires, 1991.

Grojnowski, Daniel. *Aux commencements du rire moderne. L'esprit fumiste.* Paris: José Corti, 1997.

Grosswiler, Paul. *Method Is the Message: Rethinking McLuhan through Critical Theory.* Montreal, New York, London: Blackrose, 1998.

Guglielmi, Nilda. *El Eco de la Rosa y Borges.* Buenos Aires: Editorial Universitaria de Buenos Aires, 1988.

Hartman, Geoffrey H. *Minor Prophecies: The Literary Essay in the Culture War.* Cambridge, Mass.: Harvard University Press, 1991.

Hartshorne, Charles, and Paul Weiss, eds. *Collected Papers of Charles Sanders Peirce.* Cambridge, Mass.: Harvard University Press, 1931–5.

Hebel, Udo J., ed. *Intertextuality, Allusion, and Quotation: An International Bibliography of Critical Studies.* New York: Greenwood, 1989.

Hernàndez Martìn, Jorge. *Readers and Labyrinths: Detective Fiction in Borges, Bustos Domecq, and Eco.* New York and London: Garland, 1995.

Hirsch, E.D., Jr. *Validity in Interpretation.* New Haven and London: Yale University Press, 1967.

Hjelmslev, Louis. *Essais linguistiques.* Copenhagen: Nordisk Sprog-og-Kulturvorlag, 1959.

Holland, Norman L. *The I.* New Haven and London: Yale University Press, 1985.

Horowitz, Jeannine, and Sophia Menache. *L'humour en chaire. Le rire dans l'Église médiévale.* Geneva: Labor et Fides, 1994.

Horton, Susan R. *Interpreting Interpreting.* Baltimore and London: The Johns Hopkins University Press, 1979.

Hutcheon, Linda. *A Poetics of Postmodernism: History, Theory, Fiction.* New York: Routledge, 1988.

Inge, M. Thomas, ed. *Naming the Rose: Essays on Eco's 'The Name of the Rose.'* Jackson and London: University Press of Mississippi, 1988.

Iser, Wolfgang. *The Implied Reader: Patterns of Communication in Prose Fiction from Bunyan to Beckett.* Baltimore and London: The Johns Hopkins University Press, 1978.

Jameson, Fredric. *Postmodernism or, the Cultural Logic of Late Capitalism.* Durham: Duke University Press, 1997.

Jencks, Charles. *The Language of Post-Modern Architecture.* New York: Rizzoli, 1977.

Jewell, Keala, ed. *Monsters in the Italian Literary Imagination.* Detroit: Wayne State University Press, 2001.

Kenny, Anthony. *Aquinas on Mind.* London and New York: Routledge, 1993.

Kierkegaard, Søren. *The Concept of Irony, with Continual Reference to Socrates.* 1841. Trans. and ed. Howard V. Hong and Edna H. Hong. Princeton: Princeton University Press, 1989.

Kristeva, Julia. *The Powers of Horror: An Essay on Abjection.* Trans. Leon S. Roudiez. New York: Columbia University Press, 1982.

– Σημειωτκη. *Recherches pour une Sémanalyse.* Paris: Editions du Seuil, 1969.

Lachower, Fischel, and Isaiah Fishby, eds. *The Wisdom of the Zohar.* Oxford: Oxford University Press, 1989.

Lacy, Norris J., ed. *Text and Intertext in Medieval Arthurian Literature.* New York and London: Garland, 1996.

Lakoff, George, and Mark Johnson. *Metaphors We Live By.* Chicago: University of Chicago Press, 1980.

Landrum, Larry N., Pat Browne, and Ray B. Browne, eds. *Dimensions of Detective Fiction.* Bowling Green: Popular Press, 1976.

Lang, Candace D. *Irony/Humor: Critical Paradigms.* Baltimore and London: The Johns Hopkins University Press, 1988.

Lehmann, Paul. *Die Parodie im Mittelalter.* Stuttgart: A. Hiersemann, 1963.

Lumley, Robert. 'The Sea and the Mirror: *The Island of the Day Before* and *The Search for the Perfect Language.*' *New Statesman & Society,* 6 Oct. 1995, pp. 39–40.

Lyotard, Jean-François. *The Postmodern Condition: A Report on Knowledge.* Trans. Geoff Bennington and Brian Massumi. Minneapolis: University of Minnesota Press, 1993.

Magli, Patrizia, Giovanni Manetti, and Patrizia Violi, eds. *Semiotica: Storia, teoria, interpretazione. Saggi intorno a Umberto Eco.* Milan: Bompiani, 1992.

Manetti, Giovanni, ed. *Leggere I promessi sposi.* Milan: Bompiani, 1989.

– *Le teorie del segno nell'antichità classica.* Milan: Bompiani, 1987.

Marin, Louis. *Le récit est un piège.* Paris: Editions de Minuit, 1978.

– *Utopics: The Semiological Play of Textual Spaces.* Atlantic Highlands, N.J.: Humanities Press International, 1984.

Martin, Jorge H. *Readers and Labyrinths: Detective Fiction in Borges, Bustos Domecq, and Eco.* New York and London: Garland, 1995.

McHale, Brian. *Constructing Postmodernism.* London and New York: Routledge, 1992.

Melling, John K. *Murder Done to Death: Parody and Pastiche in Detective Fiction.* Lanham, Md., and London: Scarecrow, 1984.

Molino, Jean. 'Interpreter.' In his *L'interprétation des textes.* Paris: Editions de Minuit, 1989.

*The Name of the Rose.* Film directed by Jean-Jacques Annaud. Cristaldifilm, 1988.

Nietzsche, Friedrich. *The Gay Science.* 1882. Trans. and ed. Walter Kaufmann. New York: Vintage, 1974.

Norris, Christopher. *The Contest of Faculties: Philosophy and Theory after Deconstruction.* London and New York: Methuen, 1985.

Ockham, William of. *Summa logicae.* 1339. Ed. Philotheus Boehner. New York: Franciscan Institute of St Bonaventure, 1957.

Pansa, Francesca, and Anna Vinci. *Effetto Eco.* Rome: Nuova Edizioni del Gallo, 1990.

Pareyson, Luigi. *I problemi dell'estetica.* Milan: Marzorati, 1966.

– *Teoria dell'arte. Saggi di estetica.* Milan: Marzorati, 1965.

Pearce, Lynne. *Reading Dialogics.* London: Edward Arnold, 1994.

Peirce, Charles S. *Philosophical Writings.* Ed. Justus Buchler. New York: Dover, 1995.

Perec, Georges. *La vie mode d'emploi.* Paris: Hachette, 1978.

Pertile, Lino. *La puttana e il gigante. Dal Cantico dei Cantici al Paradiso Terrestre di Dante.* Ravenna: Longo, 1998.

Pezzarossa, Fulvio. *C'era una volta il pulp. Corpo e letteratura nella tradizione italiana.* Bologna: Cooperativa Libraria Universitaria Editrice Bologna, 1999.

Pozzato, Maria Pia, ed. *L'idea deforme. Interpretazioni esoteriche di Dante.* Milan: Bompiani, 1989.

Prince, Gerald. *Narratology.* Berlin, New York, Amsterdam: Mouton, 1982.

Puletti, Ruggero. *Il nome della rosa.* Manduria: Piero Lacaita, 1995.

Raffa, Guy P. 'Walking and Swimming with Umberto Eco.' *Modern Language Notes* 113 (1998): 164–85.

Raimondi, Ezio. *Letteratura barocca: Studi sul Seicento italiano.* Florence: L.S. Olschki, 1982.

Reed Doob, Penelope. *The Idea of the Labyrinth from Classical Antiquity through the Middle Ages.* Ithaca: Cornell University Press, 1990.

Reim, Riccardo, ed. *L'Italia dei misteri. Storie di vita e malavita nei romanzi d'appendice.* Rome: Editori Riuniti, 1989.

Riffaterre, Michael. *Text Production.* Trans. Térèse Lyons. New York: Columbia University Press, 1983.

Rubino, Carl A. '"Oh, Language Diabolical and Holy": Notes on the Extravagances of *Foucault's Pendulum.*' *Modern Language Notes* 107 (1992): 828–39.

Santa Cruz, Ines, Adriana B. Martino, and Nora Castiglioni. *La Edad Media y la Postmodernidad. A propóposito de El Nombre de la Rosa.* Buenos Aires: Centro de Estudios Latinoamericanos, 1988.

Schiffer, Daniel Salvatore. *Umberto Eco. Le labyrinthe du monde.* Paris: Editions Ramsay, 1998.

Scholem, Gershom. *On the Kabbalah and Its Symbolism.* Trans. Ralph Manheim. New York: Schocken, 1965.

Searle, John R. *Speech Acts.* London: Cambridge University Press, 1969.

Sebeok, Thomas A. 'Give Me Another Horse.' *American Journal of Semiotics* 4 (1991): 41–52.

— *Semiotics in the United States: The View from the Center.* Bloomington: Indiana University Press, 1991.

Sebeok, Thomas A., and Jean Umiker-Sebeok. *You Know My Method: A Juxtaposition of Charles S. Peirce and Sherlock Holmes.* Bloomington: Indiana University Press, 1980.

Segre, Cesare. *La parola ritrovata.* Palermo: Sellerio, 1983.

Smith, Wendy. 'Umberto Eco.' *Publishers Weekly,* 27 Oct. 1989, pp. 50–1.

Spalding, Henry D. *Joys of Italian Humor and Folklore: From Ancient Rome to Modern America.* New York: Jonathan David, 1980.

Stauder, Thomas. *Umberto Ecos 'Der Name der Rose': Forschungsbericht und Interpretation.* Erlangen: Verlag Palm & Enke Erlangen, 1988.

Suleiman, Susan R., and Crosman, Inge. *The Reader in the Text: Essays on Audience and Interpretation.* Princeton: Princeton University Press, 1980.

Tani, Stefano. *The Doomed Detective: The Contribution of the Detective Novel to Postmodern American and Italian Fiction.* Carbondale and Edwardsville: Southern Illinois University Press, 1984.

Tarasti, Eero, ed. *Musical Signification: Essays in the Semiotic Theory and Analysis of Music.* Berlin and New York: Mouton de Gruyter, 1995.

Tesauro, Emanuele. *Il cannocchiale aristotelico.* 1670. Facs. repr. ed. August Buck. Bad Homburg, Berlin, Zürich, Gehlen, 1968.

Testi, Marco. *Il romanzo al passato. Medioevo e invenzione in tre autori contemporanei.* Rome: Bulzoni, 1992.

Torrell, Jean-Pierre. *Saint Thomas Aquinas: The Person and His Work.* Trans. Robert Royal. Washington, D.C.: Catholic University of America Press, 1996.

Vico, Giambattista. *The New Science.* 1774. Trans. Thomas Goddard Bergin and Max Harold Fisch. 3rd ed. Ithaca: Cornell University Press, 1968.

*Voices: Writers and Politics.* From the Channel 4 Television series. Ed. Bill Bourne, Udi Eichler, and David Herman. Nottingham: Atlantic Highlands, in association with The Hobo Press, 1987.

Williams, David. *Deformed Discourse: The Function of the Monster in Mediaeval Thought and Literature.* Montreal and Kingston: McGill-Queen's University Press, 1996.

Wilson Carpenter, Mary. 'Eco, Oedipus, and the "View" of the University.'
   *Diacritics* 20:1 (1990): 77–85.
Zanardi, Mario. 'La metafora e la sua dinamica di significazione ne *Il
   cannocchiale aristotelico* di Emanuele Tesauro.' *Giornale storico della letteratura
   italiana* 157 (1980): 321–68.
Zumthor, Paul. *Langue, texte, énigme.* Paris: Editions du Seuil, 1975.

# Index